"Ever wonder what happens at America's most iconic showplace, Radio City Music Hall? From picking a new costume for the Rockettes to navigating around piles of camel dung during the legendary Christmas Spectacular, Bonanni keeps you entertained and engaged with stories that continually surprise. He is a wonderful guide on this unique journey backstage. You don't know what you don't know until you read these wonderful stories by the man who was there."

—B. Jeffrey Madoff
Author, "*Creative Careers*"
Theatre Producer, "Personality, the Lloyd Price Musical"

"Bonanni bleeds greasepaint. This book reveals a love affair and passion for those who have dedicated themselves to both the show and its business. Throughout his career this man behind the curtain straddled that fence with great deft and politic. His voice delivers an insightful account of personalities and stories with a very special backstage pass."

—Rob Schiller
Emmy Award-winning Director,
Professor, USC School of Cinematic Arts

"Author John Bonanni's writing vividly captures the soul of the "Showplace of the Nation" – accurately describing the majestic and awe-inspiring landmark's beauty while perfectly bringing to life the passion and the humanity of the people who make Radio City so magical. 1260 Avenue of the Americas is more than a building. It is a community."

—Kent Fritzel
Executive Vice President, Creative
American Christmas

"He walked the walk, which gives him every right to talk the talk. At RCMH, when the inmates ran the asylum, Bonanni was the only adult in the room…which is very scary. A very enjoyable read from someone who shared the experience."

—Eric Titcomb
Master Electrician &
Chief of Stage Elevator Operations, Radio City Music Hall

"John Bonanni creates nostalgia for a bygone slice of Americana in Just Off, Stage Right. More than just a theatre story, John stirs a curiosity for a world few of us know anything about. If you've ever wanted to enter through the stage door, this is the way in."

—Ron Farina
Author, "Who Will Have My Back?"

"My company, American Christmas, worked for John at Radio City Music Hall for many years. His warmth and professionalism made dealings with him a pleasure. John's anecdotes and insider's view provide for a unique, behind the scenes peek into the theater world."

—Fred Schwam,
former Owner and CEO,
American Christmas, Inc.

JUST OFF, STAGE RIGHT

Just Off, Stage Right

A memoir

by

JOHN BONANNI

Adelaide Books
New York / Lisbon
2021

JUST OFF, STAGE RIGHT

A memoir

By John Bonanni

Copyright © by John Bonanni

Cover design © 2021 Adelaide Books

Published by Adelaide Books, New York / Lisbon
adelaidebooks.org

Editor-in-Chief
Stevan V. Nikolic

All rights reserved. No part of this book may be reproduced in any manner whatsoever without written permission from the author except in the case of brief quotations embodied in critical articles and reviews.

For any information, please address Adelaide Books
at info@adelaidebooks.org

or write to:

Adelaide Books
244 Fifth Ave. Suite D27
New York, NY, 10001

ISBN: 978-1-956635-23-2

Printed in the United States of America

To Carol,

My greatest critic and friend

Contents

Prologue	A Fabulous Obsession	**11**
Chapter 1	American Dream	**15**
Chapter 2	David Merrick, Jelly Doughnuts, and The Countryside Impresario	**42**
Chapter 3	The Bohemian Princess with Five Birth Certificates	**63**
Chapter 4	The Little Kingdom in the Woods	**74**
Chapter 5	Taylor-Made In-Laws for Theatricals	**93**
Chapter 6	Between Seasons and the Department of Labor	**106**
Chapter 7	The Arena Show from Hell	**127**
Chapter 8	To Have and Eat Cake: Broadway & Metro North	**140**
Chapter 9	Me, Don Imus, and a Guy Named Mort	**159**
Chapter 10	The Biggest Christmas Show Ever	**170**
Chapter 11	Showplace of the Nation	**181**

Chapter 12	Cablevision Culture Club	***193***
Chapter 13	Bloody, Bloody Monday	***210***
Chapter 14	The Rodent and the Cougar	***224***
Chapter 15	Those Rockettes	***234***
Chapter 16	And the Award for Best Supporting Instructor Goes To…	***249***
Chapter 17	Fire at Will	***260***
Chapter 18	A Cauldron of Community Theatre	***269***
Chapter 19	No Worries, No Filter	***282***
	Works Cited	***291***
	Acknowledgements	***293***
	About the Author	***295***

Prologue

A Fabulous Obsession

Addiction begets delusion, and Victor succumbs every time.

He stands by the hemp lines, ready to raise the curtain as if he is ready to raise a flag. He is not the stagehand I expect to appear next to the stage manager's desk. Calfskin work gloves match the hue of his Harris Tweed sport coat. Professor patches hug his elbows. Canary threads pierce the scaly vamp of Lucchese leather to his soles. A cornflower Stetson compliments his spotless, creased jeans. He is an ad man's dream. The Marlboro Man of stage right. The Gentleman Cowboy gatekeeper of the fourth wall.

Victor is a carpenter, once an actor, when a less wrinkled face promised a shot at a soliloquy, alone and center, onstage. Here he is now, steps away from onstage, hearing that delirious bliss of adoration from another tour de force performance. But he is not onstage. He stands with his face pressing against the black steel trough of the fire curtain track, just off right of the proscenium that offers lucky others the privilege and elixir of a captive audience.

Victor works backstage at the Royal Alex Theatre in Toronto.

I tap his shoulder to raise the curtain and start the show. He pulls on the offstage line, slow and even. The curtain leaves the stage, rising above our heads and higher. He watches for the red ribbons pinned to the ochre hemp warning him to slow down the speed to a stop. The bottom of the curtain, at our feet just seconds before, is now hurling toward a 45-foot-high trim. Like a seasoned mariner, Victor grabs the crimson ribbons traveling opposite each other, catches them when they meet, and ties off the ropes with a sailor's hitch.

Fly cue #1 complete. Curtain out to the red. Top of show.

Victor's job is done until the last act when he repeats the procedure. He spends most of the time in between downstairs, chuckling at the comedy of the Carol Burnett Show and interrupted by TV commercials hawking dreams. He reflects on what it might have been like to hear applause for his voice, his art, his enactment. At the end of the show Victor comes alive again to perform his final task for the evening. There are times when the audience reaction requires an extra curtain call or two. He enjoys those unrehearsed moments when we anticipate a second raising of the curtain. In that instant, we share a fleeting camaraderie, an immediate call to action. Victor "bounces" the curtain by slamming the bottom pipe to the stage deck, riding the rope with all his weight to jump start the curtain back up. He is a master at hauling this 1/2-ton cloth up and down at the order of the show caller's cue.

I call the show. I am a natural barking out cues to produce a sequence of movements in concert with music and actors. I imagine it like sailing a ship through a narrow, shallow harbor. I am ready for the possibility of adventure, a sudden squall in the form of jammed scenery, forgotten lines, or a missed sound cue to move the plot. I am not paid to sail on a sunny day. I manage risk. I weather the storm at all costs. Risk is what makes life worth the effort, especially when it is make-believe.

I thank Victor for a good show. He accepts my compliment in place of the standing ovation he dreams of in his heart, in his vision of a different, earlier life. Victor lives with his illusion like a lifelong medication that keeps him going but never cures.

I move on to the next city, to the next Victor I meet. I am disturbed by his compromise. I wonder how he copes. I am quick to dismiss it. My work is my adventure. Changing clothes and wiping make up off my face is not my idea of a career. Managing the sensibilities of others appeals to me more. Tending to vulnerabilities, administering a dose of self-esteem to an actor with damaged confidence moments before their entrance gives me purpose, admiration, trust. I am comfortable playing father even to those older than I am. There are plenty of people around who need guidance, direction, and parenting in this spacious, dark, hollow workplace.

Doubt returns to my mind. I worry if there is a little bit of Victor in me. I am fortunate to have escaped concession in my young career. I feel at home tucked in the dark corner of a proscenium opening. I find my grit, my tenacity under a tiny light illuminating a script that holds the battle plans of the next two hours. I belong here, in the stealth behind the curtain just off, stage right, not in the Brooklyn I left behind.

Chapter 1

American Dream

I keep my fantasies under the table.

I write the secret code of entry for visitors on the underside of the dining room table where I hope no one will look. My father's wax pencils produce neat lines of any color I choose. I emerge from under my mahogany bunker only to secure my favorite sweet cake, a whipped-cream-topped Charlotte Russe. I adjust my Astro Command helmet as instructed in the last episode of *Space Patrol*. I enhance it with wire hangers from the dry cleaner next to my father's jewelry shop. I keep the paper wrapping around the edges to boost the radar strength. The hangers retain the smell of the new and improved French Dry Cleaning method, just like they advertise on TV. Outer space and TV are synonymous with the future. The world is discovering what I already know.

Flying saucers. Spaceships. *Satsies*.

Satsies are from the outer reaches of the universe, somewhere beyond my kitchen window. "The Satsies! The Satsies are coming," I proclaim. They come from Palenti Tempi, a far away, happy place, and very similar to my living room. I am sure of it. My mother looks bewildered, amused.

I can see the Satsies through the kitchen window, appearing over the elevated subway tracks of the Manhattan-Brighton Beach Line Express train exiting the tunnel at Carroll Street. The ship glides over to the fire escape outside and floats through the glass panes like vapor, landing under the table. I greet every member off the ship, each with a blink of my eyes. They sound like turkeys gobbling. I blink 50 times, maybe 100, to accommodate every guest. Blink and gobble, blink and gobble.

The Satsies visit me exclusively. They are my height, three feet tall, and I can see through them. They have one big eye that protrudes out of the center of their forehead, like a round magnifying glass that stands out. They walk rapidly, in a hopping jump, and their facial expressions look like they are about to unleash a big burst of laughter. They are very noisy, like the schoolgirls I hear from the other side of the big brick wall that separates the boys at St. Mary, Star of the Sea Elementary.

My mother cannot hear the alien chatter from underneath the table. Just like the force fields in the "Barrier of Silence" episode of *Science Fiction Theatre,* she cannot hear the Satsies. They high-five each other 20, even 50 times as they pass me exiting their ship.

We discuss many important things. The real intentions of Klaatu and Gort in "The Day the Earth Stood Still." How to pack *Little Debbie's Oatmeal Creme Pie* for Palenti Tempi so they stay in one piece. Why the tops of their see-through heads look like jellyfish. When the Satsies prepare for their return journey, I send them off with the best gobble I can muster. My mother notices.

"You alright down there?" My mother thinks I am choking on my *Ovaltine.*

I get wobbly blinking so many times. Then the Satsies whoosh away, through the kitchen window, up the fire escape until I can no longer see the ship. It reappears in the distance, returning over the elevated subway two blocks away. Blink and gobble. The ship resembles a flying pigeon from the window. Everything gets hazy. I lose sight of the Satsies. I am confused for a second. I forget where I am. Everything is floating, moving. My stomach churns. Blink and gobble, faster and faster. It is getting dark.

That is the last thing I remember.

"Johnny, Johnny, wake up!"

I feel my mother shaking my shoulders. I open my eyes and see her face. She looks worried. My eyes hurt when I look to the left at the space drawings under the table. I hope she does not look underneath and discover my drawings. I am very tired. My father, a single jeweler's magnifying loop extending from his forehead, leans over and brings me into his arms. He carries me to the couch in the living room.

"Rest, Johnny. Sleep it off. You're ok. You need to rest."

My father places the Indian blanket from *Uncle Walt Disney's Frontier Town* up to my neck. It feels warm and secure. I do not understand why he is tucking me in. It is not bedtime.

"Might have been something he ate."

"I'll call Dr. Kaunitz."

There is more conversation between my mother and father. It hurts to blink. I doze off to sleep.

I think my gold star in English proves I can write a play in an afternoon, after school. I hurry home to finish my story about Palenti Tempi and mail it to the Famous Writers School. The ad in the Readers Digest shows successful TV writers offering a free aptitude test to evaluate writing ability. I fill out my application and place it in an envelope, ready to be mailed. I feel like a TV writer, just like Rod Serling.

I swallow my red-striped capsule of Dilantin with *Tang*, the breakfast of astronauts. The Satsies stop visiting. I wonder about the world outside of my family's apartment. I turn on the new RCA *Spectra-Color* television to find out. I think about the warning from Dr. Kaunitz, the doctor with the German accent, the one who looks like Commandant von Scherbach in *Stalag 17*.

"Do not sit close to the television," he warns in an ominous tone. "It will disorient you, and we don't want that to happen again."

Who are these *we* people, I wonder, the rule makers, the ones who approve things in my life? Who gives them authority? I decide that will never happen again, not from him or anyone else. I decide to stay awake from now on. I create my own normal.

I visit the television repair shop across the street from my father's jewelry store. Paul DiBonaventura owns the store. Everyone in the neighborhood looks up to him. He is a community leader, a modern man savvy on the events of the day, the person in-the-know for advice on the American Way. My father is not. My father looks like a grandfather. He has the whitest hair on his head, and he speaks with an accent. Everyone knows he was not born here in Brooklyn, here in America.

DiBonaventura changes his last name. He thinks it is cool for Italians with surnames longer than prescription medications to shorten them. Working on televisions helps him diminish his heritage and allows him to enter circles of people that seem different from him or my father. Pauly DiBonaventura identifies with Elvis Presley more than Mario Lanza. On TV, Elvis looks cool, and Mario looks old. Paul DiBonaventura shortens his name to Pauly D. He repairs televisions when they *go on the blink*. He becomes a sought-after technical TV specialist. Pauly D makes more money than college professors tweaking channel selectors and replacing thyratron tube rectifiers.

I inherit an American viewpoint on TV. Social class is strictly defined in racial and ethnic groups. Everyone in the neighborhood seems oblivious to the supposition of Italians being synonymous with comic relief. They laugh at the bumbling pizza maker of *Chef Boy-ar-Dee* and snicker at Dean Martin tripping over the furniture on his way to another martini. The swarthy Southern Italian look is in for mythological Hollywood anti-heroes, the antagonists in every TV show, the crime bosses in every police drama. Kentucky-born Victor Mature plays a Macedonian in *Demetrius and the Gladiators*. Thanks to the courtesy of *Coppertone Tanning Lotion*, he looks more like every wavy-haired Lothario out to deflower every blonde daughter in America.

Pauly D's *Buick Roadmaster* wagon is filled with receipts and screwdrivers that cover the front seat and a television in the back ready for delivery. I am told a story of how he helps my mother into the front seat, waits for my father to enter behind her, then drives past my father's jewelry shop and some neighbors well-wishing my mother's outcome. My father does not have a driver's license. Pauly is my father's good friend and guarantees transport when my mother needs it. He drives over the Brooklyn Bridge, up the East River Drive and exits on Houston Street. Pauly D maneuvers through the fruit and vegetable stalls on the streets of Lower East Side and arrives at Columbus Hospital on East 19th Street and 2nd Avenue. It does not look like Italians live on this block. He drops my parents at the hospital and returns to Brooklyn. Two days later, Pauly D cleans out the backseat entirely to accommodate three of us. My mother, my father, and me, a new- born.

"And that is how it happened, Johnny. Your pop was very excited you were born. Your mom said you took your time comin' out. You were a special event. You wanna eat?"

Pauly D orders two ham and provolone heroes with shredded lettuce, tomato, and onion drenched with olive oil and vinegar. We gulp down a *Coke* with lunch. I am glad we choose Coke. The new diet soda is no match for the real thing. *Tab* tastes like flat seltzer.

In Pauly D's shop, gray metal shelves support glass-domed tubes set in heavy black plastic bases from which clusters of needle-like rods emanate in four-, five-, and six- point configurations. They are inserted in various outlets of the platform on which the glass tubes rest. When Pauly D hotwires one of the units to a wall outlet, they begin to glow and buzz until a hazy array of lined images appears on the connected tubes. A whole row of televisions, probably 15 or 20, light up in pulsating shades of gray and black projecting images of different people telling their stories. The outer worlds of *Captain Video and His Video Rangers, Superman,* and *The Twilight Zone* are as magical as *Ozzie and Harriet's* suburban ranch, *Andy Griffith's* small-town countryside, and *Father Knows Best's* perfect American family. None of it seems familiar and all of it is new and intriguing. It is another world. None idolize the grit of a city street; the hoarse grinding of garbage being crushed by a trash collection truck. TV is the stage for American exceptionalism, and the understudies – the porters, the fruit sellers, the shoemakers, the chauffeurs, those with fractured accents or whose faces shine inappropriate shades – never get to be the lead. On TV, there is no outside kitchen window sporting a skybox view of the F train emerging from the tunnel off Smith Street. Sitcoms show life in split- levels in woodsy neighborhoods. Children go upstairs to bed. My bedroom is a daybed in the corner of the living room.

JUST OFF, STAGE RIGHT

Pauly D's store smells like televisions. A steely, heated mechanical odor of wires warms up, like an iron on its way to melting. It permeates the air and stays in my nose. Then the odor softens a bit, as if the metal achieves a tolerance level. Pauly D has televisions stacked five high lining the narrow store from front to back, like hard boxes, all of them inside a heavy, dark *Bakelite* plastic casing. I do not touch anything, especially on any uncovered unit he is working on. Big yellow stickers that resemble atomic fallout shelter signs warn that if you touch it, you will break apart, just like the disintegrating two-story house they show in a promotional newsreel on the nuclear war they expect to have with Russia any day now. Outer space and TV are first cousins in the atomic age of the 50s. I make sure I do not gaze upon the pulsating static transmissions of radio waves shimmering on the screen. That might make things cloudy again in my head and I am determined to stay conscious.

I see nearly every TV show of the 50s and 60s in Pauly D's store. The electronic box is the defining device for making us think we are the greatest, most invincible creatures alive. We can do anything, make anything, brand anything. We are made in America, and we know our place. There is room for everybody if you understand your assigned circumstance.

There are no TVs made in Japan or China worth owning, and as far as I know, there are still Cowboys and Indians in Oklahoma. That is what the TV is telling me. Television advertising is the great stager of our cultural conscience. TV is the little magic box of show business that delivers the American dream. I watch actors in shows about success, at any cost. The right race, the right family, the right job, the right church, sugar-frosted with all the trimmings.

America is a great play. I am sold the illusion that I can audition for any part.

In truth the play has already been cast and all available roles taken. It is as frozen as opening night, with no rewrites allowed. What began as an experiment in liberty now is a formula, a process feeding the bottom line to the bottom feeder sitting on top.

As I grow older, I question whether I am making the grade.

On Sunday mornings I know it is 6:30 a.m. by the aroma of tomato sauce bubbling in the kitchen. I prepare for the weekly ritual of the Children's Mass, the social event of the week for Catholic pre-teens. Being an altar boy provides a featured role in the event. It is an opportunity to impress schoolgirls from all eight grades of St. Mary's who are seated in a separate section of the left side pews.

Church offers more theatricality than any TV sitcom. Beyond offering eternal life and a periodic swig at unconsecrated port wine, being an altar boy provides ample opportunity for ritual, enactment, set, light, and costume design. I hear heavenly incantations echoed within a cavernous edifice built in 1884. The church is a Gothic gem that defines the showmanship in all things Catholic. The Protestants I know do not have this advantage. Their services are simple. One or two 18th century hymns, a sermon on being a good person and you are off to coffee hour to exchange the latest benchmarks one has achieved up the corporate ladder. No Latin incantations, no massive Wurlitzer organ pipes expelling open cyphers. There are no medieval costumes adorning their ministers.

A handheld sprinkler containing holy water sits next to cruets of wine. A clover-shaped set of brass bells rests on a porcelain plate. The church is filled with sensual stimulation. Burning wax from votive candles and incense tablets emit a variety of fragrances with product names like *Cedars of Lebanon, Queen of Heaven, Archangel, Frankincense, Byzantine,* and *Sweet Myrrh*.

JUST OFF, STAGE RIGHT

No one does props like the Catholic Church. Sunday service is performance art at its best.

I am staring up at the corrugated tin ceiling in the kitchen. A design of stamped florets encircles a square repeatedly. The enameled white surface turns yellow. The morning sun makes the squares resemble vanilla-covered pizzelles. My undershirt feels wet. I see brown stains on the front when I pull it up to my eyes. It smells sweet, like chocolate. I gaze over to the wall, looking up at the cuckoo clock. It reads seven o'clock. I am not fond of the clock. I do not like the roman numerals. They threaten me. I am understanding why I am lying on the floor. I wonder how long I have been here. I get up and change my shirt. My father is across the street at his jewelry shop, my mother is in the bedroom. I walk back to the kitchen and clean up the *Cocoa Puffs* soaked in milk on the floor. They still smell sweet. I do not know if I feel guilty for being messy or fearful that something inside me is wrong. I do not tell my mother what happened. No one needs to know. I dress and wait in the kitchen for my father to come home to take me to Canal Street.

I board the E train to the Lower East Side with my father every Sunday morning after Mass to buy watch parts. There are no Jews in my neighborhood, but I meet a lot of them on Sundays. Mr. Drazin, Mr. Cohen, Mr. Allen, Mr. Friedman. Open for business on Sunday, closed on Saturday. It is all very confusing, especially when I receive tins of nuts for Christmas from all the Jewish merchants except for Mr. Allen, who presents my father with a framed, glossy photo of his son.

"Hey, Daddy, can I get a big picture of me like that?"

My father does not answer me. He does not know the ways of the world in New York as well as I wish.

"Keep it," Mr. Allen beams to my father. "my son is going to be a somebody."

My father is more concerned with the watch part Mr. Allen sold him and stuffs the photo of Mr. Allen's son, Woody, in between the folds of the Daily News under his arm.

I wonder why Mr. Allen's jewelry shop has autographed photos of Broderick Crawford from *Highway Patrol* and Dinah Shore from the *Dinah Shore Chevy Show* over the counters. Through the glass top *Westclox* alarm clocks and *Parker* pens are displayed. In my father's shop, an aerial view of St. Peters Basilica and a portrait of John F. Kennedy overlook the single counter of *Timex* watches and *Fabulite* imitation diamond rings. I do not understand why Mr. Allen thinks he is a persecuted victim. Always a story about being shortchanged. My father nods in agreement, hoping to move on to buying the watch part. I think anyone who can park his *Oldsmobile Delta 88* right out in front of his store on Canal Street cannot be that much of a victim. Even though it is Sunday, and everyone in New York can park anywhere they want. My father has no car. I wish he had a *Mercury Monterey*. A four-door hardtop in two-toned blue. It is another dream to achieve. The list is getting long. After making his rounds, my father promises me a "continental" breakfast. No one makes a prune and poppy seed danish like Gertels on Hester Street. It is good enough to consider trading in the New Testament for the Torah.

"Don't touch that or anything on this table," my father warns, watching my hand extend toward the things on his worktable, especially an old brown box. The cover looks hard, almost like a box. From my view at four feet, the ends have a marbled brown design, chipped at the edges. I wonder what is inside. I imagine it to be a case filled with things I might find interesting or valuable. I want to open it, maybe when my father is asleep.

The box lives on that table permanently. It becomes part of the familiar scenery of his jewelry repair table along with jars of cleaning solutions of various shades of blue and gray.

My father is an immigrant from a mountain village in Lazio and looks older than his years. I cannot imagine him being young. There is a part of him that is so foreign, so antiquated, so permanently adult. He is unable to fully assimilate into America.

He places a jeweler's loop against the skin around his eye, squinting and squeezing the facial muscles to secure the single lens over the exposed insides of a watch as if preparing for surgery. I peer at the conglomeration of tiny, ratcheted wheels ticking in concert to keep time. He places the entire mechanism down on the work platform. The timepiece whispers and ticks, responding to the tightened force of the spring wheel. He is fascinating to watch, like a physician placing a newborn on a prepared pillow. He disassembles the timepiece, lays it out on a black cloth, and cleans every part in various solutions. The row of glass jars containing cleaning solutions offers intoxicating aromas when he unscrews the black plastic tops. When my father is involved in the tiny metal parts of the timepiece, I hold one of the jars to my nose and inhale the toxic odor. It makes me lightheaded, almost dizzy. But I stop being afraid. I think of it as a test. I push the envelope. I am my own normal.

A book remains on the worktable nestled between the jars. I notice that sometimes it is between different jars.

But it is always on the table.

There are so many parts to the watch. I do not think I could ever put them all back together again.

"Step by step, Giovanni. *Pazienza*. Concentrate," my father says.

Once he finishes cleaning the individual parts, he begins to rebuild the entire watch, securing every bridge with the tiniest of screws and placing the escape wheel that manages the oscillations of the balance wheel housing the hair-thin coil. Tweezers, clamps, clasps, and cotton hold the first parts of the ticking valve. If the spring is installed and sits properly, it produces regular rhythms of a coiled spring slowly releasing its wound-up pressure—the heart of a timepiece. The watch, now healthy and beating from a new balance wheel transplant, is ready to be put back together. He places back in the case. "*Non voglio che piu il demonio abbia ad aver dominio dell'anima mia,*" he mutters.

I do not understand him.

Everything goes well, and I am treated to an ice cream sandwich from Augie's.

Sometimes my father loses a spring. It flies into the air and lands in an obscure spot on the tile floor. Fuller brush in hand, my father falls to his knees to sweep up the suspected area in hopes of finding the tiny spring. There are times where customers think he has left the store since the counter separating the worktable and the store entrance blocks the view. "Angelo? Are you here?" A triumphant Angelo suddenly rises from the floor holding the found spring. "*Disgrazia scongiurato!*" he claims to the customer, which I learn to mean "misfortune averted!" The customer smiles politely, not quite sure of the nature of the misfortune. My father opens one of the screw-top jars and plunges the spring in the noxious solution to clean the part. Then he goes about the business of servicing the customer.

My father finds the quiet of the night the most productive. I pretend to be secure in bed and then sneak into his room by his worktable, careful not to be discovered by the spill of the sharp, blue, florescent jeweler's lamp. It casts a surreal lowlight to the room, antiseptic and fantastic, like the deep blue hues of the midnight forest in *Doctor Blood's Coffin*.

He sits on his rotating rolling stool, squished face bearing a balance of the jeweler's loop in his right eye, delicately maneuvering the tiniest of metal parts. My father begins to utter more words under his breath as he works on the dismembered watch.

I learn detail, process, efficiency watching his hands.

My father is a collector of so many variations of living. He is a farm boy brought up in a monastery, a soldier for two countries and now a jeweler in post-war America. It is quite the journey.

I wonder why he utters nonsensical things when he works.

He ends his mumblings with "…mio caro figlio, Giovanni." My father smiles at his pronunciation of my name. The brown box holds an old prayer book. He worries about my episodes. He does not approve of me watching so much television. My father, jeweler's loop still protruding from his forehead and looking like an alien, is praying for me from his book. He is concerned about my seizures. He is looking for an answer in that book.

A red Schwinn Hornet bicycle appears one Christmas morning with twenty-six-inch tires and a fender light. I lose interest in the things of my father's table. I ride beyond the cement backyard onto streets, alleys, and avenues outside of the neighborhood. I see the world for real, beyond my television.

Our apartment has a front door buzzer that sounds like the wrong answer on a game show. No one we know ever uses it, except insurance salesmen betting on my father's life, priests praying over it, or a Jehovah's Witness couple from the Kingdom

Hall around the corner pleading with us to change our ways. The buzzer pierces the quiet in the kitchen. A few moments later Guido Fratini, my father's Pennsylvania cousin, appears at the front door. He is visiting with his wife Queenie and their four daughters, Matilda, Wanda, Donna, and Joanie.

I have no intention of kissing Joanie. This calls for evasive action.

Cousin Guido's youngest daughter is older than I am. Heck, she is nearly middle aged in my mind, and meeting lips with her is not something I want to do. I am forced to watch her rendition of "On the Good Ship Lollipop" imitating Shirley Temple. She mimics every nuance, every little twirl. I am uncomfortable looking at her. She looks nothing like Shirley Temple. She has black shiny curls that smell like strawberry. I want to get closer. I am too shy to tell anyone, especially her. I can do nothing that will result in having to kiss her. In front of everyone.

"She needs practice so she can be ready when she tries out for Hollywood," Queenie claims as if she were a talent agent with a track record. Joanie's mother and father are stage parents, hawking their daughter's talent as if she were fresh tomatoes on the vine. Joanie's mother sees deliverance for her family in Joanie's success. Queenie married at 15 years of age, having been given permission to do so by her coal miner father in rural Pennsylvania.

Joanie is precocious and obnoxious, and I am not ready to share my future teen life, especially with someone who fancies herself a future teen idol.

I hide when the visiting relatives begin their goodbyes. In the confusion and excitement of departure, they do not notice me absent. When I hear the front door close, I return and go back to my arithmetic homework.

I do not mind school. I like leaving the house, getting out from under the scrutiny of my parents watching my every move. School is five minutes from my daybed. Unlike the clean yellow school buses on television rolling through the curved roads of suburban TV land sitcoms, I walk half a block, cross the street, and enter the school building. Black-robed Franciscan Brothers greet us at the school entrance. Two of them are my teachers, and the third runs the school for the full eight years I spend there. One teaching brother develops my creative side. He is open to everything, and I am surprised he is still a religious brother. We share the delirium of imagining Gisele Mackenzie, a regular on the *Ed Sullivan Show*, without clothes on. The fine arts teacher knows how to steer adolescent preoccupations toward an artistic conversation.

These conversations take away the fear of eternal damnation. Art transcends spiritual incrimination.

I watch Ann Margaret on television portraying the girl next door. She is the paradigm of sexuality on a recurring dose. I do not care about her intelligence. I worship her pedal pushers. She is the eclair for every adolescent yearning to measure their manhood. Hollywood makes her American royalty. In America, half the population accepts their objectification, and the other half exploits it. I have difficulty resisting her shimmering red tresses. She is the iconic idol of the 20th century, the standard of gender-based marketing of the American woman. I am not alone in wanting to be the head lioness tamer. There are no women in my neighborhood who like Ann Margaret. *She is loose*, they say. *A tart, a homewrecker*. I only see a goddess. Where do people like Ann Margaret come from and why do I not see them on the street outside my father's store?

In Bulger, Pennsylvania, little Joanie, celebrates her sweet sixteen birthday. In the tradition of her mother, she is bequeathed to the son of a coal miner, 21 years old, under a court approval and with the consent and blessing of her parents. From a Betty Crocker pink frosting shortcake to an RCA Whirlpool washer.

Time passes, and I am on to Annette.

I learn America's penchant for good looks. Blondes have more fun according to TV advertisements for *Loving Care Hair Lotion* by Lady Clairol. But the darling of *The Mickey Mouse Club* is a raven-haired teen whose career skyrockets as America's teen idol, passing the test of ethnic acceptance.

Annette Funicello.

The Mickey Mouse Club grows from an innocuous children's show to the premiere training ground that spawns a series of beach-party movies. I wonder how I can get on the show. Shoulder to shoulder with Annette on TV becomes my unattainable goal. Annette is no longer a little girl anymore. Even my father notices and expresses his approval in his accented, broken English. There is sweet remembrance in the sound of his fractured cadence.

Women on TV are as gorgeous as those in the movies, even when they are not blonde.

A math quiz does not prevent me from my daydreaming fantasy of how I save Annette from hurling off a cliff in Southern California, a place I visit every week only on television. A wonderful scenario emerges, interrupted by the unnerving clanging of the school bell signaling the end of the quiz and knocking me out of my imagination.

Walter Mitty has nothing on me. I fail the math quiz.

I learn that making things up is the first step in making things real. That is the attraction of show business. *If only I could...* changes to *What if?* It is the stuff of dreams. I am dashing, a hero, and super-human all in my mind. No verification or courage is needed. Weekends at the Clinton Street Movie Theatre serve up fantasy, and I draw inspiration from sci-fi flicks, *Panavision*, and *Cinemascope* blockbusters. Forging a path under the elevated highway of I-278 to the theatre becomes a dangerous undertaking. The highway cuts a divide separating two neighborhoods.

Samuel Burwell lives on the other side of the highway. I meet up with him sometimes in the schoolyard. The Clinton Theatre is in Sam's neighborhood. When I see him there, he nods to acknowledge me but stays with his friends. The only time we walk together is at school. We stay in our own backyards, in our own neighborhoods. The movie theatre is near his apartment house. When he is alone, he strikes up a conversation.

"Hey," greeting me as an acknowledgement and a question. "What are you doing over here?" as if I required permission from him.

"Yeah," I respond, attempting to level the exchange. I'm goin' to see *Spartacus* at the Clinton."

"I already saw it." A smirk surfaces from his mouth. "Gonna eat spaghetti again tonight?"

"Yeah," I respond defensively. "What do you care? What will you eat?"

"Fried chicken."

"My chicken has tomato sauce on it. We don't eat fried chicken. That doesn't go with spinach and garlic."

"No, I have fried chicken with collard greens. But you wouldn't eat that, would you?"

"Maybe I'll try it sometime."

"Yeah, I wanna be there. You and ham hocks."

"Yeah, Maybe."

"Gotta go. See you in school."

"Yeah, sure."

Hanging out with people from the other side of the highway is dangerous.

The walk back under the highway could be a weekly episode of *Vehicle Invaders from the Planet Brooklyn*. Crossing six lanes of traffic on one light change with too many cars is an invitation to escape, a risky attempt to run away, if you can make it. A South Brooklyn version of the chicken game in "Rebel Without a Cause." If I can survive to the other side, things might be different. The danger disappears. I wonder if Sam Burwell feels that way. I wonder which side feels safer to him.

I stare at the strobe light pulsating in the examination room of Dr. Rabinowitz. I try not to remember fixating on a *Buick la Sabre* front grille through an oscillating window fan. I hope the strobe does not trigger the same reaction as the grille. Unconsciousness is painless. Getting there is terrifying. The light around me is fading and I feel darkness approaching. But people who take consciousness for granted do not understand that, and never will. If it is going to happen again, it is going to happen here. But nothing does.

"Johnny, I am placing you on a dosage reduction plan for a few weeks. Some patients outgrow their tendency to seizures. You may be one of the lucky ones."

"OK, Doc, but I just don't want this to happen in front of anybody."

"No liquor. Don't drink, take your medicine and you will be fine."

The next month, I take my last, red-striped pill. I feel free and frightened, as if I drop imaginary crutches but am still standing. I just do not know for how long. No one needs to know. I manage my new normal. I have a lot of catching up to do. Learn to dance. Drink ginger ale and pretend it is beer. Avoid strobe lights. Find a dark corner if I feel strange and keep it a secret. There are more pleasant things to worry about.

Providence smiles upon Bishop Ford's All Boys Catholic High School with the Great Gifts of St. Savior.

St. Savior's All Girls Catholic High School.

JUST OFF, STAGE RIGHT

Brother Jonathan organizes a drama club and invites students from the school to audition for female roles. St. Savior's is down the street in Park Slope two bus stops away from our school.

My friend, Joe Aguanno, convinces me to audition for the drama club. The play is *The Lottery*, a harrowing tale of a beloved tradition gone evil through mob mentality. I am not cast, and I am not surprised. Acting is a terrible, uncomfortable situation, and I have enough trouble with self-esteem without adding lies around who I am. Girls seeking auditions enter the auditorium. Joe and I are there, watching every girl who comes in.

The air in the assembly hall takes on aromas of *Cutex Nail Polish, Aqua Net, Jean Nate*, and *Prince Matchabelli's Wind Song*. Girls show up to try out or seek dates, together with about 20 boys from Ford. The girls are stunning. They are lighter. They do not walk. They flow. They glide from one place to the next like friendly sightings. They exude a mystique with perfumes from the local pharmacy. Guys smell like gym shoes, like heated rubber and worse. The girls claim the auditorium this afternoon.

There are no jocks here. They are all busy bouncing balls in a hot gym or running their asses off on an outside oval track like two-legged squirrels in search of a finish line. *The Mickey Mouse Club* has come to Bishop Ford High, and I bet there is an Annette somewhere in the crowd.

In the coal mining town of Bulger, Pennsylvania, Joanie, now 18, is the mother of two.

Seeing girls in my high school is like seeing camels in midtown Manhattan. One girl enters the auditorium, running down the aisle pleading for a shot at an audition. Brother Jonathan calms her down and lets her take a few moments to compose herself. I walk over to her and offer her my handkerchief, which, thankfully, I had yet to use. Startled at first, she regains her composure, looks up, and smiles at me.

"How'd you know? Just what I need."

I freeze.

"Yeah, well I knew, I figured what you needed, I mean, like, you know, you need stuff and I have it, so I thought…"

I do not finish a sentence. I am sounding like an idiot. She extends her hand.

"Patty. Hi. Thanks."

Her blue eyes rivet through my confidence like a smelter extracting ore. I feel awkward and enthralled.

Brother Jonathan asks for volunteers to stage manage. I raise my hand, searching for a way to be part of this club.

"What does a stage manager do?"

Brother Jonathan sees an opportunity to pawn off hard, thankless work on the uninformed.

"A stage manager is a boss. They are in total charge of the show. Everybody listens to the stage manager."

"Even the actors?" I asked.

"Especially the actors. You run the show." I raise my hand. "I'll do it."

Rehearsals begin Monday. In a weekend, the auditorium is transformed into a dating center. Every track and basketball star looking for a date is out of luck, and they return to their malodorous gymnasium located on the other end of the school. The auditorium smells like Dee's Beauty Supply on Valentine's Day.

"Places everyone. Stand by for the stoning scene."

This job gives me endless opportunity be near Patty.

"OK, everyone, be sure to hold on to the stones tightly. We don't want to injure our star."

Patty likes that remark. I could see her dimples sinking into a broad smile, slightly embarrassed, totally approving, from my desk just off from stage right.

The day of the first performance is a matter of life and death. Nothing else matters. The cast and crew receive the day off in preparation for opening night.

The play is performed six times over two weekends. Patty, in the leading role, is stoned to death at every performance by the town mob cast. I protect her by rehearsing the moment before every performance. Six times I am her protector. Six times I am her knight, her prince.

This is not the usual high school drama club. The success of *The Lottery* encourages Brother Jonathan to introduce us to Shakespeare. He directs *Hamlet*. I become Jonathan's assistant and Patty is cast as Ophelia. I wonder what our children will look like.

On stage Patty is riveting. I watch her in rehearsal. Shakespeare becomes my favorite playwright. I read *Hamlet* in its entirety. I swoon over every scene in which Ophelia appears. I read her lines and hear Patty's voice. Patty is now an ever-present distraction. The costumes add to the fantasy. Costumes are the most misinterpreted invitations for affection.

My teenage life consists of simple gratifications. There is the home-grown comfort of a salami and provolone, the sensual excitement behind the stick shift of an *Olds Cutlass 448*, the relentless bliss of young women. All are guaranteed joys of a young life. Adulthood can wait while I busy myself with these simple diversions. I am all about how I feel. It is a right of immaturity.

But then I begin to care, without explanation. Calm sets in, reassuring yet disconcerting. Feelings are complex. Worry and ecstasy. Rapture and torment. Delight and disappointment. A thrilling awareness comes upon me. The sudden, immersive discovery of someone else swirling around in my mind, my heart. Patty does not share those feelings. She is not distracted as I am. She wants to be friends, and in this adolescent time of my life, I am not interested in friendship. I think of what might have been. I think it will never be. There is no exploration, no fulfillment. Only disappointment surfaces. Not making the grade again. I wonder if it is a family inheritance.

I return to my stock gratifications like they are faucets I can open at will, but they no longer provide satisfaction or comfort. A little more wary, a little more careful. Maturity seeps through a life becoming more complex. Acceptance is earned through eligibility conditions dictated by others. The right haircut, bell bottom jeans, the right curse words. I see this with my father, whose pastoral gentility from another world is dismissed because he is not American enough. Nothing he does ever makes him more American, more like TV. He endures disappointment, rejection. He becomes wary and careful.

I do not want to follow in his footsteps.

I want *American* to be an ethnicity, but I think *American* will only be a location.

A binary world leaves no room for error or reconsideration.

Something is wrong. Things are not the way they should be. I lose the girl. I lose the feeling of normal, being accepted. My father seems older than ever. I realize how much he looks like Boris Karloff in *The Raven*. His accent now irritates me. His jewelry business is not doing well. We do not have much money. My mother ignores her health, more out of lethargy than despair. Her hypoglycemic episodes occur after an argument, over saving face, not having a driver's license. My mother is disillusioned. I suspect she regrets marrying my father. She is the first native born American of an immigrant family, and the close relationship she has with her younger brother takes its toll on her relationship with my father. My uncle is more like a stepbrother. I am uncomfortable, embarrassed. My family is fractured, peculiar. I pity my father. I want to leave. The need to get away surges within me. The only place, the only chance that seems to provide relief, is beyond this home. I can begin again, from scratch, a blank page, a clean slate. I refuse to endure derision as a son of an immigrant father.

I wonder how far the F train goes, away from here.

But things change even without leaving.

No fingerprint mars the gleaming bronze coffin containing my mother. It displays a chrome bas-relief of da Vinci's fresco *The Last Supper,* an option in the long list of extras one can add to show relatives no expense was spared in honoring my mother's life. In the Italian approach to death and funerals, there are important parts. Throw an exorbitant gathering event with flowers, print prayer cards, and extend visiting hours. Friends and relatives enter the chapel. Some are not recognizable since they have not seen me since birth. I accept their stock expressions of condolence: "Sorry for your loss," and "our prayers are with you." I do not understand why they are sorry, why they would feel responsible for my mother dying. At the far end of the room lays my mother's coffin. Clusters of relatives, deep in murmuring discussions, are evaluating how much I care based on how much I spent.

"Ming. A brass box. Scotto's took them for a ride."

"Yeah, but I bet they don't have a vault."

"The flowers alone…"

"Only one limo. I guess we all take our own cars to the burial."

Only Pauly D shows genuine, if a little fractured, compassion.

"Some turn out, eh?" Pauly D mutters half to himself, half to initiate a conversation with his old friend Angelo.

My father looks up with a stone-faced expression, acknowledges Pauly D, and nods. My father is not prepared for this event. I lose my mother, but I have no idea what that means yet. My father loses his partner, his interpreter, his connection to this world of assimilation, his cheerleader. It is the first time I see my father in need, broken.

Aunt Concetta spends two days preparing refreshments for the bereaved. She seldom receives culinary accolades from the family. She sets out to change that. She serves an aromatic risotto with Arborio rice, beef broth, and mushrooms in a hand-painted, Modigliani bowl just to prove to everyone that her expertise transcends her modest Sicilian beginnings. A large ceramic vat of polenta garnished with fresh parsley and Parmesan cheese sits next to the risotto. Further down the lace-dressed table, a fresh medley of sliced tomato, handmade mozzarella cheese, and large leaves of basil float in first-press olive oil and balsamic vinegar. The final specialty is covered, Aunt Concetta's magnum opus, to be served after the final prayer of the evening. The musty odor of stale floral wreaths and bouquets typical of other funeral homes is absent here. Entry into my mother's wake can be mistaken for an Italian restaurant simply due to the aroma.

We critique the food. The event begins at two in the afternoon and culminates in a religious ceremony, conducted by Reverend Collins, a soft-spoken Irish prelate grossly misplaced in an Italian parish. He bears a striking resemblance to history book photographs of Woodrow Wilson. He evokes a distant, passionless demeanor. He probably despises us secretly. He utters Latin invocations that sound like a rain dance. Expressions of grief subside by dusk. Jokes are made to lighten up the feigned pain of sentiment. Closure is fulfilled by revealing Concetta's prized Rigatoni Bolognese. Applause rings out. Aunt Concetta has her wish, and the previously anguished entourage finally leaves for the evening.

My mother is still. From now on.

This public commemoration of my mother's death is discomforting for me. I feel invaded. My affections are laid bare, open to qualification, to someone else's assessment. The intimate trust of child and parent is thrown about like a prized trinket among family and friends, close and distant. My love, sorrow, grief is scrutinized, evaluated, critiqued. Everyone claims billing. The privacy of my affection, along with my mother, is laid to rest.

The funeral director closes the half-cut cover of the coffin over my mother's head. The disturbing feeling of this act is reconciled by watching the fractured expressions of remorse executed through mouths filled with crisp *pasticciotto*. It is difficult to manage pasticciotto as a finger food over a conversation. It is impossible to impart compassion through a chomping jowl.

The next day, I enter the church and notice a hand-made lace duvet lying over a metal stand near the altar. It stands in line with the first ten rows of pews, ready to accept my mother's final engagement with her family and relatives. The massive pipe organ expels rich chords of ceremonial underscoring. A group of older women in black lace veils congregate by the baptismal font. They are not related to my family. They attend every funeral, moaning and whimpering on cue from rows in the rear of the church. In what appears to be a second act of the rain dance, the service begins with more incantations, incense, and candles burning higher than I can reach. They flicker in line with the polished coffin. Pall bearers in *After Six* evening suits, blacker than black, escort my mother's sleek coffin slowly up the center aisle of the church. All look like they are named Joey, Vinny, Vito, or Tony. They arrive at the prepared stand, gently set the coffin, and return to a formal pose, standing as straight as their bellies will allow.

A heavy baritone is belting out "Hosea." The voice belongs to Mr. Spinner. I capture a glimpse of him from the music stand light attached to the organ. His head jerks back and forth to the rhythm of the hymn. He accompanies himself and plays as if he is attached to the organ. His moves are laborious, unwilling, as if he were an old mare being whipped up a steep hill. He strains to accompany the hymn. I imagine him the appointed greeter at some heavenly gate relentlessly imploring the newly departed, reluctant and confused, to move on.

Laments and sighs are heard among the grieving group of friends and relatives from last night's party. I have no tears. I have yet to comprehend the extent of my loss. I am intrigued by the theatricality of the whole affair.

The production features neighborhood *goombahs* in suits, the priest in an imported, embroidered chasuble and matching silk stole with repeating sequined crosses running to his knees, and everyone else in their mourning day best. The candles, the incense, the flowers, the music. It is show time at St. Mary Star of the Sea, and my mother is in the lead.

There is nothing to allay the emptiness of my mother being dead.

I am ready to leave all this once the coffin is lowered into the ground. The coolness of the night of September 21, 1971, offers a fresh alternative to the unexpected, unwanted feeling of living without my mother. I am offered compassion, lament, and pity. I am looking for answers.

My dead mother is becoming a reality.

When I return home from the funeral, I take the wooden crucifix I receive that adorned the bronze box at the funeral service and place it next to the pewter crucifix that belongs to the brother I never knew. All this religious swag needs to be in a museum, not my bedroom.

We carry on traditions for the dumbest and most selfish of reasons.

I read in the *Journal-American* that Randy Morgan, a student at my high school, is struck by the #67, the bus from

Park Slope to Gowanus, the bus that crosses under the six-lane street under I-287 to the poor neighborhood. Some say Randy ran after he robbed a candy store. Randy is a friend of Samuel Burwell. They could be brothers. I never find out the rest of the story. The highway separates us, and I am on the safer side.

It is time to move on.

My father does not understand why I choose theatre to escape.

I do not become a teacher or a railroad conductor. I tell him that such a choice keeps me in the captivity of the old neighborhood. South Brooklyn is a place where Manhattan is still a hazy backdrop view from the Smith-9th Street elevated subway station. He does not understand that I am doing the same thing he did, that we are made of the same cloth. We go beyond the given conditions of our respective lives. In his youth my father recalls boarding a steamer to leave a country for something else, anything else. I take a subway to leave a neighborhood. Both our worlds are far apart, but we share the same solution.

It takes another person entering my life to help me understand that bond.

Chapter 2

David Merrick, Jelly Doughnuts, and The Countryside Impresario

Deliverance arrives as a blindsided interruption.

I am pulled out of American History and into the General Office. I am thinking the principal has discovered my habit of inhaling the methylene solvent in the Gestetner duplicating machine whenever I make copies of test papers. My fear is unfounded. I am told that a Broadway producer's office is looking for a general assistant. The Guidance Counselor suggests I call David Merrick's production offices to set up an interview. David Merrick is one of the most successful Broadway producers of the day. He has seven productions running on Broadway simultaneously and more on the road. When I call expecting to set up an appointment, Jack Schlissel, Merrick's general manager, answers and interrupts my meek introduction. He begins interviewing me for a job as a staff associate.

"Hello, kid, want to work in the theatre? Twenty dollars a week paid as a reimbursement for transportation and lunches. You want it?"

Another day holding my own battling bullies in the schoolyard ends with a job possibility, an escape from Brooklyn. I feel like a hundred dollars just entered my pocket, which is a lot in my mind.

"Yes, I'm very interes…"

"Stop by my office and we'll talk. 246 West 44th Street, above the St. James Theatre. See you Friday at 10."

The years at Bishop Ford High School prepare me for this privilege. The Guidance Counselor praises the opportunity to work for a Broadway producer. He suggests I do it for nothing.

We Catholics are sacrificial experts.

We do great theatre at school. *Hamlet, Danton's Death, The Lottery, A View from the Bridge.* We leave *Gypsy* and *Annie Get Your Gun* to the public schools nearby. I make my way to Manhattan.

The F train rolls into the station, its screeching wheels screaming its arrival. I can tell when a Manhattan-bound train is approaching by how it blocks the daylight emanating from the tunnel entrance. The odor of axle grease from the braking train fills the station. Passengers queue up for entry. Once inside, rows of wide, four-panel fans propel stale air downward, undoing structured coiffures and waving silk blouse collars like a flag on a windy day. I enter the mix of perfumes, deodorants, newspapers, and sweat as the doors whoosh closed with a final slam.

The jelly doughnuts from Barbera's Bakery began to bleed through the thin, brown paper bag. Dark, oily splotches overtake the package. I need to consume or trash them before the interview.

The train increases in speed, shoving and colliding its occupants. As it exits Jay Street, the last station before Manhattan, I wrap my right arm around the center pole and proceed to open the bag. The powdered sugar, the jelly doughnut, and the bag have become one. It takes both hands to dismember the pastry from the bag. Successful at last, I bring the messy breakfast to my mouth and take a bite. The doughnut collapses, and the bite frees a good section but squirts jelly onto my sleeve, a button on my coat, and a final dollop explodes on the floor of the train in full view of passengers. They look up for a moment, acknowledge the mess that I am making of myself, then return to reading their newspapers, communicating their disdain with a gesture. I have no paper napkins in the bag of doughnuts. I think of how my father takes this same subway. I remember the white handkerchief ever present in his breast pocket. I have no handkerchief. I rip a page from the financial section of *The New York Times,* a section I never read and hardly understand, and rip the largest section possible without losing my grasp of the newspaper and the oily bag. I do this while balancing myself against the push and pull of this subway slalom. The train hurtles and rocks under the five-minute run under the East River like the mechanical horse race at Steeplechase Park. Lurching and swaying violently, its turns threaten to derail the train from the tracks. The underground turbulence challenges numerous attempts to wipe the jelly off my sleeve and coat button with the torn newspaper. I achieve partial success. The dark spot remaining on my shirt sleeve dries up without an obvious stain. Wiping the button is more difficult. The topside smear comes off easily, thanks to its enameled surface. It is the underside and the immediate surface of the coat under the button, a tan, faux suede zippered field jacket, which seems to ingest the blood red raspberry hue of Santo Barbera's doughnut creation.

It looks permanently stained, staring back at me like a badge of poor manners.

The F train arrives at the 42nd Street station of the 8th Avenue subway. I disembark, search for a trash can on the platform, and discard the remainder of the doughnut bag, which now resembles a well-used baseball glove. I discard the torn newspaper as well, using it to wipe as much of the grease and sticky residue of the drying jelly from my fingers. I think of taking off the jacket to hide the stain that hardens during the ride. It is too late to do anything about my sleeve. I hope for the best.

    I notice a massive vertical sign protruding from one of the buildings as I climb the last steps out of the subway. The structure's architectural style characterizes nearly every Broadway theatre built in the beginning decades of the 20th century. I see it in its entirety as I reach the street level of the subway exit at 44th Street. Thirty-watt incandescent bulbs inside the recesses of the three-foot tall letters spelling out *St. James Theatre* chase furiously around every letter like *Langoliers* eating up space and evoking a carnival midway in midtown Manhattan. *Hello, Dolly,* a long-running hit. Signage boasts rave reviews visible on every available space of the façade. Above the marquee, way above the stage house, are the offices of Broadway producer David Merrick.

    I notice Merrick's enormous 1962 Chrysler Imperial in front of the lobby entrance of the theatre. His familiar vehicle is in the newspapers for every Broadway show opening. No other theatre producer sports such a blatant expression of showmanship in their transportation. The automobile's huge rear fins make it seem capable of flight if driven fast enough. The garish building exterior and flamboyant vehicle in front of it warns me to be cautious. This is not Brooklyn. Manhattan plays for keeps. I walk into the small lobby and press a brass button polished by daily use. A dim light is seen through the dark, circular window of one of the panels of the lobby elevator doors. The burnished triple sliding doors collapse to reveal an even smaller cage occupied by an elderly operator. Cigar stub in mouth, he harrumphs and clears his throat simultaneously.

    "Where you goin'?"

"I have an appointment with the general manager for David Merrick."

The elevator operator telegraphs his expectation at the outcome of this meeting. *Here comes another one that will bite the dust*, he seems to imply.

"8th floor. Get in."

I enter and ride the tiny passenger elevator as it slowly clears the access doors for each floor by inches. Graffiti etchings grace the separations between floors, revealing dates and initials commemorating openings and closings of shows long forgotten. The elevator operator pulls back on the brass lever that controls the speed of elevation, finally stopping just short of the eighth floor. He plays with the lever, bumping the cab up a few inches until it reaches the proper level. The old codger is a pro. He nails it, landing the elevator cab even with the floor level. He pulls the steel-mesh slider allowing access to the eighth-floor door panels. He presses on the cantilevered bar causing the three panels of the access doors to fold into a single panel. I exit and walk over to the reception desk attendant to introduce myself. Clean, *Helvetica* block lettering adorns the window of the reception booth identifying the entrance as the *Offices of David Merrick*. Just getting to this level seems an achievement. Fresh from a drama club stage manager job and only a junior in high school, here I am in Manhattan, showing up for my big opportunity for $20.00 a week at the biggest producing office on Broadway. Only Alexander Cohen, whose office is just across the street above the Shubert Theatre, comes close to the importance of David Merrick's show production capacity. During the time I spend there, Merrick never has less than four shows on Broadway and five companies touring on the road. Cohen, his closest competitor, has one, maybe two shows, but he has the Tony Awards, the most prestigious event in the theatre.

I greet the receptionist, noticing the wisps of auburn hair dancing around her earrings. She radiates an elegant, sensual aura. Her starched, turned-up collar frames gentle slopes formed by timeless cheekbones. Her spectacular smile provokes a dizzying invitation to return in kind.

"Hello, I'm Sylvia. Are you John? Go down the hall on your right and enter the second door on your left. Mr. Schlissel is expecting you."

Sylvia is the second *Sylvia* I know. The first one is my friend's older sister and a high school senior. The name is synonymous with sexy.

"Thank you," I mutter, and proceed down the hall. I imagine this new Sylvia on my journey. The thought conjures up a whole concert of responses returning me to my adolescent demeanor.

I walk into a second archway, which contains two doors to more inner offices. The one on the left is open, and inside I see an impressive wall of oak shelving, a black, lacquered antique desk, a black leather chair, and everywhere else the warming embrace of blood red. The velvet couch, the walls, the carpet are all red. The phone is red. I am surprised to learn that there exists this other red phone. I only know of the original being in the Situation Room of the White House. The one that can set off a nuclear war. Both share a similar urgency.

Around the volumes on the shelves stand an intimidating number of Tony Awards luxuriating on the shelves like satisfied and confident predators resting after pursuit of their prey. Here lives the Winner's Circle, the laurel wreaths of a theatrical gladiator victorious in the colosseum games of Broadway. David Merrick is the defining Broadway impresario, the last of a dying breed of individual Broadway producers, manager of over 100 Broadway productions. I appreciate getting this eyeful before meeting the man personally. Sylvia is still on my mind. All these seismic experiences are occurring way too rapidly to fully take them all in.

Finishing off the décor are numerous plaques and proclamations of theatrical achievement. Drama Critics Circle Awards, Hirschfeld drawings, commemorative cups, trays, coins, medals, and pins crowd the extension. Over the liquid black sheen of a baby grand piano hangs a portrait of a dancer, leaning against a stool. She wears a red leotard with red ballet shoes. No one occupies the empty room. Garish becomes classy in this room that celebrates the seedy attraction of theatrical life. I wonder if I will ever meet a dancer in my life who looks like the dancer in the painting.

To the right, a more reasonable and less presentational décor graces the general manager's office. At least that is the impression I have until I fully enter. Opposite his desk, Jack Schlissel has an axe hanging on the wall painted with a representation of blood dripping from the sharp end. Next to this macabre wall art hangs a black and white photograph of an actress posing by a baby grand piano. She reveals more than I can handle, draped in a see-through teddy and assuming an alluring pose. It is autographed with a note that promises devotion and pleasure and invites the most sensuous of fantasies. Votive candles do not work here.

What an iniquitous den I enter. How delightful. The cautious jaunt in my mind suddenly flies away like a popped balloon interrupted by a forceful, throaty introduction.

"I'm Jack Schlissel, general manager. So, you wanna work here?"

"Hello, yes. I'm John."

I am too intimidated to hear myself pronounce my last name for fear of bollixing it up.

"I want to be a stage manager, on Broadway."

I am surprised by the clear, bottom-line delivery of my intentions. I wait for a reaction, feeling every moment of continued silence eroding my newfound *chutzpa*.

Jack frowns a bit, sits back in his executive chair, which shows more wear on the end of the seat than on the back. His phone rings. He excuses himself, sits up, and begins a conversation with the caller on the other end.

Show business negotiations are just a touch classier than street-corner drug deals of 1960s New York. The conversation is in shorthand, in a coded language known only to the participants and filled with equations.

"Two points after recoupment."

"I'll give you two for one after a grand."

"Minimum at preshow, ten percent at opening."

Jack spends most of the phone conversation on the edge of his seat, with one hand on the phone receiver, the other grasping a pencil and furiously running numbers on a scratchpad as he negotiates. A moist, burned-out *Schimmelpenninck* sits between his teeth, which gives his responses a tight, sharp flavor.

"What? You are fucking crazy! No deal!"

Jack hangs up, sits back in his chair, apparently satisfied with the outcome of the phone conversation. He looks back at me. I hope I have not revealed my terror in witnessing the phone conversation.

"You'll have to buy coffee every day, collect box office statements from seven theatres beginning on 52nd Street and work your way downtown. You will also have to file contracts, deliver packages to other offices, and keep the stationery closet neat and stocked. You know your way around town?"

I assure him I am thoroughly familiar with the area. I have never been here before, but I figure numbered streets on a grid should not be too difficult.

"Absolutely, been here many times."

Jake's smirk spills into a laugh.

"Okay, you got the job. You start Monday. Be here at ten a.m. with a black Sanka and a toasted bialy."

I am elated.

"Thanks. I'll see you on Monday."

As I prepare to exit his office, Jack interrupts.

"Hey kid, do you know why you got the job?"

I shake my head, too insecure to say anything.

"You said you want to manage. The others want to act. I hate actors. Don't screw up."

I nod in agreement as if it is a shared philosophy, half smiling, and walk out the door. I reverse my route exactly to prevent myself from getting lost. I have never heard of a bialy and do not have the slightest idea of what it is. I suspect it is some inner-sanctum kosher treat that former altar boys would never need or experience, but I will surely find out before Monday. I take a trip on Sunday to Hester Street to investigate the bialy. I am in show business for real.

As a staff associate, I execute every clerical and administrative whim of the general manager, the producer, the producer's secretary, and the stream of stage managers that run Merrick's eight Broadway shows. I run from theatre to theatre, collecting receipts, box office statements, visiting banks to deposit checks, delivering contracts to affluent directors and choreographers that have addresses on Sutton Place, Fifth Avenue, and Central Park West.

Every Friday, I make my rounds cashing a $500 check for Merrick and purchasing a bus ticket to Danbury for Jack. The cash is Merrick's weekly pocket money, the ticket for Jack's indiscretions.

Jack sports a smirking, disbelieving sneer that always seems to threaten a confrontation. I steer clear of approaching him directly, especially after one of his contentious phone calls with an agent or attorney. Perennially courting a *Schimmelpenninck* only makes his approachability even more distant. The gruff, tough, theatrical wise guy demeanor forms an outwardly impenetrable machismo. Nothing in his actions at work ever suggests the reasons behind his trips to Danbury.

Jack needs to get away to the countryside to pursue his life without ramification.

This is the late 60s where one's proclivities are one's business, not Twitter's.

I assume he travels to see his mother every other weekend.

I become friends with nearly every stage manager who works for Merrick's shows. I make myself available for their copying and collating needs whenever I can. One stage manager favors me and allows me to help him run auditions at Variety Arts Rehearsal Studios on 46th Street, a rundown walkup that had seen better days as a vaudeville dance club in the 1920s. I hang out backstage during a performance while he manages the show. Charles Blackwell, a towering, bearded African American man, the only stage manager of color I know, is the Production Stage Manager of Merrick's latest hit musical, *Promises, Promises*,

I am a 16-year-old kid from Brooklyn who knows little about theatre history. The theatre is a sophisticated luxury, and I have no idea of its cultural significance. I see a backstage filled with people having a great time working on a story with music. The theatre is a make-believe factory, and I want to join in on the fun.

Charlie asks if I want to help him. He may as well have asked if I want $15 million dollars, a chauffeured limousine, and an unlimited supply of Devil Dogs.

"Are you serious?"

"Yeah, I need some help at auditions. Ever been to an audition?"

I lie. "Oh sure, a hundred times."

Charlie smiles. He knows better, but he loves my enthusiasm and courage.

"Great. I'll see you at 10:00 a.m. tomorrow at Variety Arts."

No money, no fancy transportation, but I get the chance to run an audition.

Charles Blackwell makes smoking Salem Menthols literally cool. He lives in a Harlem that is real and not gentrified. He is intuitive, engaging, supportive. He makes me feel like a pro. Charlie is the man I want to be. He is a decision maker, a problem solver with a great sense of humor. Charlie has style, intelligence, and leadership. He would be a good father.

My job is to sign in female dancers auditioning for replacement positions in *Promises, Promises*. I prepare my clipboard, check my watch. The dancers begin arriving. After a few minutes the dressing area, they emerge in an array of breathtaking color and form. The olfactory dance of clashing perfumes is just a warm-up act. This type of exposure proves to be borderline dangerous and eminently uncontrollable. There is no place where my eyes can gaze upon the group without churning my inclinations.

I barely concentrate. This is not a good position in which to find myself. I am the original wallflower from Brooklyn, New York. I create a distance to hide my insecurity around everyone I meet, especially young women. Catholic grammar schools do not teach respect as much as denial, and I am trying to catch up as best I can. I cannot say no to them, and they know it. Charlie instructs me to announce the names of those dancers asked to stay for another round of auditions and dismiss the rest by thanking them. I do not have the courage to do this, so I tell the unannounced girls to go to the back of the line and audition again. I suddenly acquire a dozen potential girlfriends, all five to ten years older than me. What is not to like about that? Charlie realizes what I had done. He pulls me over.

"Johnny, there's a way to say no. Watch me."

"Ladies, thank you all for coming. We will keep all your resumes for further consideration. Meanwhile, will the following please remain to ensure we have your current contact information."

Charlie reads the list of those dancers who were still being considered.

"We will be in touch with all of you within the week. Everyone one else is free to go, and we will be contacting you."

Charlie delivers an ounce of *no* mixed in with a ton of encouragement. That is a special talent, a part of his character. Charlie's demeanor and accessible style inspires me. I do not forget this day. Charles Blackwell becomes a mentor, the standard bearer of effective management.

Merrick's smash musical of the 1964-65 Broadway season, *Hello Dolly*, is showing signs of box office weakness. Rather than reduce ticket prices or even close the show, Merrick recasts the show with all African American performers, with Pearl Bailey and Cab Calloway in the lead roles. It is 1967 at the height of racial tensions in New York, and the decision could have had disastrous results. The Broadway theatre is elitist and segregated, and this ingenious act opens a whole new market and interest in theatre for an underserved group of potential theatregoers. Society is changing and the racial and economic crises of this era affects all aspects of life, especially in places like New York where diversity is publicly acclaimed but privately avoided.

It is a brilliant stroke. It rejuvenates an aging show, and Pearl Bailey wins a Tony Award in 1968 for her performance.

The recasting is noticed nationally, and Pearl Bailey is invited to the White House as a guest of honor. There is one issue. On her way she decides that she needs her fur coat, which is in storage at Van Cleef & Arpels on Fifth Avenue in New York. She arrives in Washington, D.C. on Friday at noon, and the state dinner is that evening.

The reception desk phone rings. I pick up and offer the usual salutation.

"David Merrick's office, how can I help you?"

It is David Merrick.

"This is Mr. Merrick. I need to arrange to have Ms. Bailey's fur coat delivered to her in Washington."

"Yes, of course, Mr. Merrick."

How am I going to do *that*? I begin to look up messenger services thinking I have this under control. What an opportunity. Show the Broadway impresario what I'm made of.

"Mr. Merrick, I have a list of messen…"

"Get Jack on the phone."

So much for golden opportunities for advancement.

I have become an expert at operating a 555 PBX telephone exchange desk with long, rubberized cords that connect outgoing and incoming calls to office extensions. It is a classic setting for a Lucille Ball comedy routine. The wrong cord inserted into the wrong extension can have two people who wanted to avoid one another forced into a conversation they do not want to have. When multiple calls come in for the same person, I hold all the incoming cords in one hand, making a mental note of who is on which cord, using my other hand to screen the calls to the person on the extension, and based upon who the extension caller wants to talk to, inserting the right cord into the right recipient extension. I return to the remainder of the unconnected cords holding phone calls and manage their impatience.

I plug Mr. Merrick into Jack's extension. Five minutes passes. I notice the extension light going off, indicating the end of the phone call. Jack buzzes me.

"Johnny, come into the office. Ever been to Washington?"

"Sure. On an eighth-grade trip with Franciscan Brothers."

I remember Washington from a Columbus Day field trip for high-achieving eighth graders. *High achieving* meant I could write, add, and subtract without embarrassment. On the trip, I and the three other smart friends share a room and notice that an all-girls high school group is also at the hotel. We feel committed to the mission that these girls should not experience our nation's capital unescorted. We try to fill that need. We are caught on their hotel floor. We are the only ones escorted right out of the hotel, with the admonition that if we are ever caught in this town again, we will be prosecuted. That is a big word for a high schooler. I hope they do not remember me. Jack continues the conversation.

"You're going on an important errand for Mr. Merrick."

Jack arranges for me to pick up the fur coat, take a cab to Penn Station, and board an Amtrak train leaving NY Penn Station at 1:35 p.m. I arrive at Union Station at 5:45 p.m. As I am walking down the train platform, I am greeted by two men in suits who mention my name. I respond to them and confirm who I am. They escort me into a sedan and drive me to the main gate of the Nixon White House.

Secret Service agents have a limited vocabulary.

A U.S. Capitol Police officer waves us on at the south gate of the White House after a brief inspection of the Van Cleef & Arpels box. I stand on the top step of the main portico. An elegantly dressed lady approaches me with a smile and introduces herself. The cultured pearls around her neck seem more a statement of class than fashion. I imagine Washington, D.C. to be a huge library with the White House a giant history book standing on a shelf. I am too overwhelmed with the experience to remember her name. She thanks me then proceeds to take the box away from me. I hold on to the box.

"Sorry, ma'am, but I have specific instructions to give this box only to Miss Bailey. She knows who I am."

She looks at me for a moment. I am anticipating a brisk, curt dismissal of my claim, but she concedes.

"Very well." She turns, smiles, then walks away until I can no longer see her. Minutes later, the familiar Miss Bailey strides past the Secret Service agents and staff attendants and extends her arm toward me. She gives me a warm embrace and greeting.

"Hi, honey, you are a doll for doing this. I will see you back at the theatre. You get home safe now." She takes the box, offers another hug, and leaves. I return to the car and eventually to Union Station for the return trip. I feel I have completed my mission.

Early Saturday morning, I go to work to report to Jack on the trip.

"Everything go okay?" Jack was having his morning *Shimmelpennick* with a toasted bialy and a black Sanka. I wonder who bought it for him.

"Yes, I delivered the fur coat directly to Miss Bailey. Her dresser wanted to take it, but I told her I needed it give it to Miss Bailey personally."

"Dresser? What dresser? I didn't send a dresser. I never approved a dresser. Who was it?"

"I think she said her name was Pearl. I never met her before."

Jack is silent for a moment.

"Wait. Do you mean Perle *Mesta*?"

"Yeah, that could be it. She was nicely dressed, pleasant. Walked around like she knew the place."

"Bonanni, don't ever change. I love your innocence."

I learn Perle Mesta is no dresser. She is the premier Washington, D.C. socialite who manages and controls society parties, special events, and political get togethers for three administrations and served as the U.S. Ambassador to Luxembourg. She never pulls her well-earned rank. I admire her for the way that she handles my resolve to complete my mission. I learn the meaning of graciousness. Perle Mesta is a true class act.

I take the summer off to prepare for freshman year at Queens College. More girls, more plays. In the fall, I am required to take an acting class and as a result I am cast as Abraham Van Helsing in a futuristic version of Dracula. I am an 18-year-old playing a 65-year-old with an accent. My father's fractured pronunciations come in handy. In costume and make up I resemble Lon Chaney, thanks to my father. I am relieved the role fulfills the requirement for any more acting classes. The theatre is a comfortable environment for me and helps in my adjustment when my father succumbs to cardiovascular disease a year before my graduation. I resent my father's sudden death more than grieve for his passing. There is no fancy get together of relatives and friends over a coffin. Few show up for the wake. Refreshments are limited to coffee and muffins. The coffin is plain. The whole experience feels like a damp, grey, endless morning I hope disappears. Fatigue sets in. The familiar disillusionment returns. Disappointment surfaces. I feel abandoned again, but I am used to it. I feel relief in a strange way.

The bottle of *Canadian Club* looks at me from the shelf of the Pioneer Pub, just across the Long Island Expressway from the Queens College campus in Flushing, NY. The brown liquid for grownups. Not chocolate milk. To be spilled down my throat, not on my shirt. It is a forbidden drink. A potentially lethal indulgence. The one that might thrash my brain into unconsciousness. *What difference will it make now, anyway,* I think.

Janis Joplin is on the radio.
Freedom's just another word for nothing left to lose…

It is time. Loss is so liberating. My father's memory is fading but he is still here. I control my destiny just like he did in his own life.

I order a whisky.

I inhale it. It smells like fuel. I think I will be on fire if I light it. I take a sip, waiting for that swirling darkness that precedes the shutdown of caring. It feels exhilarating, breathy. I take another sip. It goes down easier, a bitter caramel. I look around. Things look blurry, but I am still aware of my surroundings. I finish the drink, and order another. I am an expert now, an official drinker. I can say, *I can hold my liquor.* I feel relaxed, in good humor. I am still conscious. I am my own normal.

Maybe my father's prayer book worked. Maybe the rules do not matter anymore.

Complimenti papà, hai fatto bene a me. You have done well, my father, by me.

Working for a Broadway producer, even at $20.00 a week, brings accomplishment to my show business aspirations. I meet people I would have little chance to meet otherwise. Merrick is responsible for my first Broadway job as a stage manager. Almost 120 miles northeast, Michael P. Price, the Executive Director of the Goodspeed Opera House, hawks the first of three productions for the 1975 season. It is a 1913 Jerome Kern musical called "Very Good Eddie," and it intrigues Merrick. Price specializes in producing a string of light, boy-meets-girl concoctions that are the standard fare for the little theatre. It seems all the musicals take place in the 1920s-30s and usually feature escapades of wealthy café society playboys shuttling between a Manhattan penthouse and an East Hampton estate.

A poor working girl character, usually a maid or seamstress, is introduced into the plot and eventually captures the love interest of the society cad. The servant-class girl bests the playboy's self-centered society girlfriend and wins the heart of the cad to live happily ever as one of the newly minted, flippant rich. The difference, of course, is that her big heart is deserving of her newly acquired wealth, and that fact is used to mount a closing production number with the full cast onstage as a happy ending to the show. That is the predominant theme of dramatic product at Goodspeed.

Very Good Eddie is optioned by David Merrick for a Broadway engagement. Merrick hires me as the Second Assistant Stage Manager. I receive my Actors Equity identification card, which is a momentous achievement, much like being born. I am thrilled at the title of a job that includes every task the Production Stage Manager and First Assistant Stage Manager does not want to do. But being any level assistant on a Broadway show is the reason why I live, so I embrace the opportunity. I manage paperwork, collect everyone's wallets and purses for safekeeping and record the administrative activities of managing the show.

I would mop the toilets of the Port Authority Bus Terminal for free to get this job.

I sign the one-page agreement. Emblazoned at the top of the page in ostentatious font are the words "Actor's Equity Association, Standard Minimum Production Contract." The formality of the document looks like a boiler plate for the Magna Carta. The agreement begins with "Witnesseth, this day of." This is a contract for $280.00 a week. I am surprised the contract is not printed on calfskin vellum and delivered by a tunic-clad messenger claiming liege to the Crown.

Being a staff associate from the Merrick office, the Production Stage Manager of *Very Good Eddie* suspects I am a spy and finds every reason to prevent me from assimilating into the show.

My interaction with the acting company develops reliance, trust, and an opportunity for socialization. Friendships are cultivated. Camaraderie flourishes. I fall in love a hundred times because of costumes. Coiffed hair graces alabaster shoulders, form-fitting bustiers, eyelashes highlighting lingering eyes, cheeks of blush. I am working in a wild, attractive environment away from the worry of an unfair world. In the words of Ebenezer Scrooge on Christmas morning when he realizes that he is indeed still alive, "I don't *deserve* to be this happy!" enters my mind. I want to spend a lifetime here.

Six months later, the set is loaded out of the Booth Theatre on the northwest corner of 45th Street and Shubert Alley. I need another show and quickly. Opportunity has a way of standing right behind you. All it asks is for you to turn around, but quickly. Michael Price is a frequent backstage visitor to the show during its run at the Booth. A slim, wiry man with a stiff-bristled, push broom mustache, he is an irksome joke poker. Michael looks for the angle, the edge, the best bargain, the steal. He basks in his name being boxed on the lower portion of the show card acknowledging him as the original producer of the show. The *Impresario of East Haddam, Connecticut* plays David to the Broadway Goliath. Beyond his well-rehearsed affability, he is a closer. He hobnobs with Broadway managers and producers. I hear of his tumultuous encounters with the Shuberts, the Nederlanders, the Gershwin Estate. Merrick's general manager, Jack Schlissel, avoids his phone calls. To the cast, his accessibility never lets them forget where they got their present job. Stagehands are annoyed by his recurring visits.

Michael is my next boss.

JUST OFF, STAGE RIGHT

In March, after 304 performances on Broadway and a brief national tour, *Very Good Eddie* closes in February 1977. Michael offers me a job as First Assistant Stage Manager at Goodspeed for the upcoming season. Broadway runs do not last forever. This is a promotion, despite a summer stock environment. I accept his offer knowing this may be a career-altering decision. Leaving the game of Broadway job musical chairs is dangerous unless you know where your next Broadway show is coming from. There are no other alternatives. I face a summer of unemployment if I do not take this job. There is nothing like being unemployed in the summer in New York. It is as uncomfortable as a sticky subway seat in a stalled uptown local on a humid afternoon. In New York, there is no relief, only endurance.

I board an Amtrak train to East Haddam, Connecticut, for the summer. It is April 4, 1977. I have no indication the train ride would change the course of my life.

I want to make a good first impression. I wear the only suit I own. The navy-blue velour goes well with the paisley tie and mustard shirt. It is the late 1970s and looking like a singing lounge lizard from a casino sidebar is the fashionable statement to which I aspire. I sit across the train aisle from this girl deep in conversation with two other passengers in a four-seater. I cannot see the others, but I can see and hear her incessantly. I watch her for a half-hour. The vantage point of an aisle seat provides a recurring view of her swinging blond hair slapping against her cheekbones. She never stops talking from the time I notice her. There is no conversation from the others. They are listening to her monologue. Her flailing cigarette is always in motion but never inhaled. She deftly maneuvers the burning stick of tobacco in concert with impassioned gestures of the hand holding it, leaving art forms floating in the air with a smoky blue hue, only to be redrawn by the clamor emanating from her hand movements. Constant conversation with herself and anyone within earshot continues throughout the train ride, interrupted only by intermittent trips to the restroom. I wonder if the reason for the restroom trips is a call of nature or a need to hide.

Perhaps she is just another theatrical personality who cannot stop looking at herself. I want to be her mirror.

While she uses the restroom, my mind wanders. I imagine a lake of graceful swans paddling in unison. Their feathered, white bodies glimmering from the morning sun. They coast in an ordered, demure fashion. Suddenly, the cacophonic sound of a domestic, yellow-billed duck screaming its head off makes its presence known from the weeds. The loud beautiful bird closes in toward me and I embrace it. I run my hand over its feathers to comfort it, only to be met with more quacking. Eventually, the quacking duck settles down in my mind.

The girl returns to her four-seater. I notice her companions call her Carol Ann.

If she dropped the *Ann* I could live with that name.

Chapter 3

The Bohemian Princess with Five Birth Certificates

There is no experience like Carol.

She is at the top of her game. Despite the constrained space of a four-seat enclosure on a Metroliner Express to Boston, she pulls out all the tricks of her acting trade, posing and positioning her face and body in the best light, moving her shoulders to accentuate every available charming angle. Carol is working the room, and it is working well. Her entourage giggles and gasps accordingly as if a starlet is in their midst.

Carol takes a quick breath before resuming her monologue of the last audition experience. She notices me taking investigative sneak peeks at her. My views are met with dismissive, animated looks away, suggesting total disregard for any attention I offer. My poor choice to wear a heavy, midnight-blue velour suit in springtime only confirms my social incompetence. I wish I learned how to manage this boy/girl approach better. I feel like a ripe, fuzzy plum.

I surmise through this hour-long eavesdropping that Carol is on her way to Goodspeed Opera House as well. She is a dancer/singer/actor from the Chicagoland dinner theatre circuit. Some of the venues are quite shady if I am to believe the stories I overhear. She claims to be a mezzo soprano, though her speaking voice sports a course, throaty tone. She speaks as if she has a five-page curriculum vitae of performing arts milestones. These achievements, I discover later, include back up singing for Telly Savalas' Who Loves You, Baby?" club act on weekends in between weekly filming of his *Kojack* TV series. Telly was no singer. He talked thru each song with a lollipop in hand. That is the part that intrigues me about Carol. I am attracted to chorus girls who evoke mystique by talking about limos on weekends and carrying their character shoes in a plastic bag from D'Agostino's during the week.

When we disembark from the train in Old Saybrook, I find her suitcase and help her with it. She thanks me in a way that indicates annoyance. I place it in the rear of the commuter van dispatched from the theatre to meet new hires, and she takes the last remaining back seat, forcing me to sit in the front. I am relieved to be working but now perturbed that this person seems too distracted to notice my interest. But I am thrilled we share a common destination.

The cast of *Sweet Adeline*, a 1929 Jerome Kern musical kicking off Goodspeed's summer fare, assembles onstage for rehearsal the next morning. Carol's preoccupation with her shoulders is a natural extension of her ability to telegraph her talent. In rehearsal, she stands out and maneuvers those shoulders to gain notice, and she maintains a vibrancy that flows from her personality. She is not acknowledging me. She does not return the depth of distraction I am developing for her. I busy myself with increasing the visibility of my importance when she is in the room. I check the resiliency of the dance floor right near her on a regular basis. She has something different to say about it every time I ask. There is a soft spot here, a popped nail there. Her complaints are endless, her presence disrupting and comforting. I do not want to leave her side.

Then there are the leg warmers. They flop and fold, lazily caressing her ankles. They have a girl scent of things sweet and spicy, always evocative of the last social encounter, even between washings. Being around dancers is like walking the main floor of every old-style department store at Christmas time, where crashing scents of floral and evergreen stir in the wake of every aisle. Dancers are like moving flowers, pushing the air, and those with whom you are falling in love are forever fragrant.

After fits, starts, floor creak complaints, shortened break times, and other games of evasion and coercion, Carol and I succumb to the inevitable. Walking her home one night from the theatre, I stop at the front door of her boarding house, look into her eyes, and ask, "Can we get this over with?"

Very romantic, I think.

I kiss her, and we never look back. The kiss does not have any of the usual attributes related to the moon, the stars, fireworks, or electricity. It is warm and familiar, natural, expected. It is about time, a comforting acclimation of a fact that seems to already be known to both of us.

"Alrighty then, that was nice," she offers.

A torrent of doubt sends me spinning. There is no part of me that does not feel inept. By now, I assume my ability to curry favor like a Don Juan, to be an expert, seasoned master of pursuit is my delusional fantasy. But the reality of that first kiss presents itself in a cool, distanced response from this shaky date.

A few moments pass, and I gather the remaining bits of my self-esteem to return the best response I can.

"Nice? Well, I don't think I'll ever forget that answer. I'm standing here overwhelmed by the moment, and you call it nice?"

"Well, it was a nice kiss. Really."

Her reaction is so matter of fact, so observational, like she is evaluating a new brand of yogurt. I think she invented the term *brutally honest*. Maybe now I am looking for the moon, the stars, the fireworks, the electricity. I expect something that would have indicated this is an experience that sets the stage for further exploration. A little blush on the cheek would do nicely right now, or perhaps a nervous laugh. I get nothing. She just looks at me, tells her story, and waits there, looking at me for a response or to do something.

Like I know what to do. I attempt to manage the moment.

"Look, if that's all you think there is to that moment, then maybe we should just move on, ok?"

"No, wait! Don't get so emotional. You guys get so crazy over nothing."

You guys get so crazy, I discover later, alludes to her experience with Italian boys in her Bohemian neighborhood whom she wants to date but is prevented by her father to pursue.

"You know, they have a temper, those Italians," her father warns during her high school years. Italian families are the unwelcome intrusion into her reclusive childhood Czech neighborhood. But those sons of Italy are far more exciting to Carol than any Bohemian high school jock. Tawny outdoes bland for adventurous blondes.

I recall my Neapolitan neighbor Pasquale Battista having enough of his common-law wife's complaints and hurling a coffee table out the apartment window below after a Sunday afternoon dinner. To his credit, he chooses the coffee table to vent his anger. Her father has a point.

"Come on, kiss me again." She put her arms around me.

When her lips touch mine, I do nothing. Inside, I sulk. A wall of resistance remains impenetrable for as long as I can bear.

It lasts 10 seconds.

"Kissy, kissy, come on," she sweet-talks like a little girl asking for one more of anything.

I relent, especially when she giggles. Suddenly, Carol is the girl in her home movie aggressively kissing her favorite doll. There is no reason left to resist crossing the ego-driven Rubicon I create. This time, a future surfaces beyond her front door. In the span of six minutes, we kiss, argue, make up, kiss again, and never part.

It feels like we have been doing this forever. The right thing to do. The way things should be. We leave the moon and the stars to the heavens. Looking into each other's eyes is enough.

Carol spends only one third of the season at the Goodspeed Opera House. Following the four-week run of *Sweet Adeline*, she is cast in the Broadway production of *A Chorus Line* in New York, and we spend the next year and a half dating with 120 miles between us.

Goodspeed pays the rent. For the next five summers, I stage manage 14 versions of the boy-meets-girl plot. Hundreds of love songs by Gershwin, Kern, Arlen, Porter, Berlin, Hart, and Hammerstein are performed on the tiny 26-foot-wide stage.

The 1978 Goodspeed summer season continues the tradition of presenting light musicals of Americana. Carol is on Broadway, onstage seven nights a week at the Shubert Theatre performing in the theatrical event of the decade, and her Sunday day off and my Monday day off allows for Sunday evening dinner, an overnight stay, and a Monday morning breakfast. I-95 becomes an integral part of our relationship. I think of it fondly, especially since I am never on it anymore.

Things change again when *Whoopee*, a Gus Kahn musical revival, is optioned for a Broadway run. The original show opened at the New Amsterdam Theatre in 1928 and ran for 407 performances. This inspires Michael Price, the entrepreneur of the regionals, to again seek the fame and glory of Broadway. He hires Frank Corsaro, a premier opera and stage director, to mount *Whoopee*, a light, innocuous 1927 Eddie Cantor musical. Frank is a compact, bombastic individual who directs the tinny musical comedy like he approaches *Madama Butterfly* at the Metropolitan Opera House. In the tradition of Goodspeed's penchant for despotism, Frank's statuesque, buxom, blond wife is cast in the lead. Her talent is, in a most courteous and considerate view, primarily visual. The show is scheduled out of town to test audience reaction. Our first stop is at the American Theatre in St. Louis, an aging venue languishing in a deteriorating neighborhood of downtown St. Louis. A snowstorm delays one of the three trucks carrying scenic elements. The late truck carries the decking, or flooring under which the automation system is housed that moves scenic elements on and off stage. It consists of a series of winches, cables, and pulleys, which need to be installed first before anything else can be added. This reconditioned and recertified set for *Whoopee*, originally built by technical apprentices at Goodspeed, sits frozen in three 53-foot semis outside the theatre. Across the street, the Sheraton caters to a particular clientele. Roadies and truckers make the hotel a pit stop between Indianapolis and Kansas City. The spam fries at the coffee shop is worth the danger of crossing the street.

 Carol is alone in New York, and I am alone in St. Louis. I miss her ability to reassure me, to dismiss the doubt of whether this working arrangement is worth the effort. St. Louis is listed as a theatre town but that is an urban amenity from another time. The color and excitement of a theatrical event seems faded and worn here.

The truck carrying the decking arrives eight hours late, delaying the load-in schedule and forcing an all-night installation of the scenery. The scenery load-in is completed by 5:00 p.m. of the opening performance day. I do not have an opportunity to rehearse scenic transitions or individual moves, and we start the show without knowing the outcome. The show does not run well. The highlight of the disastrous evening is the uncontrolled speed with which two rolling units travel across the stage. Two units of wooden galloping horses track across the stage with six actors straddled over the units. Both race across the stage at twice the speed and crash offstage into the wings off stage right. Luckily, the actors are shaken but not seriously injured. The resounding noise produces unexpected applause. This is musical comedy, and the expectation to stage comic moments with falls and crashes is usually received with laughter and applause as if it were part of the action. Backstage, after clearing the debris, we race to set up the next scene that includes two tracked palettes with bar tables and four chairs. They are programmed to stop just short of center stage. I call the winch cue to initiate the move. The units track on but pass each other beyond their intended destinations and continued to move off to the opposite offstage sides. Charles Repole, the lead actor, offers me a frantic look of fear from center stage as the tables saunter past him. I have stagehands grab the tables and chairs and walk them back onstage to their intended positions and we continue. Problems large and small occur with nearly every scene throughout the performance. Managing this show is like running a triage in a theatrical disaster. This is hit or miss theatre. A technical rehearsal the following day clears up the shortcomings, and we settle down to an uneventful run.

I think of how Carol, back in New York, basks in a sold-out house every night dancing at the Shubert Theatre, performing in a production with simple scenery that does not upstage her performance with technical complications. *A Chorus Line* is the theatrical hit of the season, the hottest ticket with the hippest musical score. Everyone hums the simple, memorable tunes. The whole world is in love with Broadway dancers, sympathetic to their plight, and this production galvanizes the trials and hopes of a dancing career in the theatre like no other production before it. The set is simple. A bare stage accommodates a dance bag and a resume for every dancer onstage, and a set of six tall mirrors set on a periaktoi base providing three different looks: a wall of mirrors, a black cyclorama, and a dazzling gold reveal for the finale. Carol walks on stage and dances her heart out, something she has been doing since she was a little girl. I see the childhood movies that prove it, and she maintains that insatiable need to show her talent. "Step, kick, touch" becomes her nightly routine in this latest Broadway smash, while I am busy averting scenic crashes and bodily injury every night for two and a half hours out of town in the cold of December for a show that has no guarantee of surviving the Christmas season.

I arrive at the Du Pont Theatre in Wilmington, Delaware. The sketchy neighborhood verifies that the downtown business district needs a transition. Things run smoothly onstage. I manage to mess up Carol's planned visit. I lend my car to one of the chorus members, whose family lives in the Wilmington area, so she can visit her family. This innocuous, well-intentioned act in service to my fellow Equity member develops into a tiff with Carol. I plan on picking her up at the train station. I have no car. I misjudge the time. Carol takes a cab and meets me. The misunderstanding is being ironed out until my car pulls up driven by the Equity member, Susan Stroman, who looks like she is performing in a car commercial. My car, a royal blue

MGB convertible, complements Susan's golden tresses radiating provocatively through the waning afternoon sun.

Susan parks, thanks me, gives Carol a hug, and me a bigger, longer hug, and runs into the theatre. The usually social and bubbly Carol offers no conversation. Carol, for the first time since we meet, remains silent for an extended period. It is not until we both return to New York that Carol begins speaking to me again.

Carol possesses all the attributes of an enduring partner. She is the model comforter, a flawless fit. I want to make her into a pillow and hold on to her always. It also occurs to me that that one of the more exciting things about Carol is her ability to argue. Our conversation is a contest, and we go at it, from selecting which restaurant to bringing up old girlfriends and boyfriends. These discussions occur regardless of location, and many of our friends are witness to our unabashed outbursts, which we feel are normal. Our friends think we are hopelessly in love.

"It's your dance, Carol," fellow dancer and friend Krista admits.

Krista is right. We do not give it much thought. We are too busy figuring out this irrevocable intimacy. We are still at it today.

The story of the *Blonde in the MG Who Is Not Carol* becomes part of Carol's repertoire at parties for years to come. It is usually at a party with other women who have developed a growing distaste for their husbands and at which I am not present. Many of those wives have cheating husbands, to which Carol cannot not lay claim.

Fifty years from the opening of the original production and three out-of-town engagements later, *Whoopee* finally opens at the Anta Theatre on 52nd Street. This is my second Broadway show, my first as a Production Stage Manager.

For the next six months, Carol and I achieve the near impossible.

We are making a living in the theatre in separate Broadway shows. This is quite an achievement considering that the average employment rate for AEA members during a Broadway season is 15% of the 40,000 members seeking work on a New York production.

We have a model arrangement. If we are in the same Broadway show together it results in a long-term choice: either a job or a relationship. Living and working together creates a familiarity that makes it difficult to separate performance from romance.

Having a separate Broadway show each becomes the theatrical equivalent of going steady. While other couples enjoy the ability to refer to *my place* or *your place*, we prefer the recurring banter of *my show is better than your show*.

My place and your place becomes the same apartment quicker than I can hail a taxi on a sunny day. Living in the 70s requires mastering the art of finding a taxi in inclement weather or after 4:00 p.m. There are no Ubers yet to emasculate that adventure.

Carol is out of her show by 10:20 p.m. She heads to the bus stop on 45th Street and 8th Avenue and catches the Central Park West #10 bus uptown. By the time the bus arrives at the 52nd Street stop, I am waiting for the same bus. We share the ride up to the apartment on 89th Street, between Central Park West and Columbus Avenue. She still has her makeup on. She wears the calfskin hiking boots I bought her to create that weird New Yorker look that telegraphs "Stay away!" or at least I hope it does. Walking and traveling in New York in the 70s are defensive acts of survival, and boots produce effective kicks when necessary. Life could not be more seamless for two theatre kids pretending to have responsible adult lives. But even golden opportunities of a lifetime come to an end, and it is up to me to make this outcome work. *Whoopee* closes after six months of performances. I am out of a job. I return to 90th Street and Broadway with my fellow Equity members and part-time waiters and prepare to ride out a few weeks of unemployment. I also distribute another ream of resumes to anyone who will take them, even shady penny-stock factories looking for boiler-room telemarketers.

But the only response I receive is from the Countryside Impresario from East Haddam, Connecticut.

Chapter 4

The Little Kingdom in the Woods

I approach the 110-year-old swing bridge and enter East Haddam, Connecticut's version of Brigadoon. The nutmeg state has its own way of recasting the bog myrtle, heather, and thistle of a Scottish countryside with sugar maple, scarlet oak, and dogwood. The expanse of the bridge's central span eases back from its circular excursion over the river and slowly locks back into its calling as the only access to two communities separated by the Connecticut River. Like a sentry waving me on with approval, the guard rails descend into the flat roadway and I proceed over the steel mesh road watching the opera house fill the river view. At the other end is a town square from another time.

There is more gossip than ghost story around the underlying character of this part of Connecticut. Rolling hills of natural stone fences following the hills and dips in these woods makes me forget the grainy reality of an Upper West Side known more for muggings than millennial gentrification. It offers a view of life that imagines another era. I drive by 200-year-old houses still functioning and serving their original intent as a private home. I feel like an urban immigrant, sensing the aura of a Revolutionary colonist who still lives here in the hand-hewn roughness of low hanging chestnut beams and in center hall fireplaces roaring with defiance. Artifacts from ship bells to windlasses line the walls of its woodsy taverns where everyone purports to be a shipmate or related to one in a distant past. The burgee on the flagpole by the landing dock honors a clarion call to liberty unfettered by legislation.

Standing guard over the riverbank is a Victorian structure with all the filigree of a frosted, four-tiered wedding cake. William Goodspeed, a local dry goods merchant who builds this opera house, is a descendant of Roger Goodspeed, born 1611 in British Colonial America, later known as Barnstable, Massachusetts. I am immersed in colonial history here in East Haddam. My American past only goes back to my father's arrival on the Conte di Savoy in New York Harbor in 1937. Years after its initial opening in 1876 as Goodspeed's Opera House, the building serves as a militia depot in World War I, a municipal parking lot, and a post office. Yet, the architecture of the opera house, along with the surrounding buildings, stand their ground in defiance of the mediocre tastes of 20th-century design.

A preservation committee's effort restores the deteriorating Victorian building, and the 400-seat theatre reopens as the Goodspeed Opera House. The theatre is the only major activity in an area of natural solitude and breathtaking scenery. Goodspeed is a faraway place close enough for city folk to get away. It sits in this reclusive, surreal village off a lightly traveled road in central Connecticut. The exit from the highway is unoccupied, save for a single pump gas station, a ramshackle convenience store and a threatening-looking bar filled with motorcycles.

There is a history of geological activity centered beneath Devil's Hopyard State Park in Moodus, about eight miles from the center of town and the Goodspeed. "Moodus" is a name derived from the Machimoodus-Wangunk-Algonquin tribe meaning "place of many noises." There are times when the clear sky of a starlit night is interrupted by rumblings of the earth sounding like an encroaching thunderstorm. Locals accept the condition, tourists marvel at the oddity, and visiting actors conjure up a thousand explanations from the ethereal to the macabre. The utopian promise of East Haddam is centered at the Goodspeed.

The magic behind this off-kilter glen by the river has nothing to do with aftershocks, the colonies, or tall stories conjured up by summer stock performers. The workings are the creation of the chief wizard in residence, Michael Price, the Pied Piper of theatrical froth who lures, cajoles, tricks, and maneuvers a small theatre company into a national landmark. He has been doing this for over 40 years. He has help. The original production of *Annie* in the previous summer of my arrival fills the coffers of the tiny playhouse and secures its financial future for generations.

He also has Ed Blaschik, a town native who can lay equal claim to the Goodspeed legacy. Where Price is part magician and part leprechaun ruling the four-story Victorian playhouse like a provincial Lord of the Castle, Ed is Keeper of the Realm. As theatre manager, Ed nurses the 100-year-old building and attendant properties through HVAC failures, river floods, unappreciative visiting artists, and Michael's periodic seizures of micromanagement.

Ed's handling of every crisis makes him heir apparent to the Goodspeed I know and love. Ed's loyalty to Michael's leadership becomes legendary.

"You made your life here, John B Banni," Michael reminds me, quoting the fractured pronunciation of my name by his little boy, Daniel.

He is right. It is here in this hamlet of storybook realism where my adolescent wounds fade.

Carol and I announce our plans to marry. It is the only reason Michael approves my request for a two-week vacation. We purchase our first house. It is a cottage built in 1876 by William Goodspeed for one of his nephews. I discover I am a natural plasterer and a mediocre carpenter. But there is enchantment in this messy renovation. The house becomes a jewel, retaining its original beauty. We sit in the parlor, exhausted from the work, and swear the house smiles back at us. It is alive again, freed from the discrepancies of deferred maintenance and neglect. A 19th century wood stove scraped clean with resurfaced chrome provides a cheery heat that completes the warmth and comfort of our little home.

It is here where I become a father.

There is something in this little kingdom in the woods that is unexplainable and irresistible.

The innocuous dramatizations of simple-minded theatrical fare connect visiting actor and local patron. It is a place where unabashed happy endings are dispensed through simple stories of love conquering all. Within the theatre's 100-year-old halls, the cacophonous mayhem of putting on a show is heard with the attendant crises at every turn. But once I drive away over that swing truss bridge, the hamlet returns to its slumber and its mystical aura capable of delivering dreams recede into the gloaming to hibernate from the real world until I return.

Michael Price knows his audience is the same group of people who cherish their cautious jaunts through this magical Connecticut countryside. They are the locals, the lovers of tradition, the Friday-to-Sunday urban expats seeking escape on their way to the tall ships of Mystic Seaport, the vintage rolling stock of the Essex Steam Train, the Hunt Breakfast at the

Griswold Inn, in operation since 1776. Gillette Castle, a state park attraction, is just four miles away.

The pastoral, unpretentious environment of the grounds hides the quirkiness and flamboyance of Gillette Castle. The structure is the work of a theatrical, a dubiously successful one. I do not expect in this homey backyard to find a pompous thespian, another Shakespearian aficionado expounding on the celebrity of their talent.

Just down the road into the park stands this ominous-looking stone structure resembling a fortress, somewhat out of place with the architecture of colonial homes found in the surrounding area. The builder is actor William Gillette and this hideaway is his home. It sits on a promontory overlooking the river. Today it is a quirky tourist attraction playing host to hundreds of thousands of visitors a year. Seasonal actors hired by the Goodspeed clamor to visit the site as soon as they arrive for the summer. To them, the builder is a dramaturgical saint, an American theatrical legacy. Everyone with an Equity card pledges to make the pilgrimage. The Connecticut state park is a theatre event of sorts containing this reclusive hideout of the early 20th century actor. William Gillette is famous for his performances of Arthur Conan Doyle's Sherlock Holmes. Gillette's home is as warm and inviting as the lair of a rasping, wart-ridden necromancer howling for your blood and a nip of your ear.

Goodspeed actors hold the actor in high regard, but not everyone does. Gillette, the son of a Connecticut politician who served as both a representative and a senator, made the decision to embrace an actor's life, forcing him to leave his family and fend for unpaid, minor roles in regional theatre companies from Pennsylvania to New Orleans. A friendship with Mark Twain helps the young actor secure supernumerary roles to sustain his career. But Twain has ulterior motives. He does not think Gillette has "the slightest aptitude for acting." He later admits that his concern and support to get Gillette on the stage is a heartless game of manipulation to enact a joke on a despised theatre manager. "I don't know which I like best—having Gillette made a tremendous success or seeing one of my jokes go wrong."

I shudder at the experience any actor has enduring an audition for Watson.

A few miles down the river road is another small village where the promise of quaint, picturesque, and charming converge. The place is where restoration gave birth to gentrification. Chester, Connecticut boasts Federal and Colonial homes outdoing each other's color schemes. Wallpapers in their respective interiors recall local waterfalls, murals of foliage, repeated silhouettes of the Gadsden flag, the letters of George Washington reproduced in various sizes. Ship helms, spinning wheels, both functional and as decorative art, evoke a living museum. In Chester, everyone is a closet colonist.

Except at the Cove Road Inn.

No one speaks of the dive bar identified by the number of motorcycles leaning against each other outside the main entrance. Harleys rule here. There is not a Suzuki in sight. If one waits long enough, James Dean just might show up in this black hole from the 50s.

This bar is for locals who identify with the way things were. Americana for them is tanning their tattoos at 45 miles an hour on a sun-drenched afternoon without a helmet. American flag bandannas waving in the wind, the two wheelers converge in the Inn to drink about their exploits on the open road.

The trouble at the Cove Road Inn centers on its extra hour of operation. The place gains a reputation as host to alfresco altercations with losing participants leaving the establishment bloodied and drunk. This is no place for an urban theatrical or the Gillette Castle crowd.

But that does not stop Carol and her stage cronies. Carol, Pam Dawber, the future *Mindy* of television's *Mork & Mindy*, and rocker Meatloaf's former girlfriend, Candy Darling, stop by the Inn for something new to do after the show to stave off the overdose of historical quaintness.

I drop them off and wait outside, grateful that I can avoid the threat of a bloody evening at the bar by playing the designated driver. My spineless streak disguised as wisdom comes in handy at times. Moments become interminable. I worry that I may be an accomplice to an evening of horror. But before I open the car door to face an anticipated ugly reality the girls have exited the Inn and are walking toward me. It seems their *Coyote Ugly* urge is short lived. Being a bad ass in a dive bar requires poor taste and high stakes. Acting it out does not work. This is one nasty bar.

We all return to the bland safety of the Gelston House Beer Garden, which rests on the architectural bones of the Riverside Inn, built in 1736 by Jebez Chapman. Chapman's son grows to become a colonel in the Continental Army. Fantasyland is restored with steamers, pinot grigio, and a commanding view of the Opera House, as the sun sets behind the veranda of the Goodspeed.

In this cozy retreat of a town, the bohemian nature of a theatre life becomes the norm, and the art and craft a constant adornment embracing its local history. Carol embarks on a major redesign of the galley kitchen in our cottage on Creamery Road. Restoring the antique home is a labor of tough love. I discover a unique talent in wallpapering, and the proximity to the theatre allows me to be homeowner/renovator up to the half-hour call for show time. I am three minutes away.

A wooden tulip is the finishing craft decoration after the installation of a three-paned, stained-glass window over our kitchen. It stands out from the endless array of arts and crafts hiding the imperfections of 100-year-old windowsills and settled walls. Every native-born Connecticut resident is, or considers themselves to be, a discerning artisan. Whether it be needlepoint, patchwork comforters, scrimshaw, crochet, woodworking, there is a constant supply of inspired handcrafters alluding to the founding state motto of the "land that plants and sustains."

George, a Queens College classmate, meets Katie, a New York native and Wisconsin transplant who catches George's eye on a Jamaican weekend. George is the oldest friend I know. Carol meets Katie for the first time at our wedding. Carol has a new best friend. They are permanently committed to their agenda of critiquing their respective husbands. George and Katie take on the management of that summer's Goodspeed company of actors. The four of us relish this working life together. Life is good and get togethers plentiful. We are not two couples as much as a foursome. When wine pours, it is not only imbibed, but thrown over my head. Carol is making a point, and Katie is right there to defend her right to do so. George admonishes Katie for her support of Carol. I mend any torn fabric between Katie and George.

The foursome remains intact.

"I was planning on Italy, but I arrived in Holland," Katie proclaims. She is celebrating the birth of her son, Eugene Joseph. EJ is a particular surprise. The assignment of "special" to describe EJ's Downs Syndrome offers feeble lip service to the depth of managing a child in a world that casts aside the diversity of the human condition. It is a society that designates inequality to everything from ethnicity, race, wealth, sexuality, and even an infrequent chromosome. That chromosome becomes a saving grace. EJ brings his brand of personality to light in his manner, his enthusiasm, his compassion, and his kindness. He is a blessing. EJ grows to be a staff associate at the Prospector Theatre in Ridgefield, Connecticut. EJ is one great stagehand. He is my godson. His brother Alex grows to become a strapping fireman and honors his older brother with a request to be his best man.

Fate reveals itself in the most misunderstood of circumstances. We strive to identify our destiny in ways that are most comfortable. That is because we are not confident that any other way would be any better. Happenstance, luck of the draw, divine intervention. But in that lonely moment when we chose to trust, favor extends a courteous offer to more than we can imagine. It is real and it is an act of our connection to one another. It is all in how we react to it. George and Katie, momentary captives in an unnerving act of trust, grow to become the best parents I know. I cannot imagine a world without EJ. I do not know George and Katie any other way.

Carol celebrates Katie's motherhood by presenting her a handcrafted wooden tulip to match the one in our kitchen.

We are excited this season to do a new musical instead of another period revival. We can give a rest to the straw boaters and shoulder-strap flappers that seem to surface with every vintage musical. But with every opportunity there is risk, and assimilation from one artistic discipline to another is never an easy transition. Sometimes, it is a first-rate, unconditional disaster. There is no common sweet spot when it comes to performance disciplines. Theatre is not opera, TV is not film, and directors are not interchangeable.

Bert Convy, a dapper presenter and All-American game show host of the 70s, teams up with Allan Katz, a television writer/producer/actor and former advertising copywriter. The idea of developing a musical on the life of Mexican resistance fighter Emiliano Zapata promises to be an artful, powerful, and innovative opportunity. Bert's personable TV charm and subtle, objectifying demeanor toward women are more a broadcast industry standard than a character flaw. The foursome, Bert, Allan, composer Harry Nilsson, and composer/arranger Perry Botkin, all highly successful West Coast heavy hitters, descend upon the Goodspeed Opera House in the summer of 1980.

This group, all friends, share a few iconic moments in their respective careers. Bert establishes a niche playing in TV and movie roles as the loveable cad; Allan is a senior writer on M*A*S*H; Perry Botkin, a successful music arranger, composer, and lyricist; and Harry completes the California A-team. The pastoral town of East Haddam, Connecticut endures the endless antics of Goodspeed's Michael Price creating an industry visibility for the little theatre. This latest group adds another level of celebrity gossip. This summer, Price sets his sights on Hollywood and brings in talent so far removed from summer stock that local news stations become regular visitors during the rehearsal. There is certainly a news story here, and ultimately it turns out to be different then what Price had in mind.

Early in the rehearsal process, it becomes evident that Bert's knowledge of putting on a stage show requires resources the little theatre cannot provide. There are no 20-year-old pages running around attending to craft tables filled with refreshments. There are no broadcast trucks, no energetic young apprentices positioning themselves in brazen positions seeking fame, romance, and fortune. This is semirural Connecticut, where many roads are not identified by street signs. This part of the state practices a peculiar version of laissez-faire. If you do not know what road you were on, chances are that you should not be there anyway, *so it is best that you move on from here.* I discover this fractured provincialism does not sit well with the San Fernando Valley bigwigs. But for Carol, any second thoughts about having left a hit Broadway show is cast aside as she prepares to meet the new creative staff from Hollywood.

    Carol is now employed as assistant choreographer to Dan Siretta, the choreographer hired by Michael. Michael names his son Daniel, probably after his newly hired choreographer. Despotism is encouraged at the Goodspeed. Seasonal couplings help in this matter. True to summer stock tradition, hints of carny decadence permeate the summer theatre allure, and one cannot leave the summer without having a juicy story under their belt or skirt. Unique developments occur in this Nutmegger version of an ethereal Highland village. Presbyterian pastors from Manhattan arrive for Sunday matinees to support their parishioners who happen to be members of the cast. Quite the complement, all around.

    "So, where's the Coke machine?" one of the interns assisting the entourage asks Carol.

    "Oh, there's one in the basement, but it only takes coins, no bills," Carol replies.

    The handler smirks with gentle condescension.

    "No, I mean, where is the *coke machine*?"

    I feel great relief in knowing Carol has no idea what the page is asking for. I am not aware of drug dealers beyond the outskirts of New Haven or Hartford, and both are an hour away, but I would not be surprised if we have inadvertently imported them from New York in our casting decisions. Carol answers.

    "I think we are late for a meeting," and walks away.

    Perry, Harry, and Bert are summoned to a technical meeting with the set designer, John Jensen.

    We all enter Michael's office, which resembles a Cracker Barrel restaurant lobby filled with notions, gifts, and other merchandise. An overwhelming array of bibelots, trinkets, and show effects greet us. Price's desk sits kitty-corner to the square room. That placement seems to be a warning of the ambiguity to follow. A red Victorian loveseat adds to the eccentric flavor of the Executive Director's office. The revealing centerpiece of Price's time warp collection boasts an antique barber chair with sharpening straps hanging off one of the porcelain arms. This crown jewel of Price's amusement-museum-as-an-office swivels and reclines. Occupants, anticipating the most comfortable and empowering seat in the room, can be seen attempting to maneuver the various positions of the chair while still maintaining a decorum during a meeting. In actuality, the chair becomes the seat of cross-examination for the unfortunate occupant. Inevitably, production issues that surface always revert to the responsibility and fault of the barber chair occupant, regardless of the nature of the problem. Surveying the room challenges one's focus not unlike the experience in a "Where's Waldo" search. In the center of an overstuffed bulletin board is a rather disconcerting photo of a younger Michael in white chinos, red-striped blazer and straw hat goofing it up as a participant in a barbershop quartet. I am hoping it is a publicity stunt and not a performance.

John Jensen unrolls a huge set of ground plans. Bert takes the cue and feigns understanding of the thousand industry abbreviations and notations on the plan. He convinces everyone else that he is taking in the details seriously. I suspect he has no idea. I watch too many segments of *Match Game* and *Tattletales*, the game shows he hosts, to believe a TV host beyond the cue cards they read. The truth finally comes out. If is not on a teleprompter, it is not in their brain.

"What's a gaze-bo?" he asks, articulating the word with only two syllables.

"Sorry? A gaze-bo?" Jensen replies, imitating the director's erroneous pronunciation.

Bert points to the word and the attendant illustration. Jensen withholds his incredulity.

"Bert that is a ga-**zee**-bo. The structure is the center of the set. All other scenes emanate from configurations that add to the gazebo."

Silence. Throat clearing. The eyeglass adjustment creates an opportunity for recovery.

Bert finally responds.

"Oh, you mean the ga-**zee**-bo, I didn't see the 'e' in the print.

I wonder how I am going to get through this.

Harry Nilsson's fame begins back in 1967, when folk rock songwriter Fred Neill pens "Everybody's Talkin'." Two years later, Harry performs the song and it immediately becomes a best seller, winning a Grammy when it was featured in *Midnight Cowboy*. The association creates friendships important to Harry's future success. He meets songwriter and arranger Perry Botkin. He meets and becomes friends with the Beatles. Harry is riding high in the 70s. Harry's guttural, offbeat lyrics in his various releases over the decade allude to an underlying dysfunction of life experiences. His repertoire includes lyrics that surprise, shock, and glaring.

You're breaking my heart, you're tearing it apart, so fuck you.
I sang my balls off for you, baby.

Harry is developing a uniquely personal style; the critics say. I am thinking all this is quite cool. I'm working with the Hollywood elite. I am also embarrassingly impressionable.

This is the Harry who arrives in East Haddam in September of 1980.

To prepare for *Zapata,* Dan Siretta sends Carol to the Lincoln Center Library for the Performing Arts to study the indigenous origins of Mexican dancing. Hour after hour Carol reviews and studies the *Jarabe Tapatio, La Conquista, Danza del Venado, Los Voladores de Papantla*. Dances for children. Dances for lovers, politicians. Dances for old men. Dances for old men commenting on the ruling class. Mating dances. Carol returns ready to stage a Mesoamerican Spectacular.

The next two weeks of rehearsal is more a demonstration of how a game show is assembled. Intent, motivation, character building, and dramatic conflict are cast aside to ensure timeframe, punch lines, and joke set ups. Mexicans become caricatures. Every available Mexican cliché is employed. Emiliano, played by Sean Elliott, is forced to declare to a Habanera beat:

This is a tortilla, it used to be free,
But now, not even frijoles are free anymore…
So, this means war.

Aside from his preoccupation with maintaining his celebrity, Bert's inspiration for a musical about a historically prominent figure of early 20th century Mexico evolves into creating a two-and-one-half hour sitcom. Structural weaknesses in the script are solved by getting to the punch lines sooner in a speed rehearsal. Bert feels that blurting out bad lines faster makes them funnier. It only helps the listener get it over with sooner. Everyone who witnesses the event seems to appreciate the brevity. This is directing at its bravest. This is stage managing at its most difficult.

Just in case the dubious staging of the first act fails in its zeal to get a message across, the top of the second act begins with a full house extravaganza. Dan Siretta, with Carol's extensively researched material, creates a cymbal-clashing, cacophonic house entrance with a mariachi band meandering down the aisles with the entire cast creating a fiesta parade onto the stage. Down the two aisles of the theatre come violins, guitarróns, trumpets, guitars, vihuelas. Sombreros fill the house, musicians in charro suits, dancers flailing, undulating in every available corner on the stage. Maracas intensify the already deafening production number. Danny, a holdover Broadway chorus boy from the early 60s, creates complex movements that have nothing to do with the plot or the period. Danny checks the effect of the excessively gaudy second act opening through the eyes of the matinee subscription regulars in the first rows. But their eyes are not open. The blue-haired matinee patrons are discovered nodding off despite choreography, the noise and Bert's snazzy broadcast aura.

Danny does not exhibit a capacity to collaborate with anyone in the theatre. He never learns to give up the barber chair at production meetings, so he becomes the scapegoat for everything that goes wrong with any show. Danny always returns for another show. Michael Price tolerates his antics like a friendly divorced couple. Danny is more interested in the Mexican chorus girl from the Bronx. Minorities are always welcome in pastoral East Haddam, but not everyone in town feels that way. Tolerance survives only until the show ends its summer run.

I am always busy cleaning up disorganization and neutralizing the crisis of the moment. Carol becomes a regular visitor to Danny's apartment as Danny's assistant choreographer. The meetings usually devolve into making pounds of fresh pesto. Despite his fractured approach to collaborative staging, Danny's charm is infectious to Carol, but his process still enrages me. He lays claim that he is the one who pairs Carol and I together by providing a private and secluded space for our trysts. It is for this claim that I love Danny despite his undermining creative process.

Opening night brings a Hollywood style ambiance to the little theatre. Harry Nilsson's friendship with the Beatles produces Ringo Starr in the tiny lobby. Michael, brimming with excitement of the gala opening, dances around Starr like a heart-throbbing teenager. Starr declines the offer to sit in the barber chair. At the Gelston House next door, West Coast cognoscenti fill the bar anticipating the arrival of broadcast TV royalty. Young Beatle aficionados clamor around the bar seeking autographs. They learn of Starr from their parents. Starr refuses any autograph requests.

In Hollywood hoopla, the truth of talent inevitably reveals its spurious nature. When a dream team operates under expected conditions not available in a regional theatre environment, their capability is compromised. The country theatregoers expect Harry Nilsson to be a Beatle, Bert Convy to be Alex Trebek, and *Tattletales* on par with *Jeopardy*. Perry is a fine arranger, and Allan Katz is a good copywriter with big ideas. The group's qualifications to create relevant content through a theatrical social statement is unattainable. The town is tripping over fake celebrity.

The press finally puts the venture to rest. What started as a potentially powerful musical drama devolves into a badly written, poorly directed series of offensive one-liners. Thor Eckert Jr. of the *Christian Science Monitor* castigates the creative staff for going "straight for the gag and the hollow core at each and every opportunity, making trite material unbearably cloying and utterly wanting in credibility."

So much for Hollywood expertise and cultural sensitivity.

Zapata goes nowhere, and the person most relieved is the wardrobe master, John Riccucci. In the perilous world of sensitive costume designers, John handles every tiff, every blowout, every expression of anguish originating from botched designer collaboration to inaccurate period research. John also maintains an inexhaustible supply of cookies. Michael, Ed, and

John protect the signature mission of the opera house despite the constant stream of innovative foolishness from arty outsiders.

TV presents its view as an irresistible truth verified by a participating sponsor. In television, it does not matter what you say. It is all in the casting, all in the punchline, all in how you deliver, not what you create.

The following season brings Will Mackenzie, a likable character actor who charms the Broadway stage when he replaces Charles Nelson Reilly as Cornelius Hackl in *Hello Dolly*. His claim to fame rests with his successful 20-year television career as a director of prime-time sitcoms: *Too Close for Comfort, Dharma & Greg, Everybody Loves Raymond, Scrubs*, and *Reba*, among others. After the Zapata debacle, I am not looking forward to another aptitude test of fitting the square-peg mentality of broadcast function into the round hole abyss of regional theatre crisis management. The show selection does not help. *Funny Face*, a 1927 musical composed by George and Ira Gershwin, originally earns such poor reviews in its initial Philadelphia tryout in 1927. The reaction prompts the writer to walk out of the project. The reworked show eventually manages a 227-performance run on Broadway, initiating the opening of the new Alvin Theatre, now the Neil Simon, on 52nd Street. For Goodspeed, this is yet another breakout of Gershwinitis, that recurring condition of falling back on tried-and-shelved content when searching for new theatrical properties produces a void. Boy-meets-girl musicals in posh and tony settings of privileged New York society is the staple of summer programming at Goodspeed, and no creative team fills the bill like the Gershwin brothers.

On the second day of rehearsal, Mackenzie asks for a rolling cart on which to place his script. He wants to wheel it around when he directs. I do not believe there is a need for a cart on a

22-foot-wide proscenium stage for a POV, or point of view. That is like walking your creativity around in a wheelchair. Mackenzie needs to look no further than ten feet in front of him. The Gershwin artistry makes the Hollywood TV director expendable.

John Corry of *The New York Times* concurs: "Will Mackenzie's direction is a little short on coherence. Sometimes the style of the show gets lost, but you can't have everything and maybe the Gershwins are enough."

Dinner, Goodspeed, Gillette Castle and a possible celebrity sighting. What a pleasant weekend.

Show business courts the ego like the devil courts moral turpitude. Gillette, like Convy, Mackenzie, Corsaro, and others like them, assume they can deliver more variations of their talent pie for which they are noted. But it is not their talent which is questioned. It is this little haven in the woods that dictates the quality and length of one's stay. Dream teams do not work here. The magic dust of the Goodspeed must fall upon you, and if it chooses not to, talent is irrelevant.

The ego always wants another date and show business creatives are forever looking for thespian validation. They seek to be trendy, quirky, inventive, and do weird things like William Gillette, who constructs a fortress-like haunt in the Connecticut woods and still has the time to build a narrow-gauge railroad around it. When did Gillette have the time to rehearse? Gillette is the classic self-centered thespian. He is the favorite guru and theatrical foil for every impressionable performer seeking justification for their folly.

It is all in the presentation.

The last non-stop carrying West Coast creatives out of Bradley to LAX is now airborne. The visiting creatives are gone and their summer of stock theatre fading. The usual brilliant reds and oranges of the fall Connecticut hills produce their annual color extravaganza for the fruit-orchard-and-pumpkin-patch crowds. East Haddam is still a destination, even without the periodic celebrity visits at the Goodspeed. Along with apple cider and hayrides come that unrelenting end-of-season nemesis, unemployment. I return to New York to do the thing most show businesspeople do more than anything else. Look for the next show.

This time, I take Brigadoon along, over the bridge. She is sitting next to me.

Chapter 5

Taylor-Made In-Laws for Theatricals

It is during Carol's Broadway run of A Chorus Line when I meet her parents for the first time. Job opportunities are not looking good for me, and Carol adds to my angst by announcing her parents are planning to visit soon. They are not aware of our living arrangement and, wanting to maintain her reputation of being the chaste good daughter, we eliminate any indications of my daily presence in the apartment just until they get into their hotel. My toothbrush, my shoes, and toiletries all disappear from the bathroom. My socks and clothes leave the bedroom. A jar of three- bean salad replaces cans of Ragu. I imagine my mother's wrath at the sight of the jar. Every hint of ethnic male occupation is eliminated. Our apartment is transformed into a single occupancy. At 30 West 89th Street, I no longer exist.

Carol's parents plan to arrive on a Thursday afternoon when an understudy rehearsal is scheduled for her show. She asks if I could meet them and unlock the door to the apartment to let them in. She promises to meet up with them when she finishes rehearsal. Walking down West 89th Street toward the apartment, I notice an older couple standing right by the doorway. As I approach the stoop, I surmise these are Carol's parents, Joe and Lorraine Marik. Lorraine is obviously the source of Carol's inherited effervescence. She is engaging, pleasant, and animated. Joe Marik is reserved but charming, cordial, and on a potential father-in-law's best behavior. I do not believe he knows of our intentions. He introduces himself with bon vivant fanfare. His introductory conversation leads to his lifetime honorary membership in the Greatest Generation. During the next ten years, he presents me with a trove of photographs, testaments, military medals, and scrapbooks attesting to this hallowed association.

But Joe Marik is not the stuffy, Greatest Generation curmudgeon he purports to be. Joe is a closet actor harboring a desire to in show business. On the surface, he is the somber, heavy-hearted funeral director tending to the sensitivities of his bereaved customers. He looks the part, toupee and all. When I first visit the Marik home in suburban Riverside I notice an array of hair pieces that grace five head molds on the master bathroom counter at 334 Downing Road.

But after the second martini, periodic bursts of vocalization allude to his nightclub-standup-emcee demeanor. When Joe speaks, he proclaims, delivering every word with bravado and gravitas as if the end of the day were a proclamation waiting to be announced. When Joe Marik enters a room, the house goes to half and the show begins.

Standing by the front door of the apartment, I think he is a general-in-waiting. A cashmere Borsalino cap covers his head. Tartan slacks suggest country club membership. Carol, the apple of this general's eye, falls devoutly close to the tree. She holds five announcements celebrating her birth. The hospital, the town, the city, the state, the church all confirm Carol's existence. Every controlling authority of God and country recognizes, in beautifully crafted parchment and gold-leaf-edged proclamations, the arrival of this daddy's little girl. I can only imagine what is in store.

The Mariks, excited to see their daughter in *A Chorus Line*, expect her to greet them at the apartment. They see me. They assume I am the super of the building. I introduce myself as Carol's friend.

Just who is this New York guy who happens to have a key to their daughter's apartment?

Carol and I execute the plan. I open the apartment and carry both pieces of luggage up three flights of stairs. I give the key to her father to indicate that the key came from Carol and not me. I spend a few moments with them in the apartment, make sure they are comfortable, pretend to not be aware of where anything is stored, and go on my way. I assure them we will get together soon. I assume they will be there until Carol comes home from rehearsal. Then they will settle in at their hotel. We are quite proud of this plan.

They stay for two weeks. In the apartment.

Millie Fulton, our forward-thinking, big-hearted landlord, allows me to stay in her unused basement bedroom for the duration of Joe and Lorraine's stay. My only challenge is to avoid them in the hallways and show up periodically as if my presence is a casual, periodic event. This is only the beginning of a lifetime of concessions required to be a future son-in-law on good terms. Years of securing choice seating to the most popular musicals helps immeasurably. Good restaurants add to the mix, especially when I pay. But at this moment in time, I am an unemployed stage manager living in a New York basement, pretending to be a successful and promising theatrical.

On Monday, Carol's day off, we meet for dinner. Wanting to impress her Midwestern parents, she chooses Windows on the World, the restaurant that sits at the top of the World Trade Center. The complex had been open for only two years and is a popular tourist spot. Waiting lists control entry into the three restaurants, and the longest list is for the restaurant she selects. Carol knows a theatre manager at *A Chorus Line* who has connections. Connections are a way of life in New York, and the practice permeates every economic level of city living. Being in the cast of the Theatrical Event of the Decade has some clout, and we all benefit from Carol's connection. I am assuming the Mariks treat us for dinner, so I am not too concerned.

Joe Marik's martini arrives, along with Lorraine's vodka tonic and lime, Carol's white wine spritzer, and my merlot. What a new normal. Drinking with drinkers 110 stories in the sky. The view is breathtaking. The clear evening allows the setting sun to shimmer over New York Bay. Cruise ships looking like rowboats skim past historic Castle Clinton and the Battery, out into the bay past the Statue of Liberty and Governor's Island. The spatial effect is dizzying and overwhelming. I feel just fine.

Dinner arrives with steaks for Joe and Lorraine, broiled salmon for me, and a salad for Carol. The conversation is courteous in a first, best-impression sort of way. Joe Marik has a talent for listening to a conversation and responding by redirecting it to his own experience.

"So, John, your family is from the New York area?"

Joe Marik's use of the word "area" suggests an excessive air of cosmopolitan aplomb, the kind flight attendants convey in their welcoming announcement upon landing. Unbeknownst to this midwestern-bred bon vivant, being born and raised in New York creates a myopic view of the world. There is no "area" or sphere of influence where things gradually became less New

Yorkish at the borders. New York knows where it ends. The streetlamps stop, the sidewalks cease, the subways terminate, the never-ending, ever-changing "No Parking" signs are no more. To a New Yorker, one step out of Queens or Brooklyn is the country. There is no tentative variation like the "Chicago area" of Joe Marik's world. Where Chicago vies for being first in everything, New York does not even play the game. It does not have to. That fact is my conversational leverage.

The contest is set. Man-of-the-world father, who is just a local business merchant, meets daughter's man-of-the-world boyfriend, who is just an unemployed stage manager.

The face-off begins.

"Yes. I was born in Manhattan, my mother in Brooklyn, and my father was born in a little town in central Italy. He settled in New York after a stint in the Army."

Joe Marik picks up on one word.

"Army? I was a captain during the war." The attempted focus grab of the conversation to the other camp begins immediately.

"I see. Were you engaged in any conflicts?"

"I was stationed in San Francisco."

Really? I think. *Not Dunkirk, Omaha Beach, enemy territory in Germany?*

I respond to defend my father.

"Being a native-born Italian and a naturalized citizen, my father was not allowed to ship overseas, so he remained in the states. He trained medics."

Joe Marik picks up on another word.

"Well, I trained in rehabilitation procedures for returning wounded soldiers."

"Overseas?"

"I was first to receive the wounded from overseas for rehabilitation."

This captain never left stateside. The-tit-for-tat banter lasts throughout the evening. It is courteous, careful, guarded, and all very pleasant. And it is going nowhere. If the score ties, I will consider myself lucky. I also realize Joe Marik's propensity for making impressions.

But I have my own issues.

Toward the end of dessert, I feel Carol's hand on my leg under the table. I can only imagine what she is up to. I turn to her, and she gives me a reassuring look as if to say, "Take it." She had hands me a roll of bills. She is out to make an impression to her father that she is secure in New York. I take the cue and offer to pay the bill with the money Carol gives me.

Joe Marik does not resist. In fact, I sense an expectation on his part. I anticipate the complexity that ensues in getting to know and manage my potential father-in-law. Joe Marik is a big shot in suburban Riverside, Illinois. But in this city where spectacular views from high-rise restaurants are matched only by the bigger-than-life aspirations of the people living in it, Joe Marik is a small fish in a very big pond.

Two weeks later, after sending them off to the airport and finally returning to the apartment, I discover that furniture is rearranged, pictures on the wall are moved to different areas, and any familiarity I remember in the apartment prior to their arrival is gone. New bric-a-brac and art prints have been placed in both the living room and bedroom. Then it occurs to me. I put only one suitcase in the cab. They arrived with two. The second suitcase contained all this new stuff I had never seen.

"Oh, it's Mom and Dad's care package for stuff I needed," Carol explains.

I survey the array of vintage items that belong in a novelty shop.

"You need, plastic fruit, depression glass, and a Thumbelina doll?

"Well, they usually bring things that I used when I was younger."

"When was the last time you baked?" I point to two antique sets of sugar and flour canisters next to a dozen cookie cutter molds. Carol responds with a perplexed frown. She feels she does not need to explain. I acquiesce hoping there are cookies in my future. It never happens.

This seems more like someone is cleaning out their basement and depositing all their unwanted items in our tiny apartment. I come to accept this as a recurring behavior with every future in-law visit. One shipment includes a dozen packages of My-T-Fine tapioca dry pudding mix doing double duty as protective packaging. The pudding boxes embrace a three- gallon glass punch bowl sitting in the box. The recurring inheritance of midcentury memorabilia becomes a seasonal regularity and our apartment a burgeoning repository of knick-knack curiosities.

My unemployment lasts a month. I return to the Goodspeed Opera House for the summer season. Carol returns to the Shubert Theatre every weeknight at 8:00 p.m. and I spend April through November at the Goodspeed two hours away. We see each other weekly. I head for my car following the 8:00 p.m. performance on Saturday. I drive to the New Haven train station to meet Carol who has taken the 11:05 p.m. out of Grand Central after her 8:00 p.m. show in New York. It is 12:30 a.m. Expecting a romantic evening, Carol falls asleep by 1:00 a.m. on the way back to East Haddam. On Sunday morning, Carol wakes up and devours everything bagels and a brick of cream cheese. I go to my matinee, and Carol does the usual weekend getaway ritual of antiquing in the Connecticut countryside. The delayed and intended romantic evening finally culminates in appetizers, soup, salad, steak, an oversized baked potato with mounds of sour cream and room for cheesecake.

"Don't look at me like that. This is my once-a-week meal to offset tuna and bean sprouts." This is our weekend date night. On Monday morning, my day off, I drive Carol back to New York for her Monday night performance. I drop her off at the stage door, then pick her up at the end of the show. Carol has the comfort of private transportation, and I am picking up a Broadway performer. Onlookers do a second take as my two-seater maneuvers out of Shubert Alley onto 44th Street.

The second installment of our weekend date is spent at Charlies where I get a burger, fries, and a warm brownie ala mode while she returns to a spinach salad. After 300 miles, watching her gorge over a steak house dinner, midnight rendezvous in dark train stations, Carol finally agrees to a few moments of intimacy. Repeating this routine for the whole season infers that we are going steady.

Carol and I decide to formalize our relationship, and we set a date for July 1st. I resist her request at first to call up her father and ask if I could have permission to marry his daughter. Carol's family traditions are so numerous and tedious I begin to suspect she is secretly Amish. If we ever decide to call ourselves a pair, I fully expect her to arrive at the church on her wedding day in a horse-drawn surrey sporting a handmaid's bonnet. This "good girl from the Midwest" frame of reference is going a little too far for this city kid from the Big Apple. My New York City urban arrogance and her Great Plains politesse will either solidify or sever our growing relationship.

After two Manhattans and a bowl of cashews from the Gelston House bar, I call Joe Marik.

"Mr. Marik?"

"Call me Dad, John."

This is not easy to do. My father has been dead for six years. This would be the first time I call anyone *Dad* since his death. It does not seem right.

"OK, Dad." The shallow, patronizing sound coming from my own voice feels like a knife slicing through my self-respect. Perhaps it is his way of warming up to what he probably surmises is the purpose of the call. How am I going to word this?

Can I have your daughter's hand...
I would like to ask your permission...
Would you be kind enough to...
Now that you are forcing your own daughter into an archaic tradition of servitude, will you sell your daughter off to me?

There rises inside of me a resolve to win the affections of Carol and still maintain my own terms. I have been my own person for a long time. I determine my own life without consultation. I am used to making my own decisions and making them alone. I do not need a replacement father. My real one suited me just fine. How dare this man assume that he can take my father's place, that he can man the helm, continue in his comfort zone of Big Daddy at my expense?

"Dad, I would like to marry Carol. I asked her, and she said 'yes.' I hope you don't have an issue with that." That is the best I can do. I can sense the bellows working overtime to inflate future father-in-law's patriarchal ego.

"John, I would be delighted to give you Carol's hand in marriage."

Give me? I do not realize she is on lease.

"Thank you. Thank you, Dad. Carol will call you later today, I am sure. See you soon. Goodbye, Dad."

I say the word Dad four times, primarily to get used to the sound of it. I try for the next twenty years. It never feels right. I feel I am a traitor to my father.

Joe Marik is not surprised to receive my phone call. In fact, he is expecting it, since he and his lovely daughter plan the whole thing.

I am relieved over the successful accomplishment of making her daddy happy

Expectation occurs when routine settles in. The privilege of doing a Broadway show slowly evolves into a daily grind, and her attention is more focused on planning a wedding. The truth is that she is sick of salads, and she wants to eat. She does not admit this until after the wedding ceremony. She admits she has just as much passion for hot dogs, pizza, and ice cream as I do. We celebrate our love in restaurants. At Emilio's, a venerable pizza joint in the village that offers a backyard with al fresco dining, where intimate square bistro tables are covered with that iconic, red-checkered standard of Italian pasta nooks. Candles embedded in empty Chianti bottles are wrapped in wicker, adorned with layers of dried wax bearing witness to countless proclamations of undying love. The red-and-white lattice design of the cloth napkins hide the accidental dollops of marinara sauce spilled by the last couple suffering a refusal of affections. Overhead, a trellised ceiling holds an encroaching forest of ivy and keeps the sweet sentiments uttered by lovers from traveling beyond the intended recipients. There is the Starthrower Café on Bank Street, also in the Village, where blue lamps over glass tables transform a simple lemon chicken breast into a sensual, oozing invitation to a long and passionate evening. Carol falls in love at that table. Carol speaks of that night to this day. The azure shaft of light catches the shimmer and bounce of her blond locks. I am already there, and it is great to know she feels the same way.

Carol has no idea how she saves me, transforms me. Chocolates and valentines do not telegraph the swirling depth of caring that consumes me. How do I tell the person who lifts me to where I never believed possible that her existence in my life is irrevocable, a non-compete, final? How futile it is to explain that she has descended into my mind, taken up residence in my heart, that there is not a moment when she is not present in every thought?

"That's all very nice, but can we stop at Smilers on the way? I need a nosh and a ginger ale."

We grow assuming every day is a continuation of that forever instant of choosing each other. There is no remembrance, only endless, joyous days to experience, year after year, for a lifetime. Love makes time irrelevant.

Those places where trysts and declarations occur nightly now fade away. Favorite hangouts close. *Emilio's* on 6th Avenue becomes a garish, florescent CVS. The *Starthrower Café* on Bank Street is long gone and can only be found in a one-line reference on the *Forgotten New York* website. Spinach salad with warm bacon dressing at *Charlie's*, the pub where patrons go to see Broadway eat between shows, is now rubble in a dumpster making way for a hotel. Only the *Elephant and the Castle*, the tiny eatery on Greenwich Street specializing in omelets remains. Of course, it is the place where Carol endures my love of omelets, while I never know her distaste for the dish. Points of interest become commonplace. For over forty years, through love, marriage, two children, show business careers, and nine cars, there is one constant.

Pepe's Pizza, the original, in New Haven, Connecticut.

There is no other pizza in the world. It is the center from which we celebrate every good moment in our lives. It is that part of Neapolitan that Carol accepts unequivocally without reservation. Since its establishment in 1925 on Wooster Street in the heart of a one-block, diminished Little Italy, Pepe's has nourished more Yalies who become senators, and high-powered attorneys than any other comfort food establishment in Connecticut. One can gaze at the row of photographs of recent presidents chomping down a slice. Privileged frat men and sorority women rub chairbacks with hordes of tourists seeking refreshment in the shadow of the venerable university a few blocks away. We owe a large part of our American politics and nutrition to baked tomato and melted mozzarella. Perhaps this may be the source of our present dysfunction.

Nevertheless, we are at *Pepe's, The Original*. It all starts here. Everything else comes after. Friendships, marriages, children, parenthood. Everything that matters.

In show business, you are only as good as your last show. Carol's last performance of *A Chorus Line* eventually occurs. One afternoon, on a bright, sunny, beautiful Wednesday matinee day, Carol experiences a catharsis. Preparing for the performance that day, she lays claim to a transformative realization.

"If I did this show once, I've done it a thousand times. And why would anybody want to be stuck in a stuffy, rank, dark theatre when they could be out in the sunshine on this beautiful day?"

Carol leaves the show soon after, relieved and liberated.

The show is still selling out. It becomes a permanent tourist institution. Not everyone is happy about Carol's decision. Her colleagues think she is crazy for leaving a hit show. But there is a good reason why Carol leaves the fabulously successful musical. She wants a personal life, and many of her friends are living their lives through the show.

Years later, she meets up with some of her *ACL* colleagues. They are still churning the umpteenth edition of the show somewhere in the world. They still wear their show jackets, beautiful satin windbreakers with the show logo emblazoned on the back. It speaks to their commitment, the exclusive club of do-or-die allegiance to the show now and forever. It becomes their total identity, and that is Carol's issue. They fail to realize that this business, this privilege of making a living creating a live event is special and temporary and for the younger part of our lives. Carol's colleagues regret being dismissive to her so many years ago. They sheepishly admit in a backdoor sort of way to having given their whole lives to deteriorating knees, bunions, torn meniscus cartilages, and salads for dinner with no one at home to share them. Carol endures the same scars of show business, replacing knees and hips. Her decision to leave the business rewards her with two children, a working partner, and a home instead of an aging show that offers diminishing relevance with every retread. The green satin patina on Carol's show jacket fades. It is placed in the farthest reaches of the closet. The $1,500.00 champagne-colored, beaded, crystal-studded top hat she wore in the finale now overlooks her curio cabinet of well-earned memories.

We both learn that there is always another show but only one life, and it is a shrewder decision to leave the former when it is still a hit and enjoy the latter when there is still time.

Carol walks out of Shubert Alley, hails a cab to Penn Station, boards an Amtrak train to Old Saybrook, Connecticut. When she exits the train, I am there to meet her, steps away from where I had picked up her luggage on the first trip to Goodspeed years earlier.

Chapter 6

Between Seasons and the Department of Labor

Making a living in the theatre in the early 1980s requires a gumshoe's sixth sense. I sniff around for a job like a bloodhound on the scent of a serial killer. Anything will help. Carol and I are married for about a year, and we go about theatrical job seeking as if the next audition, the next interview, will be the theatrical blockbuster of the decade. I think that way to offset the daily rejection from producers' receptionists shooing me out of their offices or directors yelling "Next!" after Carol sings her heart out on an empty stage. A vacation week sub, a two-day load in, a limited engagement deters the anxiety of being sighted on the unemployment insurance line for more than a week. The scene at the New York State Unemployment Division at 90th Street and Broadway serves as an uptown social club for actors and stage managers. I run into the same people I see at auditions earlier in the day. Later, some of them might show up as waiters at Charlie's, the hangout in the theatre district on 45th Street near 8th Avenue. If they do, they are paid in cash, and I doubt they report the transactions to the uptown social club at 90th Street and Broadway.

There is no online registration. Upon approval of my unemployment claim, I receive a record book in which I enter details of job searches for the week. I also enter the times I worked. These bits of employment help me through these cold winter months.

Fortunately, Carol is cast in two commercials, one for *Parent's Magazine* playing a young mom, which she has yet to become, and the other for Dr. Pepper, which she does not drink. But that does not stop her from drawing on her acting resources to play the successful, vivacious stroller pusher who has it all together or the hip, trendy, thirty-something who keeps her figure by drinking carbonated aspartame. It pays the rent, especially while I am knocking on backstage doors dropping off resumes to everyone in the theatre industry. She loves the attention, the feeling that she is still a vital part of the business. Accolades of how attractive and talented always feels great even if some of those compliments came from creepy producers.

I deliver so many resumes to stage managers, general managers, producers. I would not be surprised if I discover one of my resumes in a city trash can or taped to a corner phone booth by a snarky prankster. This is the 80s. We have phone booths on street corners, and they are centers for socially questionable encounters and contacts. Posted on many a glass-enclosed pay phone are variations of a message's promise: "For the time of your life, call xxx-xxxx" or "Solve your problem, call xxx-xxxx. No questions asked." The original phone numbers are blacked out and replaced with a phone number of a jilted paramour seeking payback from a former boy or girlfriend. Other messages stalk the lower depths of our urgings.

Living in New York is not an easy proposition. The murder rate surpasses 1,800 victims, the crack epidemic contributes to a treacherous quality of life and unreliable transportation is the expectation. There are more color renderings of interpretative art on the interior of subway cars than the Metropolitan Museum of Art. The Upper West Side, a grid of early 20th century brownstone homes anchored by corner apartment buildings, is habitable during the daytime but threatening at night. Muggings and smashed car windows produce emptied wallets on the sidewalk and stolen car radios in the morning. Car sirens are the area's music of the night. Dawn seems to elicit a truce. The aural reality of a city trash collection truck grinding garbage into a gray, wet purée provides a hint of order around the civil turbulence. Our apartment is a tiny haven run by a landlord who had witnessed the transition of the wild West Side mayhem of a gritty New York City neighborhood.

Millie Fulton, our feisty New England landlady from Pittsfield, Massachusetts, is a founding member of a city rehabilitation program in the late 1960's. Once a deteriorating brownstone, she purchases the property from the city for a below market price on the promise to live in the building for at least five years while repairing the property to meet building codes. Millie loves theatricals and rents apartments, two to a floor, to every actor who asks. We have the front apartment, on the fourth floor. At $278.00 per month, I can afford the place and still eat three times a week. With Carol's new gigs, we never starve.

Spring arrives and Goodspeed's new season begins. We pack up and return to Michael's theatrical fiefdom. I begin rehearsal. Carol is rehearsing how to nest. She is focused on her own show. A baby. I am summoned periodically, according to her ovulating schedule, to perform those requirements that support her agenda. Romance takes a back seat, and successful implantation is the focus. Sex, for the first time in my life is on demand, and weirdly stimulating.

One of the many visitations from the in-laws coincides with Carol's baby making schedule. Carol invents a story that sends them to a Memorial Day parade which has in truth been cancelled due to the rainy weather. To lengthen their time away, she suggests that the scheduled bands will be playing at the local high school. There is no such plan. She orders me from rehearsal. I comply and we engage. Her parents return earlier than anticipated. We hear them pull up the road. Our intimate moment still holds the record for the fastest engagement of a married couple trying to have a baby under duress while laughing uncontrollably.

The event produces a successful outcome.

I go back to rehearsal. Carol goes out for a bowl of steamers at the Gelston House. The season flashes by. I am on automatic and the shows are an afterthought. My focus is Carol, the baby. The event is becoming more real every day, especially when Michael's wife Jo-Ann throws a baby shower where there should have been a rehearsal.

At the celebration, my first child-to-be is deemed the "Goodspeed Baby."

Carol and I are now the source of breaking news.

The 1983 season ends with a 1917 Kern antique, *Oh Boy!* which joins the list of romantic musical comedy output that defines the Goodspeed. While most of the cast are on their way to the Amtrak station in Old Saybrook, I am at Dahlstrom's for the third time in a week reviewing wallpaper samples that address Carol's peace of mind. I develop a new craftsman vocabulary. Sizing, dado, accordion folding, blister, aeration, half-drop, and the most feared, repeat. This is the size of the pattern that recurs and determines the wasted rolls required to adjoin strips to an exact match. My weekends are transformed from restoration specialist to baby environment designer. Brown-toned woodland creatures from raccoon, beaver, fawn, squirrel, and fox dance with a chair rail border and ceiling frieze covering the imperfections of 100-year-old walls.

Carol deciding on the wallpaper pattern is the defining accomplishment of the season.

We spend the winter in East Haddam preparing. Carol makes one trip to New York to perform in *A Chorus Line*. The show is celebrating its 3389th performance, making it the longest running Broadway show at the time. An expectant Carol dons her finale costume and joins former members of the Broadway cast onstage at the Shubert. *Step, kick, touch.* This time *kick* is a response from Carol's baby bump. She is elated her first-yet-to-be-born is already on the Broadway stage.

I no longer spend my time restoring filigree or installing copper ceilings in my aging cottage of high maintenance. I now shop for cribs, cradles, questionable devices called Kang-a-rock-a-roos, cabinet child locks, fences, gates, something called Stimulation Activity Centers.

I am learning that becoming a father requires learning to shop like a mother. I dig deep into my feminine side and openly compare prices and read warning labels. It is painful at first, but nearby female shoppers egg me on.

Their giggle is not charming. They are warning me. After a mad dash to Yale-New Haven Hospital, Joseph is born to Carol. In that hurried, happy morning, I forget Carol's suitcase for the hospital and return to retrieve it after Joseph's arrival. On the way, I turn on the radio and hear Cat Stevens singing "Father and Son." How can I not feel blessed?

Joseph is born on Saturday, February 25th. The cast of the first show arrives on Monday, February 27th. At rehearsal, I pass out scripts, pencils, and baby pictures.

Goodspeed's addition of a second theatre in an abandoned knitting needle factory in Chester doubles my work and adds a daily drive to access both venues. New shows are added to the season including a puppet-based musical with child performers.

Take Me Along, the 1984 season closer at the Goodspeed, shows signs of an afterlife. Meanwhile, at the theatre in Chester, Sid and Marty Krofft, West Coast producers of televised puppet shows, add 17 tap dancing children to their show, along with their parents. The show is called *Broadway Baby*. They hire two original cast members from *A Chorus Line*, Tommy Walsh and Baayork Lee, friends of Carol, to direct and choreograph. I am naturally inclined to work on and stay with the show.

Take Me Along is scheduled for a pre-Broadway tour. *Broadway Baby* begins rehearsal. Michael wants me on the tour. I want to stay with the Krofft show.

I find myself in the barber chair in Michael's office. Michael demands I leave Broadway Baby and work on the tour of Take Me Along. I decide otherwise. Michael bans me from the theatre until I agree. Its Christmas time in the country again. *Merry Christmas! Season's Greetings! Happy Hanukkah!*

I concede. I end up on the road again.

I prepare Joseph for a pre-Broadway tour.

Hello, little Mister. So glad you're here.
Ready to go on the road with Daddy?
Look, Joseph, we're at the Shubert, back in New Haven!
There's the hospital you were born in.!
Joseph! We're in Washington, D.C.
This is the Kennedy Center.
Ooh Joseph! This is New York! You are on Broadway!

Isn't this fun, Buddy?

One of the advantages of a regional show with an ensemble cast is the absence of stars and their needs. It allows me to claim the star dressing room of the Martin Beck as a stage manager's office. It is large and has an alcove that accommodates Joseph's portable playpen. He gets to use it eight times. Seven previews and one opening night. I become aware of this by the absence of the producers at the opening night party. No reviews, yet. Then the death knell. I get a call from the producer's office offering me the use of the white stretch limo for the next four hours. It is paid for, a kind of severance for bringing in my first Broadway opening/closing night flop. Refreshments and expectations being what they are at this death of an opening night party, I take Carol and my two assistants, Brian and Andy, and head for a night on the town. Up through Central Park, Fifth Avenue, and Central Park West, past the Museum of Natural History, through the traverse road of Central Park, pass the Guggenheim, down to St. Patrick's Cathedral. The night is still young. Well stocked bottles of champagne in the service tray of the limousine are ready and willing. Down the West Side Highway, through lower Manhattan, up the FDR Drive.

"Just keep driving," Andy bids the driver looking for a destination, "On to the Triboro! Next stop, Cape Cod!"

Carol adds, "All I want is a patty melt…"

I respond, "There are no patty melts in New York."

"Any greasy burger will do. I'm starving."

The driver realizes none of us are decision makers at 3:00 a.m. in the morning. We cap the night in the South Bronx at the 24-hour White Castle on Bruckner Boulevard and feast on the most delectable blend of onion and gray meat in New York. At this time of night, it is an exquisite pairing with Veuve Clicquot. We all sense a new beginning.

Despite the one-night Broadway stand of *Take Me Along*, the show fares better than *Broadway Baby*, which does not survive the run at Goodspeed. The experience becomes my point of departure from the Opera House, East Haddam, and regional theatre. I outgrow the little theatre in the woods. It seems a childish enjoyment, affectionately remembered, but from another time that is now closed to me.

The Department of Labor welcomes me once again with open applications.

Central Park is at the beginning of our apartment block, and little Joseph becomes part of a small group of children of the Upper West Side that include struggling and not so struggling theatrical parents. "Play dates" become a social necessity, where parents and children meet at assigned times in the Central Park playground near the 86th Street entrance. Toys are shared. News of upcoming auditions, show closings, dance classes are the topics of the afternoon while the children play on the uniquely New York idea of a children's play station: monkey bars, sand boxes, steel swing planks suspended by chains, and, during the summer months, a circular cement wading pool with a center spigot emitting a water spray. Upon entry, parents inspect the monkey bars for rust erosion, the sandbox for cigarette butts, and the benches for drug paraphernalia. This is New York, and as much as we like to look away, it is dirty and dangerous. Somehow a job offer would seem to make things cleaner and more tolerable. I long to exchange concrete for a lawn.

I learn to accept nearly every job offer regardless of where it is or if it occurs at the same time. Usually, only one would come through, so the rule is to never say no. I become well-versed in landing the job that lasts. This is a dangerous game of musical chairs where losing means not working.

Until this one time.

I run into a dilemma. I have an opportunity to manage two shows that overlap by at least a week. One is in Washington, D.C. The other is in New York. Both have the possibility of employment beyond that overlapping week. I must decide, and I have learned to never say no.

I invent binary employment. I do both.

The limited engagement of *Carousel* at the Opera House in the Kennedy Center is tentatively booked for more cities. Tentative is the key word here. As usual, there is talk of "going on to Broadway," which I have heard countless times before. That possibility occurs only once in my career of road shows. I do not believe the hype, even if the schedule is printed. It just does not work that way in the theatre. We live on miracles and last-minute dreams, fully expecting some incredibly foolish person to invest some cash to keep the show running until reviews the come out.

We count on investors who succumb to the excitement of being in show business. Investors are in the same Neverland as critics. Critics usually do not have the talent to be on the stage but desperately seek recognition. Ignored in prep school, critics become Shakespearian aficionados who delude themselves with relevance. I remember the type in school, the ones in Advanced Placement English Lit who claim bizarre, self-appointed literary authority on every theatrical production.

If only I had been nicer to them when we were classmates.

Carousel stars Tom Wopat whose claim to fame is creating the role of Luke in the 1980s sitcom *The Dukes of Hazzard*. He is a competent enough actor who can hold his own against the elite Broadway airborne noses who dismiss him as television trash. The issue is that Tom is playing a role of complex character, a strong-willed roustabout prone to violence. Tom calls on his comfort zone of TV acting tricks to portray the 19th century New England roustabout with his 20th century *Dukes of Hazzard*,

Southern good old' boy, charming cad approach. He certainly adds a unique interpretation to the role.

The production is directed by Jamie Hammerstein, son of Oscar Hammerstein II, the creator of some of the most successful iconic musicals of the era: *Oklahoma, Showboat, The King and I, South Pacific, The Sound of Music.* Apples and people do not fall far from the family tree I guess, but brains and talent are one's own. Jamie is well connected and from a renowned theatrical family, but his claim to fame is directing anniversary productions of his father's musicals on the road, in summer stock, everywhere but Broadway.

Children of accomplished people have a unique challenge. They are at a disadvantage despite the abundant resources provided for them by successful parents. They must prove themselves, and if they follow in the footsteps of their parents' successes, it can be daunting. I can thank my own father for not raising the bar so high. He would have been happy if I were that teacher or train conductor he suggested a long time ago.

Jamie provides the sense of celebrity, but he does not provide an efficient, collaborative environment for the creative staff. He never visits the vocal and dance rehearsals. He knows the show from his father, not from his creative staff. No one can convince him to change his routine.

At the final run in the rehearsal hall of the Opera House, Jamie has staged Nettie Fowler, the kind, loving, Cracker Barrel-sized character on the wrong side of the stage for "June is Bustin' Out All Over," the big production number that involves the entire cast. It does not come of his own conclusion. Peter Martins, the choreographer, a seasoned ballet star, watches the run and panics.

Jamie's response is to bring his right hand to his right buttock, and mutter, "Oh shit," quietly. For the next five hours of rehearsal, three of them unscheduled overtime, manic theatrical surgery is performed on fixing the production snafus. We correct many staging issues that afternoon, which turn into night.

The fixes do not help the show. *The Washington Post* reviewer is lethal. He begins with the star. "Wopat comes up short in nearly every category." He suggests the "supporting players belong to the sore-thumb school of performing arts," and the sets "underscore director James Hammerstein's inherent clumsiness." The critic covertly signs off as a "Washington Post Staff Writer."

Meanwhile, back in New York, the Leo Burnett Advertising Agency is producing a Dealer Announcement Show for the Oldsmobile Division of General Motors. This is a yearly event revealing the new product line to sales managers and dealers across the country. For a stage manager, it is a six-week gig and a very lucrative one.

Of course, I sign that contract, too.

I arrange for six days of prepaid tickets on a no-frills airline, People's Express. Every day for a week, I leave my hotel near the Kennedy Center, take the Metro from Foggy Bottom Station to Washington National Airport, and board a 6:00 a.m. flight. I land at Newark, take a commuter bus to Port Authority in Manhattan, then walk twelve blocks to the facility where the *Oldsmobile Show* is rehearsing. The show that year rehearses in the large rehearsal room in Radio City Music Hall above the theatre. It would not be the last time I work there.

At 4:00 p.m., I leave rehearsal to the assistant stage manager, and reverse the trip to arrive at the Kennedy Center by 7:30 p.m. The general manager of *Carousel* has just been hired to do a new London import called *Les Misérables*. We speak many times about the possibility of joining the company once *Carousel* is over. Of course, I have already learned that nothing is certain with talk, so I do not think much of it or the GM either. The general manager's soft, round face reminds me of the Stay Puft Marshmallow Man. He shares a smiling and sinister look at the same time. It is difficult to determine whether he is genuinely pleased at my work or smiling at the thrill of potentially firing me. Managing a discussion with him requires taking everything he says and evaluating it later. Empty, crushed boxes of Entenmann's Fine Pastries protrude from the trash can beside his desk.

On Friday night of this insane week, the People's Express flight back to Washington National is delayed by a half hour. Both the New York rehearsal and the Washington, D.C. performance are covered. I arrive at the stage door of the Opera House just before showtime. All is well, and the curtain is about to rise. The general manager sees me, overnight case in hand, walking toward the stage manager's desk as my assistant calls the house lights to half. He motions me to come over.

"Where have you been?" he asks.

"I just came from the airport." I had not told him of my "day" job.

"Have you been commuting all week?

I could not lie to him.

"Yes, I think it worked out rather well." I figured I would assume innocence as a preemptive strike at controlling where this might be going.

He says nothing. He nods as if he had heard what he had been searching for, then walks away.

Carousel never travels beyond Washington, D.C., and I never hear from the general manager again. He never returns my calls. After the Kennedy Center run, I finish the Oldsmobile gig and spend the next three months watching *Les Misérables* rehearse and open to theatre history. I am not hired. I find out, through conversations with other colleagues, that the general manager did not feel I could guarantee staying with *Les Misérables* exclusively. He also considered me a weak personality for the job. I disagree, but I am confused. I believe leadership is awarded to you by the people whom you lead. But the general manager's preoccupation is with a pencil, not relationships. Whatever the reason, my balancing act of two-show employment backfires.

In theatre, every so often, things that can break you, truly devastating things, can bring you to an astounding realization that is so unexpected, so terrifying that you are at a loss to respond. *Les Misérables* is not possibility anymore. It becomes a death in the family. I can no longer claim the show as my own. I cease following its development. It no longer captivates me. It stings me. Its musical score is stirring, sensual, relentlessly passionate. This musical is now an unrequited love. I have lost it in a moment of opportunistic ambition. I question why one incident should scuttle my chances. I have a right to work. I face an unbearable fact of messing up, making a bad call. I breach some unforeseen deference to how things work in the Broadway employment game. Working one's way into a "stable" of stage managers regularly hired by general managers is not on my agenda. I think of myself as a free agent. Apparently general managers are as competitive as actors. You work only for one general manager, and they keep you employed in the proliferating companies of Broadway hits. *Les Misérables* has numerous "national companies" or tours that crisscross the country. Everyone else is the "competition." I get over harboring lament. I muster up enough resolve and self-esteem to find ways to make it right again. I learn to never, ever give up. I move on. I find another job.

Those who do commit to working only for one general manager secure a good living but at the cost of stifling their career growth. I recall the follow spot operator who opened with the show and spent his career illuminating the character of *Javert* eight times a week for 16 years. If you could see where he worked , you would suspect his emotional makeup to be a bit reclusive with hints of sociopathic ideation. He never does anything out of the ordinary. Having lunch with him is uncomfortable. He maintains this glazed stare directed just to my left which seems to indicate activity behind me. But there is never anything behind me. He chews gum while smoking cigarettes. I cannot imagine the taste of that. One day, he leaves his workstation and never does anything else in the theatre again. I find it difficult to accept his walking away from a show I wanted to do desperately. I never see him again.

The catchy theme of the Oldsmobile Dealer Announcement Show this year is "There is a Special Feel in an Oldsmobile." No Shakespearian aficionados are to be found here, just hard-driving closers looking to sell cars by filling the stage with jazzy dance numbers. We travel with six new Oldsmobile car models, five musicians, and twelve dancers. While the cars travel in carefully padded 53-foot semi-trailers, and the cast and crew travel with their regular luggage, I travel with 12 red-spandex hot pants with matching gold lame halter tops, 12 pairs of red sequined two-and-one-half-inch character shoes and a rolling cart of hair and safety pins, Aqua Net, Kotex, Tylenol, and Pepto-Bismol. I am ready for everything. The show budget does not allow for the hiring of a wardrobe attendant, so I double as costume caretaker and provider of the dancers' well-being. I take care of their every need.

We tour Chicago, Atlanta, Las Vegas, New York, and East Lansing, Michigan. East Lansing may seem out of place on the list, but it is the home of the Oldsmobile Manufacturing plant, where all Oldsmobiles are made. The people of East Lansing worship Oldsmobiles. The police cars, taxis, fire chief's cars are all Oldsmobiles. There is not a Ford or Chevy sedan to be seen. It is the home of Michigan State University, and the energetic young backstage crew picked from the theatre department put the "pros" from New York to shame. They put on a great show.

Five weeks later, I am out of a job, but I have added a lifelong friend.

Henry Aronson, the music director for these car shows, shares in the ridiculousness of making a living involving dancing showgirls and shiny automobiles. We sneak periodic glances of disbelief during rehearsals. There is nothing like sharing the limelight with 4,000 pounds of hulking, polished steel twirling center stage on a revolving turntable. It is truly a once-in-a-slow-Broadway-season experience, but this gig is memorable for its attempt to make a boxy sedan sexy enough to buy. When we run in to one another at an audition, on the street, the inevitable jingle making big bulky cars look attractive surfaces in our heads simultaneously. *There is a Special Feel in an Oldsmobile* reminds us that beyond one's artistic calling, rent must be paid.

Twenty-five years later, Henry and I share my last Broadway show, a revival of *Grease* at the Brooks Atkinson. Back as a stage manager, I enjoy the energy of those onstage who are half our age. Henry is a triple lifetime threat. From the Broadway productions of *Rent, the Rocky Horror Show, Little Shop of Horrors, Rock of Ages, Tommy, Rocktopia,* and more, his accomplishments span from legendary Broadway to ear-bending rock. One of the most sought-after conductor-musical director-composer musical artists on Broadway, Henry still retains a seasoned blend of rocker and maestro. To call a show with Henry is permanently cool and nailing the light cues off his tempo is proof I can still call show with the best of them. We celebrate our addiction to keeping our theatrical chops. Henry continues to work on wilder and louder shows to which I became a regular visitor. He helps to maintain my contemporary relevance despite advancing age. He and his lovely wife Cailin share memorable dinners with Carol and I, especially when Henry provides complimentary tickets to his shows.

I resign myself to not being part of *Les Misérables*, which turns out to be the theatrical event of the century. I deal with passing by the theatre on the street where it plays. The show keeps on breaking performance records and is defining a theatrical era. The production plays forever, its signage becoming part of the permanent streetscape of Broadway. Meanwhile, I do car shows, award shows, endless hit musicals that turn out to be flops, even a show with the oldest working man in the theatre.

George Abbott is 99 years old when a revival of *Broadway*, his 1926 crime drama, is revived as a regional theatre production at the Great Lakes Theatre Festival. The idea that Mr. Abbott is alive, kicking, and working prompts the producers to mount a limited run of *Broadway*, the play, on Broadway, the street.

I am hired to monitor and advise the stage managers on the show who had not had Broadway experience. I approve their daily schedule, point out possible pitfalls in overtime and missed cast members in rehearsal calls, and suggest they tone down their constant enthusiasm.

Mr. Abbott is the unofficial representative of the American theatre for the entire 20th century. His theatrical and film career spans 75 years. That is more than three generations. He earns the nickname Mr. Broadway, there is not much anyone can say, do, or tell the living icon. My biggest task turns out to be keeping the cast and staff from cooing and pleading with him for advice and autographs. The stage managers temper their provincial gawkiness by reducing their penchant for treating Mr. Abbott as a theatrical deity. I am focused on ensuring he does not trip over wires and on stairwells. My job is more akin to a resident aide in assisted living than managing a workplace with a sage. As a wise old press agent for "Hello Dolly" quips when he helps an aging Ethel Merman out of a cab, "Got to make sure the lady doesn't trip over her age and fall on her baggage." I watch the rehearsal proceedings from the tech table located in the fifth row of the orchestra.

The show opens on Mr. Abbott's 100th birthday and closes two days later. I could have remained in the fifth- row tech table and not impacted any patrons. It receives mediocre reviews and does not sell a ticket. The hoopla subsides, the cast returns to the unemployment line, and Mr. Abbott returns to Florida. Yesterday's hits are today's flops, and that is the stuff of a theatrical life regardless of one's celebrity.

I wait for my phone to ring.

In June, Jamie Hammerstein asks if I would speak to his students in his summer class in directing at Columbia. I agree and wonder how I am going to skillfully avoid the collaboration issue I had experienced with their professor.

I get lucky. He wants me to discuss why his directing students should not be stage managers. I could have taught a whole semester on the reasons why. The first lesson would be how to clean up after your boss's creativity.

Les Misérables, the show I did not get to do, is now a Broadway institution. I begin to identify with Cossette, the character that is the advertising signature of the show. The waif is from an 1862 giclee print by Emile Antoine Bayard, a French illustrator who created the artwork for the original book by Victor Hugo. That forlorn look of being victimized looks like a mirror to me. I avoid it as much as I can.

My phone rings.

Bruce Nelson, a producer with Leo Burnett Advertising asks if I am interested in doing another industrial. The

Maytag Appliance Company is launching a new product line, and they contract the advertising agency to create a product announcement for its sales force. Maytag recently purchases the Admiral Refrigerator Company of Galesburg, Illinois, and wants to create a show around the announcement. This is the same job as Oldsmobile. The red spandex hot pants with matching gold lame halter tops, pairs of red sequined two-and-one-half-inch character shoes and a rolling cart of hair and safety pins, Aqua Net, Kotex, Tylenol, Pepto-Bismol, adding Kaopectate to the mix. The first aid case from the Oldsmobile show comes in handy. All I need to do is hire just six of the twelve original dancers from the automobile show.

Conjuring up sales excitement by stimulating libidinal emotions around cars is one thing, but making refrigerators look sexy is quite another. The conservative Maytag sales representatives wear mandatory charcoal or navy suits with black wingtips. This is a hard sell.

How to make six white rectangular boxes marketable is the challenge. We decide to make the refrigerators dance partners. We place them on casters and the ladies dance with their "male" partners. This is an unbelievably sexist solution that receives a standing ovation from the charcoal suiters. I suspect that it is the golden halter tops and red spandex pants that draw them to their feet. It has nothing to do with the cubic foot capacity of refrigerators.

After five days in the only hotel in Newton, Iowa, I drive to Des Moines and return home, wondering where the next offer of employment takes me.

My phone ringing becomes a welcome regular occurrence.

Jerry Kravat, a music producer, is looking for a stage manager for a tour of a one-woman show, which appeals to me. The performer is Barbara Cook, the original Marian the

Librarian in the 1957 Broadway production of *The Music Man*. Barbara's voice is heavenly, exquisite. At sixty years old, she still retains the sweet ingénue beauty of her youth in her face and her voice. This looks like an easy gig, with additional duties required.

Barbara's work regimen includes culinary management. I take the job.

I oversee the search in finding sources for delivering a healthy, well-balanced meal for every rehearsal and performance. The rehearsal schedule for the day includes selected food items in specific, weighted amounts. "Gluten free" occupies my dietary vocabulary. Eggplant Parmesan and meatball heroes are the sustenance of a working lunch for me. I become the unofficial resident dietician for five weeks.

We rehearse at 890 Studios, a converted warehouse on the corner of 18th Street and Broadway that had been purchased by a choreographer, Michael Bennett. Michael made a fortune from his work in *A Chorus Line*, one of the most successful Broadway shows of the 1970s and Carol's claim to Broadway fame. Nearly every Broadway show rehearses at 890. Just working in the building feels successful, as if the original success of *A Chorus Line* permeates the gray plaster walls and rock maple dance floors.

Squeezing into one of the pair of tiny elevators, I run into stagehands on their way to constructing set mock-ups, stars shading their eyes from autograph seekers, dancers piling their dance bags over their heads to make room for another passenger. With one space reserved for the operator, the elevator cab holds seven people. The mechanical spaghetti of oily cables, sheave pulleys, and greased tracks of the lift system are easily visible through the steel mesh walls of the cab. Passengers with vertigo are immediately identified by their concentrated stare to the floor, seeking some semblance of focus for the ride.

I meet Wally Harper, the talented and gracious music director for Barbara Cook, in the lobby of 890. We ride up to the fourth floor and enter Studio B, a 20-by-20-foot corner space overlooking ABC Carpet across the street and Paragon Sports across Broadway. I peer through the southside windows and notice the busy display of activity in progress directly facing me inside the windows of the ABC Carpet store building. The work is so close and identifiable. Workers rolling and unrolling carpets and restacking them. It is work so different than what is occurring on my side of the street. I think of Alfred Hitchcock's *Rear Window*, a 1954 thriller where actor Jimmy Stewart's voyeuristic peeping inadvertently causes him to witness a murder in a window of an apartment building directly across the alley from his own apartment. I look away. I have more pressing things to do than to entangle myself in a crime mystery of an imagined criminal act. *The Rug Roller Murders*. *The ABC Carpet Murders*. I make note of the titles for future use.

Wally's piano testing pulls me away from the window. I focus on my day job of stage and nutrition management for a mature Broadway celebrity.

At 10:00 a.m., Barbara enters the room, a silk afghan draping over her alimentary indiscretions. She greets Wally and me at the grand piano. A few minutes of small talk, a small throat clearing, and Wally begins to play the introduction to "Dear Friend," a sweet love letter ballad from the Broadway hit *She Loves Me*.

Barbara begins to sing.

The sun illuminates the room with light and warmth, and I witness a command performance attended by a single patron, me. Barbara fills the air with her clear, sweet, lyrical soprano voice. Privileged to be in the room, I realize how memorable experiences such as these define a performance standard delivered only by the best in the business.

The sublime brilliance of Barbara Cook's voice inspires the producer to book a tour that begins in Providence and continues to Chicago and Washington, D.C. Everywhere Barbara sings adds to the history of great performances of every venue. Her voice is a mystical experience. I follow her every note, anticipating light cues in tune with her performance. Though it may just be sentimental conceit, I feel I am performing with her.

But it is at Ford's Theatre on 10th Street NW where my frivolous musings and the venue's historical reality form an unsettling aura. The interior of the theatre is surreal. Restored to its original look as it appeared on April 14, 1865, it evokes a calming mood and seems to resist the intrusion of the commerce of theatrical presentation. The raked stage creates an intimacy for the audience, bringing everyone together as if in a great room unobstructed by a proscenium. The violation of that night over 150 years ago persists and has taken permanent residence in the house right theatre box, still adorned with bunting, an American Flag, and a framed rendering of George Washington. It was placed there for Lincoln's arrival by the theatre owner, John T. Ford. In the shadows of the ghost light on center stage, the haunting view commands reflection.

Barbara's delivery quiets a full house, beginning with "Come Rain or Come Shine," "Stars," "We'll Be Together Again," and the moving "The Rose." In the somber venue that has become a resting place for a national, historical wound, her poignant ballads sound like hymns.

On her service table, I refresh the crimson seedless grapes and reflect on the depth of the moment made timeless by art and circumstance.

Chapter 7

The Arena Show from Hell

Carol tucks one-year-old Joseph into his crib. Her responsibilities become a different kind of performing art. Now, Carol dances, sings, and pantomimes to Joseph's delight. Carol is a natural mother, and I do not realize this talent until after she has Joseph. We agree on how we are going to manage this growth of family. Two parents in show business is not in the cards. She stays home, I work. In our midcentury environment, that remains the best option, and the healthiest environment for our children. Joseph has a constant parental presence in his life, and he has a constant financial support system if I have a job.

I am getting better and better at securing one despite the gnawing reminder of the *Les Misérables* new signage atop the Majestic Theatre.

The few leads to cover vacationing Broadway stage managers come to nothing. I need work. Alan Hall, a premier stage manager who manages every David Merrick English import brought to Broadway is busy setting up third-tier road tours. He is managing a children's bus and truck show disguised as a rock concert. The story is set in outer space on a planet called *Eternia*. The chief attraction of this extravaganza is a world-clash conflict between *He-Man*, protector of all that we hold dear, and *Skeletor*, the evil, black-light-illuminated antihero out to capture Castle Greyskull and rule forever in his iridescent Halloween costume. *She-Ra* is *He-Man's* trusted mate, a role created to provide eye candy for all the good fathers taking their kids to a Saturday morning show at 9:00 a.m. *She-Ra* has lines, but her character never evolves into more than just a supporting role for *He-Man*. Her character does empower her, and it is one of the first attempts to include credible female roles in live-action cartoon content.

Everyone is on roller skates.

Alan Hall is a veteran of the theatre. His career spans over 40 years. He manages everything from the West End of London to imported limited engagements on Broadway. His opening nights are performed in a tuxedo. He is now lugging a one-nighter roller derby tour in jeans on the other side of 6th Avenue at Radio City Music Hall. It runs eighteen consecutive sold out performances, a record that still holds over twenty years later. Following the initial run at the Music Hall, it is scheduled to a 60-city tour through the heartland of America.

Carol's demeanor evokes concern and a subliminal warning. She looks for an answer from me about how we are going to pay our bills. I hope for a solution.

My phone rings. It is Alan.

He invites me backstage at *He-Man and She-Ra, Masters of the Universe*. Alan asks if I am interested in taking the show over by Monday in Nashville. It is Thursday.

Needing work and seeking relief from Carol's burning eyes, I say yes.

It is the arena show from hell.

JUST OFF, STAGE RIGHT

The whole production fits into five, 53-foot semis and tours cities every three days. Keith, the sound engineer, cannot make the show any louder. He thinks it sounds just fine.

"Third tier" refers to population size and access to cultural events. Unlike the East Coast where there is a cultural event every ten feet with a wine tasting and a Starbucks close by, some cities have limited consumer demand and venues that translate into profit potential. Running a performance for 15,000 patrons in one night is far more profitable than running a performance on Broadway for 800 patrons. An arena show can be a cash cow with merchandise sales soaring far above the already inflated ticket price. For patrons who cannot afford a trip to Disney, it might be the only entertainment available.

I arrive at Nashville International Airport on Sunday night. This is one of those airports that claim a different meaning for "International." It is nice enough, except the ads for travel boast Louisville, Charlotte, Knoxville, and Chattanooga. The tunnel connecting the arrival gates to baggage claim offer a display of guitars, discount ticket offers to the Grand Ole Opry's Ryman Auditorium, and a bus tour of the Parthenon, a full-size replica of the real thing located in Athens, Greece. But there are no ads for trips to Greece. It is not that kind of International.

I check in at the Red Roof Inn. It is the 1980s version of Motel 6, where your shady neighbors are alcoholics instead of drug and human traffickers. The room is clean, with Johnny Cash-compliant references in wall art and music selection and with 100 brochures for free delivery ribs. I call Carol to let her know I arrive safely. She claims the wood stove in the back room offers a cozy warmth on this chilly Connecticut evening and wishes I were there. I kiss the receiver of the phone hoping it will travel and hang up. I drop off my gear and leave for the theatre.

I pass the home of the Grand Old Opry, the Ryman Auditorium, and Tootsie's Orchid Lounge. I think how prestigious this historic theatre would look on my venue resume, but the show is booked down the street at the Municipal Auditorium, a faceless, block-wide box arena built in 1950. It boasts of being the first air-conditioned public assembly building in Nashville when constructed. The sign is still there with frosted letters resembling inverted ice cream cones.

I enter the building through the stage door, past an alley lined with the five tractor trailers. Some drivers are in their extended cabs, drawing electric power from the facility and living their road life in a four-by-eight box on wheels. That, for a moment, seems appealing to me. The set consists of a 40-foot-square steel truss loaded with automated Varilights, CO_2 emitters to accentuate the take-off to our journey to Eternia, and numerous woofers, tweeters, and speaker arrays guaranteed to provide permanent damage to the future auditory capability of everyone in the arena. Hanging from the grid of the arena ceiling is a massive cargo climbing net where the final battle is waged fifty feet in the air, with *Skeletor* meeting his doom in a pool of green soup illuminated from below.

Alan is standing in the oval skating track, which forms the bulk of the scenery. At seven feet above the floor, it seems sparse, but hidden within the structure is a series of trap doors, pyrotechnical stations, mineral oil fog makers, and strobe lights that flutter color and light to detract from the reality of the illusions created for the intergalactic fight for survival. This is big-time smoke and mirrors. *Star Wars* on the road.

Alan and I meet, exchanged industry banter, and begin a tour of the production set up. As we walk around the set, he familiarizes me with the cast and crew.

Most of the stagehands are lifetime roadies. There is Leo, a head rigger, who displays death-defying agility in wrapping burlap around steel beams before placing the cables that will hold trusses holding special effects. Leo is five feet tall and angry about it. I do not think Leo ever travels further north than Daniel Boone National Forest.

Davy is a show electrician. A true patriot, Davy maintains the All-American Jack Daniels stash on the crew bus for extra-long rides between venues. Davy is not short for David. "My name is Davy. It ain't short for nothin' else," the technician proclaims. The last Davy I recall is Davy Crockett. I do not think anyone named their kids from Disney characters anymore.

Matteo, assistant to Leo, runs prop and costume setup. His long hair extends only from the sides of his head. He is otherwise bald, except for the shrub-like carrot hedge horseshoed around his ears. I never bring up his doppelganger Bozo, and I think he appreciates that.

The assistant stage manager is the daughter of the producers. She is very pretty and very useless. They are a Bible Belt family who feel their mission is to provide the country with family entertainment through morality plays. At $25.00 a ticket, the arena can gross $400,000 in one performance. This seems quite lucrative for the moral of any story. These folks are nice enough, but I know I am not in my comfort zone, and being from New York, I am sure they find me quite odd.

I am beginning to think no one in this group has ever met or worked with anyone from the East Coast. I meet Stack, the production manager. Stack's demeanor is pleasant enough. But that is before I see the Stars and Bars inked on his back at a load in. There is no landsmanship here. Stack is a braggart, which is a dangerous thing to be when you are responsible for loading in and out five truckloads of scenery. Stack is charged with putting on a show with people rappelling from scenic pieces hanging from the rafters within seven hours. There are no shortcuts in accuracy allowed here. There is no room for bravado.

I learn this is his first day on the job.

The cast begins to assemble on the track to warm up for the next show. The person playing *Skeletor*, sans his ultraviolet-sensitive ghoulish cloak, practices his routines of fouetté turns. The actor playing *She-Ra* appears and stretches to practice her arabesque. She is a body builder by profession like her real-life husband, who plays *He-Man*. A supporting actor joins the cast warming up. Another actor joins the group. The actor is a cocaine user. He always keeps his sunglasses on.

Sound check destroys any attempt at continued conversation. Keith begins generating pink noise, a process by which all frequencies are played out at full volume at the same time to ensure a balance of amplification within a confined space. It is a loud, persistent hissing that raises blood pressures and frazzles nerves.

This is Keith's favorite thing to do.

This might turn out to be the most revolting show I will ever work on in my career, I begin familiarizing myself with the sequencing of the show. Cues involve lighting, truss motor moves, pyrotechnical, trap door, and sound calls. The production is partially automated. There is taped music, taped dialogue, taped explosions, robotic light cues, all tethered to a SMPTE time code, which is a standard of synchronization developed by the Society of Motion Picture and Television Engineers. The control system allows various activities to be executed against a timing device. The result is a recurring sequence of events that are automatically implemented. It is very much like autopilot, allowing things to run consistently every time, until it does not.

The system is both despised and loved by stage managers. It is used on the road to reduce labor costs.

Broadway show people distance themselves from theatrical events beyond the jurisdiction of 6th and 8th Avenues to the north and south, and 42nd and 59th Streets to the east and west. Any other production is assumed to bear cracks of imitation in varying degrees of unprofessionalism. Unless you are working for Disney, recreating cartoon characters for a live presentation, and taking it out in the road is just about the bottom of the industry barrel, slightly above traveling ice shows, which is slightly above warm-up acts in casino lounges.

I have never had a more depressing, more debilitating attack on my self-esteem than having a drink in a casino lounge. It is the birthplace of alcoholics.

The arena gates open, and throngs of families spill out onto the thousands of unassigned seats. Aromas of deep-fried grebbel, corn dogs, and caramel popcorn coerced children to pull their parents toward concession stands placed every 25 feet. Massive speakers blast the Oak Ridge Boys, Randy Travis, and Hank Williams, Jr.

The 44-foot-square truss illuminates its sixty automated varilights and strobes as heated mineral oil sends a cloudy fog of vapor in the air. CO_2 tanks spew white thrusts, creating the illusion of a huge spaceship taking off. Keith, now threatening everyone's aural health, turns up the sound console pots to a guttural, thunderous punk rock underscore. The whole place feels like an assemblage of ambulances at the scene of a multi-vehicle pileup on Route 80. The kiddies eat it all up along with their supersized sugar treats.

"What's a grebbel, Daddy?"

"It's like a pretzel. It's good for you. It's German."

"What's the white stuff, daddy?"

"Powdered sugar. Just the way you like it."

I thought for a moment how Carol feeds little Joseph codfish squares at home, claiming it to be something else.

"It's chicken, Joseph, just the way you like it."

I wonder how many parents sitting in the arena go to that extreme to maintain nutrition.

The truss rises slowly and reaches a 60-foot height. On a musical cue, a circular pod preset in the rafters began to descend with a shaggy-haired, generic pop/rocker sporting a futuristic guitar. Being the talented, lip-syncing songster, he mimes his way down until the pod reaches the roller derby track. He disembarks, mouthing all this time, waves his sequined cape-like garb like a Metallica warm-up wannabe. His character's name is *Songster*, quite an original moniker considering the creative arc of inspiration found in this production.

The ad for hiring brokers in a penny-stock boiler room is looking attractive right now.

Utilizing every available special effect to the fullest, *Songster* is drowned out by a crescendo of pyrotechnic ordnance accompanied by a thirty second spray of fireworks emanating from the truss above. The sparks are magically designed to extinguish upon contact with the arena floor. Some do not, bouncing across the stage like drunken fireflies, but no one seems concerned. I am ready to evacuate the facility.

Songster continues synching his lips to the automated track: "Boys and Girls, help me give *He-Man* and *She-Ra* a big, loud, warm welcome!" The overcompensation of the actor's arm and body gestures telegraphing the excitement of his lines reveals a major synchronization issue. It becomes apparent that the timing of his voice tape and his acting are nowhere near each other.

Squeals of delight of the same decibel as screams of fright pour from the vast spread of young voices now fully energized and needing to work off the powdered sugar grebbels.

He-Man, glistening in body oil to accentuate his remarkable hulk, descends the Grand Steps of Castle Greyskull and greets the audience by waving his steely looking sword like it is a toy. It is. He gestures toward the top of the steps as *She-Ra*, shimmering in a white-and-gold winged cape adorned with a matching winged helmet found only in lavish European opera productions of *Die Walküre*. She steps down, takes her place next to *He-Man* and waves her swordette, a weapon a fifth smaller than the manly size of her co-star. Here is feminized inequality to fit the feminine hand. *She-Ra* greets the crowd as if she were catapulted with bouquets. She is just being screamed at by thousands of little voices.

The acting has no relationship to the audience. The actors can only feign awe at the crowd's reaction for twenty-five seconds, the allotted audience reaction time before the next taped line played and the actors are forced to lip-sync pre-taped script. Later in the performance an extended crowd reaction drowns out the exposition of the actor's dialogue because the screaming and applauding continues beyond the recorded space of twenty-five seconds. Toward the end of the first act, a less energetic, quieter audience ends their reaction ten seconds into the star's entrance, leaving our heroes to feign responses in silence until the silent space of the tape plays out to the next line.

The crew spends my first week sizing me up. I am as foreign to them as they are to me. They do not appreciate me hanging around for the load ins and outs after the performance. They feel spied upon. Attitudes change in Louisville when the breakfast caterer fails to show up, and I order take-out from the local Waffle House in time for the 7:00 a.m. break.

Springfield, Tulsa, Kansas City. We work our way through the heartland of America, in places I have never been. My East Coast cultural privilege is suppressed until I arrive at the State Fair in Wichita. A 15,000-seat arena stands in the middle of cornfields with a chrome-plated bull overseeing the main entrance. All five trucks each have their own bay, which cuts the load time by two hours. This is a clean, new facility. Preinstalled carabiner hooks eliminate the need to spot points in the grid from which to wrap cable around the rafters. We are scheduled for three shows followed by a load out. I am convinced this is the place where they capture all the cornfield photographs for the boxes of Kellogg's Corn Flakes. I decide to go for a run to see how it feels to pass acres of corn. For a while, it is invigorating. Then I get lost.

Two hours later, I return. I tell no one how I incredibly inept and stupid I am in the middle of thousands of acres. My East Coast upbringing does not allow it, and I can't afford it in front of the crew.

The show works its way through Kansas City, Vancouver, and Oakland. Things settle down quite a bit, and most of us are now used to a routine road life. We perform at the University of Nevada arena in North Las Vegas. It is not the 107-degree weather that overwhelms me. This is what it must feel like to arrive in downtown Sodom, just outside of Greater Gomorrah. We have a three-day stay here, and it gives me a chance to see the sights. I have never been here before. The garish promises of food, drink, and sex makes me think I am never going home again. The pseudo-sophisticated East Coast New Yorker in me gets homesick and I become a wallflower.

I travel most of the time with the cast, but on this last leg, Clive, one of our truckers, invites me to ride with him to Los Angeles, the next stop. After the last show on the last day, we are anxious to get on the road. A sandstorm begins to kick up speed just as we are heading out. We are fortunate the storm is due east.

We leave Las Vegas around 2:00 a.m.

The moon on a clear night in the desert is breathtaking. Its light creates a stunning, shimmering foam over the landscape.

I take in the pristine aroma of air heated by the day's sun. The earth is untainted by human habitation for endless miles. Clive settles into the numbness of the ride. We exchange bits of conversation, but the peace and serenity of the earth claims my interest more. We both take in the silence, the timelessness, the deadening contentment of just being and breathing. He is well-versed in this silent life. I am a beginner. There is nothing to learn here but patience and an unfettered appreciation for living on the planet. I think that explains those truckers I first saw in Nashville resting in their cabins while in between hauls.

We stop at the Flying J Truck Stop in Jean, just at the California-Nevada border. I stumble in, now being one of the boys, and order eggs, grits, and biscuits with a pot of coffee. I call Carol, mumbled a few words, something to her like, "I'm in the middle of the desert and I was thinking of you," then hang up. I stumble back out onto the bus. The moon invites its silence again, this time with friends. The crew decides it is time I join them on their bus. I thank Clyde and enter the crew bus. I approach the back-lounge area. The whole crew is there, and I have no idea what to expect. Jack Daniels is poured. I am offered a glass.

Matteo leads everyone in a toast.

"We've been watching you, and we think you have become one of us," he announces. "Welcome aboard."

There is a good feeling in my mind and in my throat.

I am a roadie, at least for now, in the middle of the desert.

As the sun visits the passenger side of the bus three hours later, we exit Route 405 and head southwest on Beach Boulevard on our way to Huntington Beach. We have not slept, and the warm sand is a welcome mattress for the next three hours. No one thinks about sunscreen here, and everyone falls asleep to the sound of the early morning sea gently crashing on to the shore.

Setting the thermostat at 50 degrees and closing the drapes to block out any sunlight helps to reduce the pain of a three-hour California sunburn. Layers of aloe salve begin the long process of my skin returning to normal. My Mediterranean heritage saves me from sun poisoning that day. I thank my Neapolitan and Roman heritage.

The decisive moment of my roadiehood comes when we arrive at the Cow Palace just outside San Francisco. A tractor and cattle pull convention is booked the night before, and when we pull up for a 6:00 a.m. load in, bulldozers are still scooping the last mounds of topsoil mixed with cow dung which had been installed over the arena floor. The debris is removed, but the aroma remains.

I call Carol.

"Hi, Honey. How are you this morning?"

"Fine. What's up with you? When are you coming home?

"Oh, soon, I'm sure."

"The show is closing, isn't it?"

"Oh no, no, nothing like that. I just wish you could be here to take in the fragrance of the Midwestern plains. It's so inspiring."

"Are you trashing the Midwest again?'

"No, no, I'm just trying to get used to the bullshit. I mean the real thing. They had a tractor pull here last night, and its smells like a methane spill or the Bronx Zoo. I can't decide."

She did not respond. I try to be funny.

"Hey, they need a dancer in the show. Want to sign up and do the road together?"

"No, thanks. Come home soon. I'm getting tired of this."

"Really? But I was having such a good time with the last trashy waitress in the Nevada desert."

"No, you didn't. Come home and I'll wear my Howard Johnson's cocktail waitress uniform."

"Love you."

"Love you, too."

I hang up and take a deep breath, which makes me skip breakfast that morning. I am certain that any remnant of Carol's desire to re-enter show business is at an all-time low.

I realize that live presentation is an elective for some. Out here where there are few choices, a traveling road show about the forces of good and evil is a cultural necessity. It might be difficult to manage weak plots and one-dimensional characters against a physical production that belongs at the midway of a carnival, but it may be the only social event a rural family can experience together. It may not be for the Starbucks crowd back East, but it recognizes the farmers, ranchers, and one-horse town folks who need live entertainment's life reflection as much as anyone.

I am always ready to leave this ridiculous business, until I sense the value of an arena show to the people attending it. There is no alternative career that tastes better.

That is the problem with addiction.

Chapter 8

To Have and Eat Cake: Broadway & Metro North

I survive the roller-skating extravaganza of He-Man and She-ra. My next job is ringing on my new cell. My older phone weighs nearly two pounds and is slightly smaller than the Signal Corps radios used WWII. Its ring resembles a warning of an impending explosion and fishing it out of my briefcase is like unloading a car battery.

Stephen Zweigbaum, the stage manager who replaced me on the Broadway run of *Whoopee,* offers me a job replacing the Second Assistant Stage Manager on his new musical, *Singin' in the Rain.* Finally, a rescue from the road life of truck stops, arenas in the middle of nowhere, and fantasizing trashy waitresses that I have begun to entertain. I jump at the chance and look forward to returning.

Back in New York, the signage of *Les Misérables* increases, attacking my self-esteem like a relentless gnat on nearly every corner.

Theatrical design trends of the 80s rely on spectacle. *Starlight Express* features a series of tracks with actors on roller skates, transforming automation design both onstage and backstage. Not to be outdone, *Singin' in the Rain* boasts a rain curtain pipes and a water trough. Both shows test the limitations of backstage space, forcing carpenters to piggyback scenic elements over each unit and store them in the air. A sequencing of scene preparations delivers required scenic elements on to the stage when needed. The backstage storage plot becomes a crucial organizational element of a smooth-running show.

Singin' in the Rain is playing at one of Broadway's newest and largest theatres, the Uris, now known as the Gershwin. Built in 1972, the theatre seats 1,900 patrons and is accruing a history of major theatrical events. *Sweeney Todd*, the New York Shakespeare Festival Production of *The Pirates of Penzance*, and the Tony Awards all play there. The building is cavernous and sleek with a modernist look reflecting the minimalist approach to public architecture styles of the era. The theatre lacks the warmth and intimacy of the older theatres surrounding Shubert Alley, mostly built in the 1920s. Those buildings feature neo-Gothic trimmings of limestone carvings, gargoyles, and tiled friezes, with the average capacity of 1,000 patrons. The structure of the Uris allows for more complex theatrical design applications and with nearly 2,000 seats it has the largest seating capacity of a Broadway theatre. Outside, it looks like a big box.

The producers take advantage of the space. The scenic elements of the show include a full-sized, operable locomotive prototype, a movie studio within the stage set, an exterior street scene, and 11 minutes of a rain shower for the famous dancing rain scene. The execution of the street scene requires exact timing, visual and musical coordination, and technical management coordination.

The theatre management structure evolves because of this technology. Head carpenters morph into technical supervisors. Stage managers, listed as the "executive instrument in the technical running of the production," according to Actors Equity Association, evolve into production managers and organizational designers. They run the show, meaning that they organize and order a series of physical production moves, i.e., changes in light, scenic moves coordinated with musical timing, to achieve a cohesive sequence of events. Before audio technology gave us headsets and wireless communication, stage managers called instructions out loud to technicians ready to execute the order. This is where the term "calling the show" originates. Wearing a headset then was quite unique. I consider wearing my *Sennheiser* double-muffed receiver with padded microphone extending over my face to be unique. Today, I could be mistaken for taking orders at McDonald's.

The calling of the rain sequence is the highlight of *Singin' in the Rain*. The preparation in setting up the sequence is just upstage of the production number being performed downstage. Near the end of the first act, a huge, waterproof tray, stored on its end and hanging on a reinforced pipe, is brought to the stage level and rolled downstage as stage carpenters let in slack and technicians guide the front end. Once the unit is secure, it is positioned over two downstage drains. The drains lead to a retrieval system for the water about to shower over the unit. Overhead, three water pipes descend closer to the stage and the water tray, at about 15 feet, just out of sight of the audience. Once secured, I call a test cue for the pipe nozzles and do a ten-second test of the water spray. Electricians check for leaks and drainage. Carpenters add the walls to the exterior set. A prop man plugs in a lamppost and completes the exterior street scene set up. The scene is ready for the actor playing Don Lockwood to perform his title number and get wet for the duration. All this is happening just upstage of the actors playing Don Lockwood, Kathy Selden, and Cosmo Brown, who are dancing over a sofa in "Good Mornin'," an acrobatic number where all three actors are required to balance over the top of a sofa and apply just enough pressure to force the sofa backward to tip and then jump over the fallen sofa without injuring themselves.

Toward the end of the production number, the transition going into the last scene of first act begins with the three rolling decks, or palettes upon which the "Good Mornin'" number is performed, being winched offstage, unlocked and stored. Two stagehands lift the fallen sofa and walk it back upstage to its storage position. Next, more stagehands immediately hook up each palette on all four ends and hoist them up in the air, one underneath the other, as the first onstage water pipe is cued. At this point, the water tray is not yet in its final playing position, so it is crucial that the activation of the right water pipe be turned on to avoid spraying the stage floor. The wrong pipe activation would short-circuit the winch pulley system that is incorporated into the stage deck—the system that sent the "Good Mornin'" palettes on and off stage.

I worry where this might have gone, but it never does.

As the water tray moves downstage to its final playing position, the second and third water pipe is cued, so that by the time Don Lockwood begins his vocal, the effect produces a fully engaged shower, brilliantly lit. It always works.

The scene also calls for a police character to be strolling the beat of the wet street scene while Don Lockwood dances in the rain. A marketing strategy is employed to use the role as a celebrity cameo appearance. Executing this idea adds to the tight backstage area when then New York City Mayor Ed Koch is scheduled to appear one evening. This adds a City of New York

Police Department detail backstage as well as television reporters and camera crews running lines of cable and equipment crates.

Despite the creative public relations efforts, the production suffers from mediocre reviews. Millions are poured into innovative technology to make the production palatable to an increasing spectacle-hungry audience. The show closes after 367 performances, not enough to recoup the magnitude of the original investment.

Thanks to Steven, *Singin' in the Rain* brings my employment score to three respectable runs vs. a one -night flop. He asks me to assist him on a new English import, *Me and My Girl*. I spend the next four years at the newest theatre on Broadway, the Marriott Marquis.

I meet Arturo Porazzi, a premiere stage manager and excellent teacher. In another life, Arturo is the professor I yearn for in college. Patience, accuracy, follow up, and an engaging personality. We three become fast friends. The show has a strong box office. It provides a welcome financial stability. Arturo and I look to improve our home life from city apartment to suburban living. Steven seeks a weekend getaway. Being stage managers, we begin to chart our house buying progress. We review progress reports every week. I claim the first bid on a house in Ridgefield, followed by Steven in Redding and Arturo in lower Manhattan. Carol responds by announcing her pregnancy as a housewarming gift. I am ready to exchange the two-seater MGB for a Volvo station wagon. Carol has an unexpected reaction.

"What's next, a tweed coat? A shopping spree at Talbots? Don't you dare sell that car!"

We settle on a Chevy Blazer SUV.

Carol gets to tour the Fairfield County countryside edition of manicured villages and crew cut lawns while I get my chance for a taste of the dashing commuter life. The gray flannel suiters are the earliest birds who take the 6:35 a.m. out of Goldens Bridge. My early train is the 11:20 a.m. It is a quieter ride, a non-peak train that carries the maids and nannies back to their Bronx apartments after cleaning their employer's very large homes and delivering their employer's children to their private schools.

I spread out across a three-seater, ready to spend the hour with newspaper, coffee and bagel. Bagels are so much more acceptable on a train than jelly doughnuts. I relate to these early, crack-of-dawn commuter counterparts. I take on their character of mover and shaker, decision maker, big-time jobber. My line of work is service. I polish the entertainment for my suburban neighbors.

In a way, Steven has more influence on my employment, my marriage, and my professional life than he may know. He has the unique talent of selecting long running shows. Working in a new theatre on Broadway is a privilege. I am looking forward to working in a state-of-the-art facility with ample room for the cast and staff.

The reality of this theatre is the fact that it is stuck inside a hotel. Access to backstage is behind a stanchion, then up a steep flight of stairs. Dressing rooms are spaces that are partitioned off behind retail windows exposed to the interior ballroom levels of the hotel. The "lobby" is on the 4th floor. The theatre is an afterthought in this hotel's construction plans.

Mike Okrent, one of the more successful British theatricals who invade Broadway, directs the show. His periodic visits are welcome. I find most directors to be emotionally problematic people. I could write a separate book entirely devoted to their insanity. Mike, however, is one of the finest, most genuine human beings in the theatre. He has an engaging sense of humor and reveals the depth of his good character by wearing it on both sleeves. It is a joy working with him.

The new theatre is the latest hotel addition to the Broadway entertainment district. Featuring a 49-story atrium, the theatre is accessible through the fourth floor. A dizzying view of the atrium can be seen outside every hotel room door. The openness of space is spectacular. The attractive upper lobby overlooks Broadway, an intimate stagehouse boasts excellent acoustics, and an air intake system that takes in outside air 15 feet above the street level and purifies it before distribution into the building. This is a unique adjustment that allows outside air to enter the backstage area without making an intrusive whoosh that would impact the quieter moments of a production.

On matinee days we notice a problem.

By 2:00 p.m. showtime, the backstage area begins to stink like the access ramps of the Port Authority Bus Station, the midtown terminal that accommodates the hundreds of commuter buses from New Jersey and points north and west of the city. Exhaust fumes from diesel-powered tourist buses parked on 45th Street keep their motors running. Their exhaust pipes run up the backside of the vehicle and bluster the warm flow straight into the accepting intake fans of the new building.

It takes a city ordinance, the Broadway League, and the NYPD Midtown South Division to keep the buses from parking there on show times. Meanwhile, complaints and health issues develop. Throat irritations, breathing difficulties lead the backstage conversation of the day at every performance. I become an expert in medical coding when filling out accident reports. I master the right ailment for everyone's irritation, physical and emotional, all for bus fumes. Things settle down when the air duct system is rerouted away from the backstage wall.

Living 60 miles north of Times Square provides an escape from 6,000,000 light bulbs chasing for attention. The Crossroads of America, New York's Times Square, is a myopic salute to this little island on the East Coast. No one here ever seems satisfied. One drink after the show is never enough. Everything in the Broadway theatre district is glaringly supersized, and tourists and district workers never achieve a feeling of satisfaction even after they stop imbibing and cavorting, even on holidays. The center of entertainment that is Broadway is a relentless lure that fails to satisfy regardless of how much I accommodate my urges. Home is the only cure.

By the time the evening performance is over at the Marriott Marquis, New Year's Eve revelers have already assembled along the "X" of 7th Avenue and Broadway that makes up Times Square. Crowds congregate as far north as 51st Street. A nearly impenetrable partying crowd stands between the stage door at 45th Street and Broadway and Grand Central Terminal located east at 42nd Street and Vanderbilt Avenue. I have trouble finding a path through the crowd to race to Grand Central to catch the 11:08 p.m. train. The show comes down at 10:45 p.m., just enough time to walk quickly to the station. This never happens on New Year's Eve. Police and security do not allow cross street pedestrian traffic through the swarm of people now fully engaged in party hats, inebriating beverages, embarrassing paraphernalia, and bitter cold. I pretend to become part of the mob and attempt to weave my way through to the east side of the crowd. It never works.

The 1:30 a.m. local becomes my only available transportation for the New Year. I board the train on Track 32 along with revelers who are more in need of a bed than a seat on the last train out of Grand Central.

At 2:45 a.m., after forcing my final goodbyes to fellow commuters who keep on reintroducing themselves many times over, I sidestep over the regurgitated excesses of overindulgence on the seats and aisles. I wave and leave the remaining revelers to the last six stops of the Harlem Line local, disembark and walk to my car. I breathed in the frozen silence of the early morning. Tonight, I feel lucky. I am grateful that it is a clear night and there is no snow to clear over the windshield. The door handles are cold but not frozen. The path to my car is clear. An open crack of the car window gradually exchanges the remnants of overdone quaffing for the fresh coldness of pine and evergreen. Whiffs of skunkweed line accompany the sweet fragrance of woods, confirming entry into my nightly escape of leaving the Crossroads of the World and all its unfulfilled expectations. No angst, no stress, no bustle, no repugnant aromas. Just the sweet smell of going home.

 I turn in to the driveway of my house to the garage doors but do not open them. It is 3:15 a.m. Not wanting to wake a sleeping family, I leave the car in the driveway and quietly enter through the front door. Out of the blackness of the row of boxwoods emerges Spats, my jet-black cat with snow-white paws, mewing his need to find a warmer spot. We both enter. The cat surveys the warmth of the living room and settles by the remaining embers of a spent fire. I close the front door, throw my coat over the loveseat in the living room, and check Joseph in his bedroom. I hear the sentient breathing of a sleeping child. In the master bedroom, Carol, managing a nine-month pregnancy by resting in well-deserved comfort and much needed sleep, seems content in enjoying the benefits of the back seat she had taken from her career.

 Walking softly, I close the door, tiptoeing back into the living room, and sink into the recliner by the fireplace. Spats complements the serenity of the moment with purring approval.

 I am home.

JUST OFF, STAGE RIGHT

Joseph's pancakes swell to small muffins, thanks to a spoonful of yeast. This may be the last day before his new role as a big brother, and I want this father and son moment to last before we both share his sister's arrival. Breakfast is cut short by Carol's contorted position on the stairwell leading to the basement. The time is sooner than we think. I place Carol in the car, drop off Joseph to a neighbor and return to I-95 in the second race to Yale-New Haven Hospital. This time from the other end. This baby is more decisive. Carol is crowning by exit 42. The hospital is two exits away.

I take a foolish stab at support and encouragement.

"Carol! You are her mother and you will not allow her to be born in this car!"

I pull up to the main entrance of the hospital. The security guard's lethargic look turns to panic at the sight of Carol in the back seat. He runs to get a wheelchair. Carol is wheeled into a post birthing recovery room, the closest room from the main entrance. The on-call doctors are still scrubbing, oblivious to the urgency at hand. A nurse and a trainee witness the trajectory of a newborn bent on being born now. The nurse literally catches my baby girl, pink as a chicken. No waiting or meandering. Lauren decides today is the day she intends to be born, and she arrives.

Carol, now an authority on delivering babies, shouts at the trainee attempting to plug oxygen into Lauren's nostrils. "Don't do that!" Carol orders. The nurse concurs with a look of approval. We now have two children.

Fatherhood is more complicated than ever. This is the 80s. The only known self-help groups are *Alcoholics Anonymous* and *Act Up*, the organization bringing the AIDS crisis to recognition. Fathers are assumed to be perfectly knowledgeable of their responsibility. One or two Lamaze classes watching your wife hyperventilate and you are a pro. The certificate you receive proves your sensitivity in separating lust from function. Will I live up to the task of my daughter's needs is an unanswered question. Is a strong father a compassionate one? How do I say 'no'? When do I say 'yes?' Will she charm me into being a fool, or will she adore me without question? I hardly know how to handle her mother. What makes me think I know how to be Dad to a little girl? I am still in training with her brother. There are no right answers. There are only decisions and acceptance of their ramifications. I wonder if I will be able to endure decisions I regret having made. I am awed by the complexity of Carol's role of mother in a stunning act of womanhood. It is so natural, not learned.

It is not like that for a father. Wonder and confusion are my emotions at birth. Women have an intimate relationship with creation. Men hunt, which is now called breadwinning. Men fight battles, which is now called negotiating. Men build shelters, which is now holding a mortgage. Nothing men do relates to the natural order of human existence other than to ignite the creative process already installed in women. Men are the fuel, not the fire.

The title of my show takes on a sentimental meaning for me.

I go home to see my new family every night. In the small middle bedroom, once my office, the hum of a baby monitor records Lauren's gentle rise and fall of a deep slumber. The happy wallpaper of smiling ducks are quiet and dark now. Lauren is a new person, and I want to watch her, to see her smile, giggle, react. Little human beings are irresistible, especially when they are part of you. Fatherhood is filling up more and more of my downtime.

My homelife is peaceful and full. I think about my neighbors. I live in the same bedroom community as IBM and

PepsiCo marketing and finance managers, attorneys, corporate executives. I am not one of them. I am a black sheep living a corporate life. They are company veterans with 15-, 20-, 30- year careers. I can only claim employment longevity up to 4 years at most, and that is from a hit show. The nature of show business and my low tolerance for long running shows is a good match. Ticket sales for *Me & My Girl* begin to wane, but Carol goes to spend Thanksgiving with her parents in Florida, unaware of the now half-filled houses at the Marriott Marquis. Her trip is a yearly ritual, and beneficial for both of us.

"I go to Floor-da," Joseph proclaims at 4:00 a.m., excited about the flight to Marco Island. Lauren is still asleep. She will awaken minutes before we leave for the airport. I am glad they have an opportunity to spend days at the beach. I am not envious, but melancholy surfaces within me, a peculiar sense of loss, an expectation that happiness is never permanent. I think of how long this bliss of a new family will be with me. I return to work.

Peeking from the side of the curtain to see how populated the house is can cause the decision to send out resumes. Stage managers check everything, including the size of the house.

The high overhead costs of a show usually require at least a 60% capacity to keep running. Checking out the empty seats 15 minutes before curtain gives me a good indication of how much longer the show will last. *Me and My Girl* gradually enters the endangered list as the weeks linger toward summer. When Steven leaves the show, I know the end is near. Steven has an uncanny ability to anticipate the performance life of every show. The question is for how long.

This employment balancing act comes with the quirks of working in the theatre. I expect it, and after a while running the same sequence of events eight times a week is not much different than an assembly line worker toiling in a car-manufacturing plant. Creativity suffers a slow death with every paycheck, just like the follow spot operator in *Les Misérables*, or *The Phantom of the Opera* or any excessively long-running show.

The closing notice is posted for the Tuesday night performance. Carol is in her second week in Florida.

"Finally!" I say to some of my coworkers at *Me and My Girl*, "If I had to hear 'Doing the Lambeth Walk' one more time, I was going to jump from the balconies of the Marriott Marquis lobby." *Be careful of what you say.* I learn that edgy humor has its disadvantages.

The interior of the Marriott features an open atrium soaring up the 49 floors of the building. One could lean over the balconies just outside the individual room entrances and scan the panorama of waterfalls, bars, lounges, and restaurant traffic. My *Lambeth Walk* remark loses its humor when the hotel management installs decorative metal screening over the ledges of each floor facing the atrium. It seems that the hotel hallways that open to the expanse of the lobby had become a favored location for those seeking to end their lives by jumping over the ledge.

As level-headed as Carol is at her career decision-making, my employment game requires unique management of information on my part. I never share the first signs of show weakness with Carol. That only initiates panic that spirals out of control by her own doing. I take advantage of her vacation to Florida with her parents. There, she is surrounded by little Joseph and baby Lauren, basking in motherhood and adoration from beaming grandparents. It is as if I am not needed in this scenario. I am almost an intrusion, and every incident of a show closing occurs when she is watching the sun set from the lanai, pinot grigio in hand reflecting on the fullness of her life. I have a controlled setting for delivering bad news. Having her parents within ear shot of a phone conversation effectively restricts the severity of her reaction. This is a great advantage for me. When she is there, I can tell her the world is ending and she will calmly reply, "Oh, ok" or "My, my, so, what else is new?" or "That's nice." The last comment is an indication that she is reaching the limit in managing her panic at the situation. Overheard by unsuspecting parents, her comments are innocuous, generic reactions that prevent skepticism of any issue or crisis. My in-laws are equally fragile when it comes to the business of working in the theatre. I have great in-laws. We are so tight and close they feel free to rearrange the paintings and decorations on the walls of my house without asking. They feel so much at home they regularly take over when they visit. Their behavior is a dysfunctional complement, which seems to coincide with my growing appetite for single malt scotch. It helps me accept the newly decorated living room and endure the endless podcasts of Garrison Keillor's *Prairie Home Companion, Tales of Lake Woebegone* "where all the women are strong, the men are good looking, and all the children are above average." Listening to this routine is Joe Marik's idea of family time by the fire. It feels more like family by fire. Acceptable behavior with in-laws who are the personification of the Greatest Generation takes patience, restraint, and *Glen Livet*.

"The good news is that there's a new show coming up, and the bad news is that my show's closing." I wait for a response after having successfully overcome the angst of calling Carol in Florida.

"My, my, so what else is new?" Carol responds on cue. Being within earshot of her parents restricts her response. She is as loaded as she could be considering her proximity to her parents.

"The management posts the closing notice as a precaution, but they say they will probably take it down by Thursday."

Thursday is the decisive day in which a posted closing notice can be taken down without penalty. Most shows wait to see if the ticket sales increase for the weekend before committing to close.

"So, Carol, no worries, I have a job either way. If the show closes, Steven said he might take me on his new show. The stage managers on the job are having difficulty calling the show, and if it gets good reviews, he will add me as a fourth assistant."

"Oh, that's nice. What's the name of the show?"

"*Double Exposure*. But they're thinking of changing the name." Changing the title of a show is a very good indication that the production is in trouble.

"Alrighty, then," Carol has added a new level of clandestine expression of frustration. She gives it her best shot. I know how she feels, and I know she cannot freely express it. I complete the dirty deed of talking unemployment, and the usual closing salutations fill the rest of the call.

I also know that Carol does not fare well with stress or confrontation. She never did appreciate my penchant for drawing a line in the sand. She is committed to a full-service, 24-hour attempt to make everything just "ok" or "nice' as she likes to say. I resent the extra pressure to create a false impression. I feel that my partner in the trenches does not prefer to access her ability to weather big storms.

My new flip phone rings. It is Steven.

"John, I can hire you for *City of Angels* on a temporary basis. If the show is a hit, then your position becomes permanent. If not, then you are out. You can stay at *Me and My Girl* for however long it lasts. It's your call."

They change *Double Exposure* to *City of Angels*. The authors work on the show and promise a better than 50% chance of making a run for it. In finance the nut to break even in the theatre is 50-50. You can lose your shirt depending on your discretionary income. Job security in show business never builds. It is all or nothing. I can lose my living on an opening night. I never have any real money to invest, so I gamble. I sign on to *City of Angels*.

I leave Broadway's newest theatre in a hotel and return to the old Anta, now known as the Virginia. The neighborhood still has remnants of Swing Street, an allusion to the numerous jazz clubs of 1930s New York. Gallagher's Steak House is across the street, a venerable meatery opened in 1927 as a speakeasy by a former Ziegfeld show girl, Helen Gallagher. It boasts a meat locker of thickly sliced aged beef as window dressing and sawdust on its floors. The place for an opening night party. The area retains that old sense of an opulent and sensual New York.

I leave a version of the boy-meets-girl formula of *Me and My Girl* and enter a theatrical adaptation of a film-noir movie filled with shady characters, broken men, and loose women in *City of Angels*. It is a difficult show to run. I can see the issues. The scenes are short and quick, and the general design utilizes a "wiping" of scenes from left to right. Quick setups and strikes on four sets of pallets in each wing. These pallets are laid down, scenery and props set upon them and secured, then sent out and tracked onstage. The scenes last five to ten minutes, then requires a quick turnaround of striking the scene just played and setting up the next scene to be sent out. The formidable, labor-intensive activity keeps everyone busy. I never stop calling cues for two-and-one-half hours. I work hard on this one. Working this show is a wild ride, loud and brassy. I have a blast of a time while fearing a train wreck.

One of the stagehands who doubles across the street at Rock Center's NBC Studio 8 on 50th Street asks if a friend of his could come backstage for a tour. I comply and tell him to show up for the Wednesday matinee. I expect a stagehand looking for another voyeuristic opportunity to ogle chorus girls up front and close. The guest turns out to be Ken Aymong, the Supervising Producer of Saturday Night Live. For me, this is like meeting the Dalai Lama. The Pope. The Great Genie of live entertainment. Working in TV, especially at SNL, is the ultimate cool. On this matinee day, my plans for him change when a stage manager calls in and I am required to run the deck moves instead of calling the show. The job requires a choreography of evading moving scenery, cueing trap doors, providing clearances for entering actors, executing gunshot cues, and escorting exiting actors through the darkness into offstage safety. Ken has no choice but to follow me through the next two hours. He has the time of his life. He rides on and off moving scenery, stands with me behind a reveal to execute a gunshot cue with a starter pistol. He even gets to call a few cues. He reciprocates by offering an open invitation to SNL. We pick up and get together on a moment's notice between years of absence. We have a friendship that transcends the fractured schedules of our respective working specialties. Working at SNL is my lifetime dream. Working a Broadway show is Ken's dream. Go figure. My children benefit by receiving reserved front row seats at SNL. I wonder if they realize how lucky they are.

The depth and endurance of friendship in show business is only as strong as the character of the individual. I never get to work SNL. I get to enjoy the pleasure of a dependable colleague and friend, and that is far more valuable than a front row seat.

Carol's concerns are not about my show business exploits. Having just had a baby, not fitting into her pregnancy wardrobe, and facing the postpartum reality of life, my celebratory preoccupations do not help. I have a New York life, and she has a *Mad Men* suburban crisis. But our challenge is distance, not extramarital affairs.

My monthly commutation ticket for Metro North is due. I worry if there will be a reason to buy unlimited transportation to New York if there is no show to pay for it. The ticket is more than entry to a train. It is a badge of suburban success, like the groomed lawn. It is my VIP pass to executive life, proof of making the grade.

Opening night approaches, and Carol is more concerned than I am. I seem to weather the life-gambling game of finding work, but we are living a lifestyle in Fairfield County more suited to a financial advisor than a stage manager. At least that is what it feels like when the bills come. My livelihood centers on how theatre critics react. In these days, television critics make or break a show. More than one bad review sends your show to a Hoboken dump.

At home, Carol stares down the TV screen. After a commercial break featuring Brooke Shields sporting a white upper lip in the latest "Got Milk?" ad, Carol starts surfing the channels of the major TV network reviewers: Gene Shalit, Joel Segal, Gene Siskel, and Rex Reed. The first reviewer she tunes into pans the show. The next is lukewarm. Carol, assuming the worst, of course, is ready to order moving boxes. She presses the remote to the next channel and walks into the bathroom. Hearing a rave, an odd superstition emerges, and she decides not to move from the bathroom for fear of breaking the theatre critic spell. She presses for the next channel, listening attentively from the bathroom. The next three reviews on TV, newspapers, and radio rave about the show. *City of Angels* makes the grade as a smash hit. Carol breathes a welcome sigh, and finally leaves the bathroom. Pinot grigio spews out of bottles, champagne flows like a waterfall. I have a lasting job in a Broadway show once again.

City of Angels brings new life back to New York. Cy Coleman creates a dazzling jazz-based score that redefines the

Broadway musical as a classic standard. Swing Street is back in a classy, sassy musical.

Carol and I are secure, Joseph is five and Lauren is just four months old. We are managing a mid-century nuclear family in this high rolling business of broken hearts and in an era of social transition. All seems right with the world, for now.

I write a check out to Metro North Commuter Railroad and place the envelope in my mailbox at the end of my driveway. I raise the red metal flag to signal a mail pick up.

For another month, I ride with the movers and shakers.

Chapter 9

Me, Don Imus, and a Guy Named Mort

This year I count eight employers on my 1040 Federal tax return. In show business, listing that many employers means you are highly sought after. In any other industry, it means you cannot hold down a job. I work for any short-tempered, wisecracking show business shyster out there. The Broadway producer variations of barking, complaining closers pushing for the deal cannot be distinguished from the shady street corner hawkers preying on the tourist from Iowa. Both are seeking the tourist dollar. It is just a matter of what you are looking for.

All these short-term employment gigs make for a living, and there is not a job offer I refuse. Employers hire me for my service, not my opinion or my support. To increase my visibility, I agree to sublet an office at 1501 Broadway, in the Paramount Building, in the middle of Times Square. I share an office with a producer friend, Gerry, who sub-sublets a desk in a 150-square-foot reception area. I get to use the el-shaped end of the desk. I am here, on Broadway, with an office. Today we call that a *virtual address*. There are more Broadway producers, general managers, and theatre owners running around the lobby of 1501. It is just a matter of time before I find myself and a potential employer waiting in the lobby on their way to our respective offices. Here is the opportunity to strike up the classic elevator pitch. Most people capable of hiring me work in the upper floors, allowing more time to close a conversation with a resume in hand. Not all elevators run at the same speed, I discover. That fact helps me hone my 45- second presentation.

My producer friend's primary renter is a merchandising maven who uses the office as a storage facility for every imaginable trinket and giveaway. Mort, whose last name I never discover, manages street fairs all over Manhattan. He visits his office only to drop off boxes of kazoos, noisemakers, an array of tacky notions all produced in a China from another generation. I can tell because the packaging is yellow with age and the same type I remember from the finger trap toys I had as a child.

After the second delivery of whoopee cushions arrives, Mort asks if I am interested in helping him set up a street fair the following weekend. He offers a cash payment. I say yes.

The street fair is the annual Upper West Side Arts and Crafts Fair, the largest fair of its kind, featuring over 200 vendors, food carts, street musicians, body painters, artists of every sort. The event stretches from 86th Street to 72nd Street along West End Avenue. Each vendor is allocated twenty feet of space to set up tenting, tables, stands with their wares. My first job is to chalk out as many 15-foot-wide spaces as the streets would allow. My second job is to argue with every vendor who claimed I am short-changing them by three inches.

Once set up, the NYPD detail opens the street to the public. I continue to monitor the activity, especially the vendors who are encroaching upon their neighbor's assigned 20 feet of space. Placement of vendors is at Mort's discretion, and having done this for several years, he attempts to minimize the potential for issues by placing argumentative vendors away from each other based on previous years incidents. The trouble is that Mort was running out of room and reasonable vendors, and he is managing a horde of perennially argumentative complainers. The end of the event is a welcome moment. I am paid well, and I have avoided the sausage and pepper trucks, the Pennsylvania powdered sugar pretzels, and the super-greasy egg rolls.

But it is Mort who has the last laugh. Not impressed with titles or status, Mort makes thousands selling all those kazoos and noisemakers to vendors just outside 1501 Broadway, the heart of Times Square, once a year on New Year's Eve.

Though it is not the Broadway show I am looking for, this next job is one of the more peculiar side gigs. This event preserves an archaic tradition of hobnobbing with New York society figures clinging to the glitz of things theatrical. I am not sure that the reason for the Theatre Hall of Fame's existence has much more to do than acknowledge arrogance and privilege to those seeking more visibility than they have earned. The event peddles the familiarity of attachment more than a purposeful initiative. I expect a costume ball to emerge with a hologram of Marie Antoinette welcoming the ruling class to a grand party. Every participant's claim to fame at this event seems to underscore a penchant for social climbing. The networking is spectacular. The venue is billed as the Home of the Theatre Hall of Fame in the Gershwin Theatre. I assume that is true if you consider the *home* to be the signage of past honorees along the stairway lobby on the way to the balcony of the theatre and a few memorabilia showcases better suited to live at the New York Public Library for the Performing Arts at Lincoln

Center. The event is an unscrupulous cultivation of old money, warming up to well-endowed individuals past the prime of their lives who seek a continued relevance in society. An array of causes of the moment hide the obscure pointlessness of the event. It is populated with dismissive social elites who live more on inheritance than achievement. It does not pay well, but I am not able to walk away from the opportunity. Honoring stuffy theatre folk and their dubiously outstanding contributions to the quality of art feels a lot like managing a horde of retiring lounge lizards convening at an after-theatre bar. One incident proves to be priceless at the installation of some venerable old theatrical codger. One individual's irritating fraternizing has an effect they never expect. As he bounces around the guests seeking accolades throughout the evening, he is approached by Lauren Bacall, the iconic celebrity. She turns to him and lashes out a ten-minute diatribe of his ineffectiveness and amateur performance in dealing with sensitive personalities such as herself. Mortified, the glowing red face of the gold-digger never returns to normal. I admire Ms. Bacall from that moment on. I watch every one of her movies. She is a woman in charge of herself before movements, hashtags and self-serving dilettantes.

These side gigs fill in the few weeks when juggling the musical chairs of show jobs result in me standing outside of the game. The jobs keep me in circulation and employed. I manage to acquire a stagehands union membership that allows me to do load-ins, loadouts and other technical work. No one knows my union local is #518, the Brotherhood of Motion Picture Machine Operators of Fargo, North Dakota. I have never run a film projector, but I carry a lot of crates. I never step foot in Fargo.

The 100th anniversary of the International Alliance of Theatrical Stage Employees and Motion Picture Operators of the United States and Canada prompts the secretary of that organization to create a celebration dinner honoring its current president.

The president is a self-made man. He works his way up the ranks of union bosses, shady producers, theatre owners who refuse to contribute to a contractual obligation providing a percentage of benefits to workers. He is a simple guy who could not understand why his staff is spending hard-earned union money to throw a party.

I secure six chorus members from a currently running Broadway show to do a segment from the show gratis. His assistant has an idea.

"Hey, you know what would really be cool? A phone call from a talk show guy, you know, like Howard Stern or Don Imus. Then they mention him on a radio show. That would be something, eh?"

The surprise plan is to install a phone line at the president's table and at an opportune time the phone would ring, and the conversation would be heard throughout the ballroom and on the radio simultaneously. The talk show celebrity would wish the organization a happy birthday, and the president would feel like a player. The chorus ladies, in their dance-hall costumes and silver tiaras perform the opening number from their show. The members of the IATSE, the International Alliance of Theatrical Stage Employees, are happy. The president is happy. The show gets publicity. We all go home.

We all go home is an industry response to the countless, endless variations of performance tactics for every event. The ridiculousness of preparing, coordinating, and executing the detail of a seemingly simple evening prompts all of us to reconfigure our focus…that sooner or later, regardless of the outcome, this is not life or death. We are privileged to work in this business, and if all goes well, we all get to go home.

The night of the event brings more stagehands in suits I never expected them to own. The sleek, glassy lobby of the New York Hilton brings the usual level of news seekers from local television stations. No one calls for them. The activity of this midtown Manhattan neighborhood and the propensity for a newsworthy incident occurring makes a newshound's presence there a good bet that something worth reporting about will occur sooner or later. Stagehands and other theatrical union members from box office treasurers, wardrobe, scene, lighting and costume designers all enter assigned tables in the main ballroom. The plan is to have radio personality Don Imus call from backstage to a courtesy phone installed at the president's table. At the conclusion of the phone call, Imus is to appear in person and hand the president a gift at the table. He has no idea of the plan to connect him with his favorite talk show host.

It is two minutes and counting to the planned Don Imus phone call. Imus's entertainment value is beyond me, but I am hired to organize this event, not to critique it.

At one minute before the scheduled phone call, not knowing that Imus is about to call him personally, the president rises from the table and excuses himself to the bathroom. One-minute passes. Don Imus arrives backstage and prepares to make the phone call. The president is still in the bathroom.

The phone rings. The ring is amplified and can be heard by all in the ballroom. The assistant considers answering. The president is not in sight. The assistant finally picks up the phone.

Hullo? No, no, I ain't the president. He's in the bathroom. Can you call back in a few minutes?"

Television and radio personalities work on a second-to-second timeframe. They may sound casual and natural, but the focus is the timing, and when programming or transmissions fail, they go crazy and lethal. They respond as if they have been personally slighted.

The president returns from the bathroom. Missing the phone call, the assistant attempts to call Imus back. There is no answer.

The president never gets to talk to Don Imus on the phone.

About 10 minutes later, Imus walks into the ballroom, asks for the president's table, and unceremoniously drops a package at his table. He walks out of the ballroom.

The next morning, on *Imus in the Morning*, the talk show we all think is going to publicize the stagehands union and plug the Broadway show I am working on, turns out to be a publicity nightmare. Imus spends the morning hour trashing the stagehands and the show, the president, the assistant who picked up the phone call, and me. He compares the event to a mob meeting of crime families complete with blonde wives present. Carol and the president's wife are both blond.

The president never listens to Imus again. I continue to refrain from listening to him. The aired attack has a positive effect. I am known in circles that I am not even aware of that I am a survivor of the infamous Imus vitriol. Celebrity by default.

New York is such an unforgiving, rough room. Then again, we all go home.

The arm of my Adirondack chair provides a stable shelf for a shot of *Glen Livet*. It is also a great vantage point to witness relationships grow. Joe and Lorraine are transitioning from in-law to grandparent. For a son-in-law, there is a relief that Joe and Lorraine are enjoying their family's legacy in action.

I watch my father-in-law work his military jargon on his grandson. Joseph is a natural peace maker. He aims to please and he accommodates his grandfather in almost any request. He salutes, does endless chores. I expect his grandfather to spoil him. Grandpa wants to play father. I adjust to my father-in-law's preoccupation to father his grandson by spoiling Joseph.

My father-in-law's approach does not work so well with Lauren. She decides one afternoon to cross the lightly travelled road in front of our house to visit her friend Carter. Her grandfather does not allow her to do so. Lauren's unique personality surfaces.

"Grandpa, if you don't let me cross the road, I'm going to kick you in the wiener!"

"Who taught you to speak such language!"

"My brother!"

Grandpa learns a grandparent lesson. He walks her across the road.

I take another swallow and celebrate my daughter's awareness of her independence.

I wonder if I am a better father to Lauren than to Joseph.

Adirondack chairs reveal the truth in exchange for comfort.

The greatest and worst aspects of the theatre business is the realization that I am only as successful as my last show. Assuming there is another show coming down the pike, my latest employment can spell achievement or failure. This is the double-edged blessing. Forgetting my failures heals my wounds. Forgetting my successes forgives my arrogance.

Show business always presents itself with other opportunities. Susan Stroman, the girl with the flowing, blond curls who borrowed my little MG convertible on a Wilmington street ten years before, is back, this time as the choreographer of a new Broadway musical adaptation of an old Gershwin musical from the 1930s. Stephen hires me as his First Assistant. The theatre is a small world. What a family. What a temptation, and Carol is watching.

Despite the fractured, backstabbing, egomaniacal world of Broadway show business, Susan earns her celebrity without sacrificing her integrity. I am genuinely happy for her success.

Roger Horchow, a successful merchandizing retailer, produces the revised and edited adaptation of the 1930 musical

Girl Crazy. Additional Gershwin numbers are infused into the remake. Horchow hires Ockrent and Stroman to direct and choreograph. Disney's Jodi Benson, the voice of *Little Mermaid*'s Ariel, and Harry Groener, an accomplished Broadway song and dance theatrical veteran star in *Crazy for You*, opening at the Shubert Theatre in February of 1992. The show is magical, popular, and I am back in Shubert Alley.

Roger attends many rehearsals and numerous performances. He loves the show so much he hires himself to replace a vacationing actor playing Jodi's doting father for a week. I help him join Actor's Equity, rehearse him, and direct him into the show. He never pulls his producorial rank while on stage. The whole experience reflects the warmth and special intimacy of a close theatrical family.

Despite things running smoothly, I find myself looking for something else. Theatricals have an extremely short attention span. Backstage, the trade paper advertising jobs seem good reading material, and even lead standby Karen agrees. Jodi, the voice of Disney's Ariel, rarely misses a performance, and things settle into a routine in the office basement of the Shubert Theatre.

Karen languishes backstage waiting for Jodi to call out sick. She seeks an opportunity to perform the role. She spends most of her time during the show visiting all the backstage areas and the stage manager's office is a frequent stop. The effort in making this subterranean cave under Shubert Alley an office is no small feat, and it becomes a consideration in whether I leave for a new job. It would have to be something special, unique and, at the very least, the same salary. Maybe a dance show or a concert at Lincoln Center or Carnegie Hall, although the hall is a hike from Grand Central. I am used to the quick, three-block walk from the theatre to easily catch the 11:02 p.m. to Goldens Bridge. Comfort, ease of transportation, Shubert Alley presence—these are the things that make a Broadway career worth the effort.

Karen visits regularly, waiting for the moment when Jodi calls in, which occurs just once over 1,300 performances. We are well into the run, and Gershwin's tunes are beginning to irritate everyone. "I've Got Rhythm" is universally despised as is "Someone to Watch Over Me." Being theatricals, we have the shortest attention span for anything that is done twice. We are looking for something new even if it is just the latest flavored latte.

Karen notices an ad in a trade paper for a Production Stage Manager at Radio City Music Hall. I never consider working there. It is a different labor jurisdiction. Performers and stage managers there are members of the American Guild of Variety Artists, the union representing standup comedians and Rockettes. It is the union of Rodney Dangerfield, a comedian whose humor is based on his hapless incompetence. The unions depends on the Rockette affiliation to maintain solvency. The stagehands operate on a different contract from Broadway as well. Radio City does concerts, events, and the Christmas Spectacular, and no one in the Broadway industry considers the venue more than just a tourist trap. It is an attraction, not a theatre, and our Broadway noses are held too high to consider it seriously.

"Just send your resume. See what happens," Karen urges, half out of needing something to do.

I comply and fax my resume without a cover. I do not expect a response. The entertainment industry is notoriously provincial and specialized. Television managers do not apply for theatrical management positions, and variety and concert managers stay within their expertise. I send my information to entertain Karen more than any interest I have in the position.

I receive a response the next day.

The Senior Vice President and Executive Producer of the Christmas Spectacular invites me to an interview scheduled for

Wednesday morning at 11:00 a.m. He is genuine, approachable, and pleasant. He details the nature of the position in a somewhat circular fashion. He delivers information without implications, always returning to the grid of the performance schedule. Regardless of the subject matter, we always return to the grid. My interest grows more out of curiosity than desire. It is 12:30 p.m. and I must excuse myself to get to my scheduled matinee. This affects our conversation as if I had interrupted the control of the interview. I realize inadvertent timing is a classic tactic. I communicated my interest in the job as a consideration. I did not come pleading for a job with a burning desire. When I am called for a second interview, I am sure to schedule it again on a Wednesday. I enjoy playing this game. I do not need a job, and I do not care whether I get this job. The interviews alone are a welcome distraction from advanced Gershwinitis at the Shubert theatre.

Meanwhile, Susan, the lively dancer who tapped her way through a string of creaky old musicals at the Goodspeed Opera House and choreographed a smash with *Crazy for You*, celebrates by marrying her director, and lives the quintessential boy-meets-girl story. Both deserve every accolade. Both are talented and the nicest people I know.

Carol's suspicions are eliminated. Two weeks later, I am offered a job as Production Stage Manager for Radio City Music Hall. It is July 1995. Corporate show business has its peculiar personality and process. I finally sign a contract and begin on October 4, 1995, two months after the offer.

I have no idea what is in store.

Chapter 10

The Biggest Christmas Show Ever

The Radio City Christmas Spectacular is a world away from Broadway. There is no intimacy here. It is massive, brassy, and opulent, representative of an age when extravaganzas needed venues to house them. The Spectacular is quite at home in the lavish, art-deco movie and stage palace of Radio City. Here, the ghost of Phineas T. Barnum is resurrected to entertain the millions who seek to be awed by the grandiosity of the event. Here in this palace, this massive holiday production makes patrons forget their troubles and lose themselves in the folly of unending entertainment of every taste.

On Monday morning, October 9, 1995, the rehearsal hall is filled with 40 women attired in every available color and style of dancewear. Perfumes clash in the wake of every twirling body, their toned athletic forms balancing on firmly grounded toes. After 15 years and seven Broadway shows, I finally cross the great divide of 6th Avenue, join my new labor union, the American Guild of Variety Artists, and begin working on the Radio City Christmas Spectacular. My job description includes managing the entire year's schedule of everything that occurs on the great stage. I learn never to forget the branding. I am told it is the only stage of its kind in the world, and I am working the world's biggest indoor proscenium stage.

The Christmas Spectacular is about size, largess, and numbers.

I miss it.

I miss hating it.

My workday begins with live music, Rockette and Ensemble dancing, everyone singing. The Spectacular utilizes every available corner of the 100-foot-wide stage, 67 feet deep, 105 feet to the grid, which is the steel frame that carries the drops, effects, and lighting for every show. On Broadway, show drops are 40, maybe 50 feet wide at most. Here they are at least 80 feet. The stage contains three huge elevators that carry scenery and personnel before, during, and after shows. Each is 70 feet wide and 12 feet deep. They travel 27 feet below the stage level and rise 13 feet above. Incorporated into the three elevators is a turntable, 45 feet in diameter, which operates only if all three elevators are exactly aligned in height. Visiting concert production managers want to use these elevators in their shows, and I work out a sequence strategy and execute it at showtime without rehearsal. I become very efficient at quickly working up a sequence of moves by the 3:00 p.m. sound check and implementing it at showtime.

I am scared to death.

The responsibility is frightening. The execution is exhilarating.

Nearly every night a concert is loaded out and a new one arrives the next morning with a different group and different needs.

Past opening night, shows are performed seven days a week, with four, five, and six show days. Seven-day workweeks take its toll. That schedule lasts during the two and one-half month holiday schedule. Soon after a week or so of rest, things start up again in February with concerts and events.

The workplace is grand, and the barrage of exotic animal aromas from Christmas Spectacular camels, reindeer, sheep and a horse, marijuana smoke from rock concerts, patron regurgitation from alcoholic overindulgence, and the general pong of 6,000 humans entering and exiting the space on a daily basis create a lasting wake of ambient air not unlike sour milk. Occurring nightly during the concert season, smoke, weed, stained velour seats wet with beer, sweat, and accidental constitutionals leave a legacy of broken class and empty glasses. Plastic beer cups, supersized mimosas called "Rocketinis," roll under the seats along with snack trash. Some patrons are abusive in their treatment of the hall. The hum of vacuum cleaners and the tinkle of glass shards dropping into huge black plastic trash bins extend into the early morning hours after every concert. The cleaning crew finishes at 6:00 a.m.

And then there is the Christmas Spectacular.

The show is an extravaganza of numbers. In the fall of 1995, there are two companies to accommodate the 225 performances of the Radio City Christmas Spectacular. Beginning in November and ending by the first week in January, the Spectacular performs as many as six shows a day, and 32 performances a week. Each company contains 40 Rockettes, 24 chorus dancers, 11 little people, 27 wardrobe attendants, 40 musicians, 10 stage managers, 67 stagehands. Then there are five sheep, one reindeer, a donkey, one horse and three camels. There are 11 separate budgets from load in/rehearsal/load out, wardrobe, stagehand labor, Rockette operations, principal, chorus budgets, new elements, recurring, stage manager, front of house, to security.

I purchase a futon and place it in my office. I use it regularly.

One morning, at about 2:00 a.m., during load in operations and in the middle of my mid-overnight nap, I am awakened by the cypher release of trapped air in the Wurlitzer organ pipe system. It sounds like the Queen Mary leaving port in distress. But it is only the organist prepping the organ for rehearsal the next day.

All this noise, all this volume, all these numbers take their toll on my family life. When I arrive at home, especially during the Christmas Spectacular, Carol knows well enough to turn off the Christmas tree lights in the living room as I enter the driveway. I sit in the darkness of the living room, thankful for the fireplace, and begin a detoxification of the commercial overload of the day.

I think of the exhilarating first days of my new job, the heady interaction with some of the most talented artists in the industry, and how to minimize the vulnerability of this group of precision dancers in an unorthodox environment. Rockettes constantly changing costumes are vulnerable to the leering eyes of just about everyone. I oversee their workplace.

I think back to Kathy Mauceri, the first girl cast for a role in my high school production of *Oh, Kay*. Being in an all-male high school play is not the most comfortable situation for Kathy. When she needs help with her costume, she asks for me. Somehow, I am not threatening to her, and subsequently I enjoy an intimacy of trust not shared by others. The feminine mystique is no less effective on me than anyone else, but I know how to behave. I remember her appreciation, that kiss on my cheek.

Now I am here with 200 Rockettes compounding the issue. Stretching muscles and extending limbs in their bathing suit costumes, requiring unique management, and reminding me to earn that trust again. On a caption under one of the photos in the rehearsal hall, founder/choreographer Russell Markert refers to them as his "dancing daughters." I think of Lauren and whether I understand her needs, her expectations. Do I treat her like just another dancer?

In my living room, the flames begin to subside in the fireplace and the reddened logs reduced to a warm glow. I think of the incident of December 21, 1995, 77 days after my first day at Radio City. The crew is preparing for the 8:00 p.m. show and I am backstage observing the routine. One of the peculiarities of the expansiveness of the space is managing a persistent western wind strong enough to enter the theatre from the lobby and force the grand curtain, a huge 3,600-pound cloth, upstage where it impacts the ability of hanging scenic elements near it to fly in and out properly. The solution is to physically page the entire curtain downstage to allow a free path of the show drop to fly to the stage floor. The issue here are the footlights, located in a trough that, when opened, creates a depression in the stage floor. Just beyond the trough is the pit elevator, which at this point in the show preparation, is down 27 feet to accept musicians on a moving platform called a band car. It takes 15 stagehands, spread out across the width of the curtain, to effectively page the grand curtain downstage to the trough area to allow free passage of the show drop. Some of the best stagehands in the country page this curtain.

On this night, a veteran stagehand miscalculates the distance to the trough and trips. He loses his balance and falls 27 feet below, landing on several music stands and chairs. He lives through the experience, but with a devastating caveat. He is permanently paralyzed from the neck down. For the stagehand, the incident changes his life forever. For me, I keep the irrevocable exposure to a horrific event within me. Watching a life ambushed by chance, bloodied and broken by unexpected circumstance is overwhelming. The incident is brought to unbearable, ironic heights by the required manufactured cheer of an overdone holiday. To say it changes my outlook does not explain the experience. Witnessing the disturbing and ruinous mangling of a human body fosters panic and rage. Minutes after the ambulance leaves, the process of accountability begins. The unending visitations of shop supervisors, vice presidents, attorneys, police, and the Occupational Health and Safety Administration, confer, concur, evaluate, propose. All the while the stagehand feels no pain because he is reduced to seeing, swallowing and never moving again. I devise an operations strategy to prevent future accidents. The implementation of stringent safety procedures prevents any serious future incidents from occurring, especially with visiting concert and event personnel not familiar with the stage elevator systems at the theatre.

But the hollow feel of emotional violation transforms me. Best practices always follow the worst incidents, and while they set a path for improvement, they are helplessly futile before tragedy's surprise visit.

The glow in the fireplace become ash. The peace, unsettled at the thought of calamity, departs. I live with this incident for the next 12 years, and it dictates every activity onstage. I check every cavalier attitude of every employee, institute safety training programs for stagehands and performers, include orientation programs for every visiting event promoter, demand rehearsal for every elevator move, set up safety parameters for every opening created during a sequence, supply trained stage manager monitors to supervise movement onstage. When I hire new stage managers, I watch for the reaction to their view of the elevator system onstage. If they are overconfident, out to impress, I do not hire them. I hire the ones who show fear, who show respect for its size and its capability for disaster. I never let go of this defense. The intimacy of glittering dancers, celebrity arrivals, and technological entertainment feats center relentlessly on ensuring that the floor is always beneath everyone's feet.

I learn that overconfidence is just off right of being a fool.

"Hours of boredom interrupted by moments of sheer terror," stage technician Eric Titcomb responds to the uninspiring question posed to him by a visiting interviewer, "What it is like to work the Hall?" Eric is right. In the first few minutes of conversation with Eric, we both realize we were undergrads at Queens College at the same time. Eric is the backbone of stage elevator operations at Radio City. He is Captain Nemo, sliding and dialing knobs and buttons off a brass console that outsizes him. He is the man behind the controls behind the curtain, the Great Oz implementor that everyone depends upon to move the tonnage of the main curtain and the massive stage elevators out of the way of exiting Rockettes and entering camels. I respect his leadership. He and the brass control console are one entity. He has a no-holds-barred, bottom-line, get-to-the-point approach to life and his peculiar line of work. He needs to. His work is exacting and dangerous. Eric's day job is akin to single-handedly taking the hill of a losing battle and winning every time. His affinity for detail irritates those around him. It also saves lives and prevents injury. I am in unshakable awe of his capability. In any one season, Eric will execute nearly 18,000 individual elevator moves without an injury or mishap.

In a corporate expansion of a cable company, *The Radio City Christmas Spectacular* becomes the property of Cablevision, then the fourth largest cable company in the nation, having leased the music hall for 99 years. When we institute a fundraising activity for Cablevision's Garden of Dreams Foundation, we think up a great idea to auction off a 20-second ride across the stage in a horse-drawn carriage during the "Christmas in New

York" production number. This is a popular event among parents who view it as a great photo opportunity for their little ones. The children are received at the stage door, taken to wardrobe to be fitted with scarves, a hat, and a vest, instructed on how they are expected to behave while in the carriage, all with the excitement and anticipation of making one's debut on the Great Stage. Rockettes fawn over them, adding to the special event. Parents are given choice seats from which to record the brief event. Showtime comes. The horse, who lives in a stall in the lower level, is escorted by an animal handler to the elevator and taken to the stage level. The carriage is brought down from an airborne storage area and connected to the horse. The excited children are placed in the carriage with two adult chorus members with the children placed on the downstage side of the carriage to offer the best possible photo opportunity for parents who had offered up to $5,000 for this charity event.

On cue, the horse begins to travel across the stage onto the wide expanse. Downstage, 6,000 audience members *ooh* and *aah*, while upstage 36 Rockettes, 22 chorus members, a pair of little people skating in snowmen costumes and a team of figure skaters work a Teflon surface. The problem arises when the activity upstage so mesmerizes the children, they never show their faces downstage toward the parents hoping for a memorable photographic opportunity. Mummy and Daddy spend a whole lot of money for the photo shot of a lifetime only to be tremendously disappointed at their children's performance.

I give them a second chance at another performance, warning the children that if they turn upstage away from Daddy's camera this time, Santa, who is in the building, will come down to warn them personally.

It's amazing how effective an iconic holiday figure in a large red suit can be when your hopes are based in delusional fantasy.

"The Living Nativity" is a 15-minute segment of the Christmas story of the birth of Jesus. It is an enactment, not a church service. Yet there are people who believe they have satisfied their weekly religious responsibilities by attending a performance and others who walk out feeling they have been subjected to a forced indoctrination. Here's the truth. It is an entertainment. Rockettes in Mideastern garb are following a narrow path of light hoping to evade the droppings from camels relieving themselves from doing a four-, five-, or six-show day. One can recognize this when one notices that a Rockette walks out of the narrow path of light, disappears for a few feet and then returns. She is not stumbling across a long journey to Bethlehem. She is avoiding camel shit.

Inside the manger, the baby Jesus rests comfortably until the moment when the chorus members playing Mary and Joseph stifle giggles because the walkie talkie nestled under the baby Jesus doll is blurting out "Feed me! Feed me!" courtesy of a prankster stagehand. Phones all over the backstage area are busy transmitting food deliveries. Most employees fit in a quick meal in the half hour before we do this all over again. And again, and again. By Melchior's arrival in the Nativity story, Santa has de-weighted, debearded, and unsuited, looking like another normal, hungry actor.

I decline Chinese take-out again. I dare not walk outside into the 6,000 exiting patrons running into the 6,000 entering patrons of the next show. I do not want the roasted chestnuts, the falafel wraps, the Rogan josh and vindaloo cart food, and the sausage and pepper heroes. I go downstairs, for the fifth time today, and sit in the makeshift commissary and have another coffee, a banana, a doughnut. I go up to my futon and spend the rest of my 30 minutes thinking. The Rockette brand, the shortchanging of attention to the non-Rockette chorus, the special needs of the little people, the quirky wants of the figure skaters, Santa's relentless Perrier stock, the maintenance of animal stalls. The first, perfume-infused day of rehearsal. All those legs, so close, so inspiring to the ambiance of my workplace. The paralyzed stagehand. What it is like to have no use of arms or legs. The churning in my stomach every time a stage elevator moves. The management style of the new CEO.

My father-in-law Joe Marik joins me at the Adirondack chairs. Our relationship evolves into a genuine mutual appreciation. We discuss our wives, our children. We never mention that time in Florida.

That Florida incident changes the dynamic from being tolerated to being recognized. Frustrated with Carol's balancing act of pleasing everyone, I dispute the constant categorization by her parents. I do not receive the acknowledgement I expect. I feel like an appendage to Carol's agenda. It is as if her marriage is a continuation of being a daughter and not a partner.

"If you don't come now, it's over!"

"Calm down, what's the problem?"

The judgmental categorization of my in-laws sends me over the edge.

"I'm done with this. They don't give me the time of day!"

I slam the door to our bedroom, waiting for Carol to enter. I hope this is enough to jumpstart her inertia. My father-in-law exits to his bedroom. Bohemians do not slam doors. That makes it even more frustrating. My mother-in-law expresses concern. Carol, good daughter that she is, assures her mother.

"Oh, don't worry, Ma. He's just a hot-headed Italian." She and her mother open a bottle of wine. The impact of my outburst is not what I expect. I am more concerned with my relationship to Carol than with my minute sense of remorse for calling my in-laws out. I eventually apologize. Things return to normal, but somehow there is a sense of an irrevocable change. My father-in-law and I have a new relationship, born from the patronizing, careful exchange of that first dinner at the World Trade Center and sealed by an incendiary moment that needed to occur. I find out how deep that change is later.

Chapter 11

Showplace of the Nation

The Teenage Mutant Ninja Turtles Tour did, and I spent a raucous afternoon with Joseph and 6,000 other children and parents watching the shelled cartoon creatures rock, bop, and shimmy their way through the world's thinnest storyline. Sitting in the last row of the Music Hall, 185 feet way from the stage, one gets a pint-sized but panoramic view of the massive limestone arches that begin at the proscenium and stack up higher and higher until it reaches over our heads. It is up to the viewer to determine when the stage wall ends, and the ceiling begins.

Radio City Music Hall is more than a structure. It is a bigger-than-life, transcendental encounter with overindulgence. From the excesses of prewar, Art Deco inspired works of art claiming social democracy to its intimidating urinals, Radio City fits just fine next to Rome's Colosseum or the Temple at Ephesus. It is a gargantuan place extending an entire city block. Radio City, in all its grandeur, is a division of Madison Square Garden Entertainment. The facility is a natural fit for MSG's heightened sense of branding. Every aspect of the physical plant is an instantly recognizable reference to irrefutable invincibility. MSG is the home of the Knicks, The Rangers, and The Rockettes. It would not be enough to say I work at Radio City. A branded employee proclaims they work at the *Showplace of the Nation* managed by the *World's Most Famous Arena*. This swaggering delusion is instilled by marketing division executives. They have us thinking what we do for a living happens nowhere else in the world.

They are right.

When I sit in the 15th row center of Radio City Music Hall, I sink into an optical illusion. I see a magnificent rows recreating a permanent sunset, especially when recessed lighting imitates a dazzling high noon array of color settling into an early dusk, right before a show begins. At opposite sides of this proscenium arch are two Wurlitzer pipe organs that are revealed through automated curtains operated by dual organists. Directly above the audience seating, beyond the magnificently carved limestone ceiling at about 145 feet, is a 40-by-80-foot room with a complete wall of mirrors on the longer side with a ballet barre running the entire length. On the remaining three walls are photos of women in various costumes caught in the action of a production number. These photos are a chronological, visual history of the Radio City Rockettes, the iconic precision dance troupe that began life as the "Missouri Rockets" in St. Louis, Missouri, in 1925, and first came to New York's Roxy Theatre billed as "The Roxyettes" until finding a permanent home at the opening of Radio City Music Hall's first performance on December 27, 1932.

The opening night of that lavish production lasted over five hours and suffered many show-stopping technical problems. The experience caused an irrevocable decline in the health of its producer, Missouri impresario S. L. Roxy Rothafel. Rothafel and "Missouri Rockets" choreographer Russell Markert, realizing the popularity of the troupe, created the brand name "Radio City Rockettes" in 1934. Rothafel succumbed to complications of angina pectoris in 1936 at the age of 53. Russell Markert continued to direct the Rockettes until his retirement in 1971.

Volume defines the scope and nature of working here. Radio City is a performing artist's port of call, a clearing house for every talent and event of celebrity and prominence. Concerts and events feature hundreds including Elton John, the Dali Lama, Larry Ellison, founder of Oracle, the Executive Vice President of General Motors, Barry Manilow, Luther Vandross, Sharon Stone, Mikal Gorbachev at Bill Clinton's 50th birthday, Time Magazine's 75th birthday, the entire faculty and graduating classes of Villanova, NYU's Stern School of Business, Pace University, the stage shows of Barney, Dora the Explorer, Doug, the Tropical Tribute to the Beatles, Tito Puente, Celia Cruz, Aretha Franklin, Luciano Pavarotti, Dion, 50 Cent, Phish, Trey Anastazio, Metallica, Madonna, Brittney Spears, B.B. King, Riverdance, Michael Flatley, Diana Krall, Andre Rieu, the Beach Boys, The Chinese Acrobats, The Russian Variety Show, Billy Joel, LL Cool J, The Grammys, the Tony's, the Daytime Emmys, the MTV and FIT Fashion Awards, Aveda, Commerce Bank. More than 300 concerts a year come to the Hall.

Show business life is a lark, an odd existence. No preparation or schooling guarantees success. For the artist or the manager, it is simply a gift of chance, and everything can tumble without reason or warning. I am privileged to support the talent. I love the intimacy of trust I develop with artists. Serving their art gives me purpose, makes me feel significant. I want to organize, to serve the shape of sequence. That is enough for me, especially when I work with people of unquestionable talent. I am happy to leave the performing to artists like Tony Bennett, a crooner who can toss away a faulty mic, walk to the edge of the stage and mesmerize a sold-out New Year's Eve crowd of 6,000 with a simple introduction of a legendary song.

The loveliness of Paris seems somehow sadly gray
The glory that was Rome is of another day
I've been terribly alone and forgotten in Manhattan
I'm going home to my city by the Bay.

On one New Year's Eve, Tony Bennett delivers an unamplified, acapella rendition of "I Left My Heart in San Francisco" with an aesthetic reverence found only in a solemn church service.

At center stage a rotund, bearded man in a folding chair sips bottled water wearing an oversized, multi-colored cotton scarf. Technicians, managers, performers are milling about, preparing for rehearsal of the 1998 Grammy Awards. Finishing the last swallows of spring water, Luciano Pavarotti rises and proceeds to the downstage edge as stagehands remove the folding chair with the empty water bottle. He greets the 40-piece orchestra's enthusiastic cheers and prepares to sing *Nessun Dorma*. This big man, with the big voice and the longest scarf ever, performs 32 bars until the music stops. He looks down to thank the orchestra and leaves the stage. As he passes, he acknowledges me with a friendly nod and moves on. This big man, whose voice stirs memories of my father listening to the *Metropolitan Opera Radio Broadcasts* on Saturday afternoon, has just given me a moment of *Turandot,* live. In that moment, I think of how extraordinary it would be if I could share this with my father.

At 30 minutes before live transmission, the DGA stage managers fail to locate Pavarotti in their initial talent checklists. The presentation begins. We are live. Still no Pavarotti. The producer of the event, Ken Ehrlich, receives a message to call Pavarotti at home. He is ill. Last minute plans are to cut to commercial and fill the down time, which messes up the sequence of events of the stage elevators for me, and costs ad money for the producers. An emergency huddle between Ehrlich, Aretha, and Pavarotti's conductor ensues in the dressing room.

Aretha Franklin agrees to sing, unrehearsed, and rises to the occasion belting out a trademark bluesy rendition of *Nessun Dorma*. The audience responds with a screaming, standing ovation. Aretha pours her Sunday morning gospel into an iconic opera star's signature solo and claims it. Real talent triumphs every time, at every impasse, and leaves uncertainty in the dust.

Just another Saturday evening show at the Hall.

Radio City is a place of astonishment and wonder. It embraces the visitor with a swelling feeling of dreams met and realized. It is a place where I meet and work with upcoming celebrities and aging stars working the big stage, heads of state being honored and local colleges using the venue for commencement.

It is where moments of compassion and integrity outshine those of ruthless competition, grueling hours, unrelenting effort to put on a supersized show, day after day. But that dichotomy is what makes the place alluring to the patron and exhilarating to everyone who works here. It is a fraternity with purpose, an exclusive club with its own shorthand operating to do just one thing-to put on the biggest, best show possible.

A maintenance call for the stage elevators requires me to spend a Saturday on stage. At 4:00 p.m. I prepare to leave for the day. Harold at stage door security asks me to come to his station. I discover six sailors asking for the manager of the theatre.

Radio City is eight sort blocks from the Hudson River. During Fleet Week, thousands of sailors roam the western grid of Manhattan seeking big city adventure. My middle age makes me realize these folks are barely adult. They are wide-eyed, enthusiastic, and have that wonderful immature sense of being invincible. To them Radio City is Disneyland, an amusement park, a contorted representation of that American quality of life for which they are told they are defending. They are from hometowns few have heard of, and their furlough from life on the water brings them to the stage door.

"Any chance we could take a look inside?"

"My friends back home would be green with envy!"

"Yeah, my parents spoke about Radio City a lot!"

"This is my first time in New York."

The empty, cavernous space is not much to look at, but the expanse seems familiar to the sailors. The remaining stage crew members cleaning up embrace the young group and join in on the random opportunity for hospitality. I bring them to the stage, and the electrician turns on the rows of house lights embedded in the arches of the ceiling. He runs a series of looks by changing colors, chasing rows in opposite directions. The sailors are enthralled. The stage elevator technician invites them for a ride on the stage elevators. Up and down they go, 27 feet down, 13 feet up in the air. We reposition them on the turntable. They ride the revolve like children on a carousel. I go to the concession store and purchase six mugs. Their tour ends. Stagehands talk of their military experiences, share old Navy jargon, complain about bad food on ships, bad food in the commissary at the adjoining AP Building next door. We discuss the similarity of aircraft carrier elevators and our own stage lifts. We all shake hands and present them with the mugs. The young sailors feel an adventure of a different, creative kind. We share our unique crafts.

The Radio City staff is like that. We know we are a welcome tourist trap, and we flaunt our golden egg with anyone who visits. We are eager to show how much we enjoy this way of life. We make the visiting sailors headliners for a day and they return the camaraderie as if we are fellow midshipmen. For a brief time, we all make believe, we all dream.

I tour the nooks of the theatre.

I explore the rafters alone. It is an invitation to escape. The network of steel stiffeners in the arched ceiling supports the grandeur below. Hand-applied plaster smudges bleed through the steel mesh that forms the huge arches. A labyrinth of catwalks leads every which way into the deeper and higher sections of space between the ceiling and the steel grid. It feels like a cave, 150 feet in the air, above 6000 seats. It is like a museum, seeing the work of laborers from the Depression of the 1930s. I find treasures here. A complete, folded up newspaper from 1937. A record book of projectionist assignments with running times of a film schedule for 1943. Old stationery announcing "The Showplace of the Nation" with an address that has no zip code. Boxes of Thyratron tubes, once new, still unused, and laden with the dust of 60 years.

The follow spot bridge in Cove D features sixteen positions. The view is breathtaking. A protective lip of six inches prevents anything from leaving the bridge and landing on a patron 150 feet below. Technicians spend hours here illuminating award show nominees and winners from the Grammys, the Tonys, the Emmys, musical artists like Roberta Flack to Diana Krall to Bon Jovi. International dance companies like Ballet Folklorico de Mexico, traveling orchestras like Andre Rieu grace this presently empty stage with color, music, and dance from every corner of the world.

I look stage right to the 82-line sets of hemp lining the stage wall. The lines hold the scenery that make this whole cavern a blazing rock show, a glittering, Hollywood-style social scene, a candy-coated Christmas holiday.

Another unplanned visit produces a former senator on vacation in New York with his wife. I am the only executive in the building on Sunday afternoon. I walk to the stage door and find John Glenn and his wife Annie looking like two midwestern tourists hoping to enter a museum about to close for the day.

John Glenn. Astronaut. Spaceman. An out-of-this-world traveler. His handshake makes me feel I have touched rocks from the moon. He marvels at the 1930s brass control panel off stage right with hundreds of dials, switches, clocks, and levers. Eric is in his glory. He explains most dials are for the elevators; some are for the 6,000-pound grand curtain. One large lever is for the steam curtain which produces a wall of steam from a perforated trough running 70 feet across the 100-foot proscenium opening. I wonder how much that truly impresses a person who flew an Atlas LV-3B rocket 130 nautical miles into the atmosphere and hitched a very hot and harrowing ride back to earth. The gentle couple from Ohio thank Eric and I for the tour and move on.

A week passes and I receive a package in the mail containing a commemorative medal of the *Friendship 7* Mission launch and a letter on United States Senate stationary thanking me for my hospitality. It is signed "John Glenn, Astronaut." The gift completes my dream of adventure.

The make-believe of "The Right Stuff" becomes real, only at Radio City.

The 4th performance on this Thursday taxes the company of Rockettes endlessly eye-high kicking throughout the day. The show is a costly endeavor. At the final curtain, Rockettes have just 15 minutes to get out of their costume before the show incurs overtime costs for the 27 wardrobe attendants. After show meet and greets are budgeted events.

I receive a phone call during the Living Nativity. The house manager has a patron request. A parent is pleading for permission for her daughter to go backstage to meet a Rockette. This happens regularly. Most of these requests are not vetted and many are denied. Most are frivolous and are categorized in the same vein as obnoxious autograph hunters. Exposing Rockettes in full costume to the general public without that 4th wall of a stage is risky. This one request is different.

This family's flight to a New York vacation arrived too late to follow the protocol established by marketing to approve a backstage visit. Nearing the end of the last performance of the day, this parent produced documentation that their daughter was a recipient of the Make-a-Wish Foundation and meeting a Rockette topped her list. I promised the house manager I would look into it.

At 9:15 p.m. there is no controlling authority in the building beyond me. I announce on the backstage intercom if there is a Rockette who is willing to come down after changing her costume to meet this little girl. I have no reason to believe anyone would want to break the rules, incur overtime costs, or extend an already grinding workday. I tell the house manager to escort the family backstage and hope for the best. If no one shows up, I can at least give them a backstage tour.

It takes about 15 minutes following the final curtain for the family to maneuver around the 6,000 exiting patrons to reach the stage right pass door to backstage. I am standing at the pass door entrance, watching the transformation of exiting patrons and entering facility workers beginning the clean-up of discarded popcorn containers and half empty soda bottles. I finally see the family being led by the house manager toward me. I greet them and gently break the news that there may not be an opportunity to meet any cast members due to the late hour, the full day of work, but I offer a backstage tour instead.

As we all enter through the door and turn into the off-stage right area, 15 fully costumed Rockettes are waiting to greet the little girl and her family. The wardrobe attendants have declined to log in overtime costs if the Rockettes are willing to do this impromptu meet and greet. I am overwhelmed but not surprised. That is the way it is at the Music Hall.

Hezekiah Walker, a South Ozone Park man of the cloth despite his gray leather suit, surveys the 52-row expanse of orchestra and three balconies at the Music Hall. His 300-member Love Fellowship Choir can easily attract enough constituents to fill the 5965 seats. His concern is how to make the most of the Music Hall's toys.

The LFC arrived at the scene fully self-contained and dressed for the event. Church members in brilliant colors, wide brimmed fedoras, head wraps, dashikis, and caftans carried aluminum trays of home-cooked Macanese casseroles, roasted chicken, Jollof rice. The group arrives at the Showplace of the Nation, and they intend to celebrate.

For many members of the choir, this is their first time at Radio City. For some older others, they remember the box office window on the side entrance on 51st Street. Beyond that window is a set of stairwells that lead only to the third balcony. The route bypasses the opulence of the Grand Lobby. It was designed to separate the inexpensive ticket holders from the expensive orchestra patrons. Savannah has nothing over New York. The dark, endless stairwell to the highest balcony is a remnant of the inadvertent racism of the 1930's rearing its nasty head in 21st century midtown Manhattan. The access now serves as an emergency exit.

We assemble onstage for rehearsal. The Reverend loves the idea of being revealed to the audience on a rising stage elevator. Just upstage, the choir, split over the remaining three stage elevators, will rise in tandem to the rising crescendo of the opening gospel number. All choir members are excited and ready to go, except for one member.

She refuses to ride the stage elevator. She is in her 80s.

"I'm not goin' on that elevator," she announces.

JUST OFF, STAGE RIGHT

The event does not require me to be stationed at the stage manager's desk just offstage right. I can call the show from anywhere with a walkie-talkie. I negotiate with her. Some choir members gather to witness the outcome.

"What if I went on the elevator with you?"

The 80-year-old mulls over the possibilities.

"Hold my hand so I don't fall off. Otherwise, I'm not goin'."

"It's a deal."

I reposition myself behind a taller member of the chorus to hide myself. I have no choral gown and I am the only white person in this group of 300 chorus members spread across three stage elevators.

The show begins. I have a walkie-talkie in one hand and the hand of the venerable chorister in the other. I wonder whether she is holding on to me or I to her. There is a greatness in holding her hand. She talks to me as if confiding a thousand secrets. Our sin is always around, she says, ever present. "Us folks are reminded every day," she claims. Her story could be a feature film. As a teenager she remembers when the last confirmed lynching of two black men occurred in Marion, Indiana in 1930. I call out the Grand Curtain to the sounds of a humming chorus. Sixteen bars of the orchestra later, I call each of the 3 elevators individually to rise in tandem revealing the entire company of singers. The twenty-minute opening number concludes with the reveal downstage on the orchestra pit elevator of Reverend Walker in shiny, leathery gray. Thunderous applause of a full house ensues.

My 80-year-old partner's hand tightens around mine as she sings with all her strength and glory. At the beginning of the second number, her hand leaves mine as she joins in a vigorous handclapping gospel number. My frail octogenarian becomes a Radio City pro. I extend my arm behind her to ensure her enthusiasm does not send her over the edge. She is the most important person in this moment. I am privileged to be her protector. She is no longer fearful. She sings with the unrestricted innocence of a child.

At the load out, there is a knock on my office door. Mavis, the company manager, presents a cd, a whole Macanese casserole, a standing invitation to the Kingdom Church of the Love Fellowship Tabernacle Choir, and a note thanking me for being an "angel." The note is from my new old friend.

Chapter 12

Cablevision Culture Club

King Kong never played here.

    January arrives at the Hall with mixed relief. The comfort I feel following my first stint in the Christmas Spectacular lasts a weekend. This is not Broadway. The football field that serves as the stage here still reeks of camels. This aroma, not unlike a zoo, offers Middle Eastern notes. A musky, Bahārāt blend finished off with tones of turmeric and cardamom. Repeated exposure makes the Music Hall retain this scent throughout the year in varying intensities. I do not remember the hall without this signature bouquet.

    The corporate environment of Radio City casts a different viewpoint from the Broadway theatre. Behind the awe and wonder of a hopeful holiday is a bottom line, a grand total, a financial reckoning. Beyond the glitter droppings from 230 Christmas Spectacular performances that remain in the elevator tracks onstage lurks a first quarter forecast meeting. Snowflake confetti appears in every crevice throughout March.

The Christmas show is now packed into 25 loading trailers in a storage facility somewhere on Long Island. I sit on one of the last packing crates on the stage. I peer out onto the open magnificence of space that accommodate 6,000 people, quiet now. The place is clear of scenery, costume racks, and towers of electrical equipment. Electricians are in the ceiling restoring and replacing color gels across the span of arches that extend a full city block. It will take a week to check and service the thousand plus lamps tucked into the massive ceiling. I stop thinking of the forecast meeting.

The stage manager's desk, now devoid of the spaghetti of communication cables, transmitters, and closed-circuit television monitors, resembles a simple workbench table. The bales of hay for the camel beds are gone. The 50 racks of costumes ingeniously stored for every performance inside the nativity temple are cleaned, packed, and stored at Ernest Winzer Cleaners, a facility in the Bronx that has been washing, starching, and ironing the famous Wooden Soldier pants for more than 50 years. The Winzer reputation does not prevent me from seeking out a better deal despite their loyalty and expertise. There is the difference between show quality and product delivery.

The stage elevators are level, locked off to insure against hydraulic sinking. The linoleum surface that covers the rock maple flooring of each elevator is clean and polished. I will squeeze another year of use from the worn linoleum on stage. My forecast report will reflect a reduction in maintenance costs, and that will guarantee another year of employment. Everything seems put away in its proper place. Order is restored and its proof is in the emptiness of the place. It is as if the Hall enters a half-life without cacophony, intensity, overkill. Goals have been met and benchmarks achieved. It feels good to finally be free of the grasp of another performance.

I rise, put on my coat, pick up my case, and walk toward the stage door, feeling accomplished but knowing that in a week I will be at it again, this time with another extravaganza. *The Radio City Christmas Spectacular* has a second but no less complicated cousin, *The Glory of Easter*. The thinking here is purely financial. Repeat what we just did for the Christmas season, only bigger.

Theatre as art has been left for dead on this side of Sixth Avenue. I manage profit and loss through 11 budgets, and I am no more creative than the general managers of sports teams and television studios that encompass Cablevision's holdings. At least for a few weeks my son Joseph gets to see his dad during his waking hours. We ride the lawn mower, build a model, do a school project. I secure the floor of the treehouse, so that it will remain strong during the times I am away. I play endless catch with Lauren who seems to take more time to satisfy. I claim my fatherhood with every nail, every drop of glue, hoping they will remember, when I am not there.

The message of the Easter holiday as a Radio City event seems rife with confusion and mixed purpose. No one seems happy with the content. Management is not happy with its financial performance. The event loses money every year. Never having successfully matched the iconic branding of the Christmas Spectacular, the Easter show suffers through revolving doors of fixes and inventions that tax the ability of the staff just reeling off the Christmas extravaganza.

We try everything in this show. We even build replicas of the Hall's actual revolving doors. The opening sequence features Rockettes dressed in a costume designed to represent a 19th century Polish Daughters of Charity habit marching solemnly to the dirge of Anton Rubenstein's "Kamennoi Ostrow Rêve Angélique." The static choreography concludes with the Rockettes forming a giant cross with their headpieces resembling newly bloomed lilies. The dark, churchy ambiance bares no relation to the intended frivolity of the spring season. I feel I am back in church again, at Lent.

This Easter show is a remnant of an old variety format where acts are patched together with no relationship to each other. This structure cranks out act after act of unrelated entertainment with Rockettes being thrown in yet another costume to dance around in between acrobats and mimes. Years of editing and nit-picking at the remaining dramatic structure leaves the show a jumble of good intent without the dynamic strength of the Christmas Spectacular. The only original piece from its inception is this opening number, derisively referred to as the Flying Nun act. The rest of the show offers a potluck evening of warm-up-act leftovers from vaudeville.

Following this morose and gloomy enactment of solemnity, the next scene presents a rendition of "Pure Imagination," an Anthony Newley/Leslie Bricusse tune arrangement from the original score of *Willy Wonka and the Chocolate Factory*. With a twist of his riding crop, the emcee, dressed like a bunny, ushers in a green laser that captures heated mineral oil, creating a smoky effect. Suggesting a transition into a world of pure imagination, the happy, dancing bunny-of-ceremonies invites everyone to come along and discover a new and wondrous experience. A curtain of steam appears from the downstage edge and rises 20 feet into the air, enhancing the murky surroundings. The special effect makes as much noise as the Con Edison street-steam exhaust from which it originates. Its unexpected effect upon preschoolers attending the happy Easter Show includes screaming and extended crying.

Once the steam and mineral smoke dissipate, the audience discovers a stylized replica of the Radio City Music Hall marquee. This fact alone raises a red flag of dubious creativity. Recreating the very building in which one is performing suggests that the audience is never going to get further than the lobby. Revolving doors swing open from the marquee set delivering Rockettes dressed as ushers. A respectable, upbeat tap number follows. The group, who five minutes earlier were solemnly treading up the steps of an unnamed cathedral in French Gothic starched wimples, are not to be outdone by a little rainwater. Those intrepid dancers brave the slick surface created by the steam curtain and manage to get through the number without tripping.

The first act offers a rotation of filler acts. I watch a hopping, jumping, somersaulting group in an acrobatic act aptly named *Anti-Gravity*. The next year features a hopping, jumping menagerie of dogs somersaulting through the air for treats. The show includes a black light act of the type usually found in funhouses at amusement parks. The Easter show tries to be so many things to so many people. It never attains the universal appeal of its big iconic sister, *The Radio City Christmas Spectacular*. We attempt to invent a holiday where there is none. Easter is a primarily religious event, which explains the spiritual overtones of the opening number. It is the answer to the Christmas Spectacular's *Nativity* scene. But Christmas is always festive and universal, and the strange bedfellows of spiritual adoration and secular celebration work well together. But the spiritual overtones of Easter are death and resurrection. It does not fit well with the ancient springtime ritual of fertility. Hence the bunnies, the egg hunt, the pastel colors all seem in contrast to the event at hand. Adjustments in the show over the years do little to improve the box office.

A splashy medley of Gershwin songs is installed in the 1970s and ends the first act. Grandly designed by Erté, a renowned but dated fashion designer, the set is immersed in blue drapes with a grand piano as the only scenic element. The scene infers a palatial mansion by the sea with high society guests milling about and gathering around the piano to sing Gershwin favorites. It feels dead on arrival but returns annually to end the first act.

The Rockettes open the second act with a salsa number dressed in costumes of synthetic fabric. They balance headpieces Carmen Miranda would refuse to wear. The second act is just over one-half hour long. The next themed segment is called "Yesteryear," a retrospective on the good old times of late 19th century America. This segment features numbers like "A Bicycle Built for Two," "Daisy," and "In the Good Old Summertime." This number is staged as far downstage as possible to allow resetting the steps used in the cathedral set in the opening number. When the audience has their fill of chorus boys donning seersucker suits and sporting boaters and the female chorus dressed in full length cotton street dresses suggesting end-of century 1890s, I cue out the giant, 80-foot-wide scrim to reveal a Fifth Avenue in New York exterior with a forced perspective of St. Patrick's Cathedral. The full cast of chorus members, Rockettes, dogs, dancing bunnies all enter to sing and stroll to the strains of "Easter Parade."

The last Easter show performs in 1997, two years after I arrive at Radio City.

Radio City operates 365 days a year, sometimes with multiple events that occur simultaneously. We stage a political event for then New York Governor George Pataki in the Grand Lounge of the Hall. Upstairs in the Grand Lobby, Commerce Bank presents their first-quarter meeting. On stage, we perform maintenance of the stage elevator system. All spaces are utilized at the Music Hall. The stage elevator's 72 moves per performance at Christmas and 225 performances take their toll on oiling, solenoids, and copper contacts of the stage elevator's mechanics. The Grand Curtain weighs three tons and operates from thirteen cables suspended from the grid, 125 feet above the stage floor. The curtain rises in an Austrian style, scalloping up to the desired height in infinite configurations. There is never anything small at the Hall other than the occasional attitude from an egocentric performer.

Some are candidates for psychological therapy.

"This is unacceptable! Where is my line producer? Get Craig here, now!"

This wailing diatribe originates from the site supervisor for the MTV Awards, every year. The only thing that changes is the name of the line producer, who is the replacement for the previous year's line producer. This guarantees that the present line producer is scheduled to be fired at the conclusion of this year's event. Finally, trucks, cables, monitors, speakers, trusses, swag, rented photocopiers, leased costumes, gowns---all the gak of broadcast show business---leaves by 3.00 a.m.

Another day, another show. The single 53-foot semi that parks on 51st Street contains all the scenic elements and special effects for the concert scheduled for one evening. Most of the equipment is the usual package. Lighting, fog machines, hanging soft goods—all the expected physical production elements of a one-person event. I question why such a big truck is required.

"Why the huge truck for one artist?" I ask John Lemac, the supervising house electrician who is a 35-year veteran of the Hall and has seen everything.

"This guy is special. You'll see."

Lemac is always careful to stop just short of throwing anyone under the bus. But he succeeds in making a point to warn of impending issues. Many one-person concerts can be contained in what is called a bobtail—a two-axle truck cab with a box integrated into the design. The second half of this semi carries pipe and drape. Pipe and drape is a free-standing system of hanging soft fabric that section off areas requiring definition but not secure restriction of rooms or pathways. It is comprised of poles with cross-support bars upon which hang drapes.

The spec sheet is the list of required elements for a show. Everything from the type of refreshments needed in dressing rooms to the temperature of soda or water is contained in this list. Most of the tech sheet requirements seem usual except for one request. The sheet calls for the setup of a pipe and drape walkway from the star dressing room to a dedicated elevator, and from the elevator exit on stage level directly to the stage entrance. Radio City employees are hidden from the recording star as he moves to or from the dressing room. From the stage manager's desk, it looks like just another quick-change dressing area. From inside it looks like an escape tunnel, protecting the occupant from any contact, real or imagined. No one can look at him, which is the purpose of the pipe and drape. Once the artist arrives onstage to perform, technicians view him only when necessary to execute lighting and special effects cues. It is as if his reveal to an adoring audience has been protected, remaining untainted and unspent until his entrance. The usual camaraderie between celebrity and Radio City personnel is nonexistent, and the performer connects only with a nameless crowd, distanced by the insurmountable fourth wall of the proscenium.

This is not the norm. When Johnny Mathis visits the Hall, he jokes and talks with the nearby technicians before he goes onstage to sing.

"All set, Mr. Mathis?"

"If I'm not ready by now, I'll never be," he quips.

Tony Bennett, LL Cool J, Eminem, 50 Cent, Meatloaf, ZZ Top—all are cool, approachable, and very appreciative of our assistance in making their show a success. Every time Luther Vandross visits, I receive a box of Padron premium cigars. Luther trusts my stage elevator management. When his overbearing production manager attempts to control the moves in the rehearsal, Luther stops him and announces, "Any stage elevator moves come from him. Let him call it in," pointing to me. "Let him handle it." Susan Lucci, a longtime soap opera diva nominated for a daytime Emmy countless times without a win, is a backstage favorite. When she finally does win after so many years, she walks offstage and holds the award over her tiny frame and celebrates for a few moments with all of us. Even *Wheel of Fortune* game show stars Pat Sajak and Vanna White embrace the house crew at the Hall. B. B. King gifts me the guitar picks he uses in his performance. My son has drumsticks from Lars Ulrich, drummer for Metallica.

Roberta Flack is concerned about riding on a stage elevator with a grand piano. I offer to ride it with her.

"Is it safe?" she asks. Her face reveals concern.

"I wouldn't be on it and I wouldn't let you on it if it weren't," I respond.

She thinks for a minute, chomping on the last of an apple. She looks around looking for a place to deposit the core.

I extend my palm to accept it.

"I'll take it."

She is surprised at my reply, and she begins to smile. We run the elevator move five more times.

She glows when the elevator reveals her to a cheering audience going wild.

There is a natural solidarity at Radio City that permeates the collective personality of the staff. It comes from professionalism, trust, and sharing in this very special way to make a living.

Another attempt to create a holiday spectacular around Easter shifts the focus to the season rather than the event. The idea is to create a spring spectacular celebrating the birth of new life. A group of creative artists are hired to develop an international theme around a celebration. It is called Carnivale, an exotic name designed to tell the story of spring around the world. Graciela Daniele, a Broadway choreographer with a long line of credits including *Annie Get Your Gun*, *Ragtime*, and *The Pirate Queen* is hired to direct. Her celebrated Broadway lighting designer husband Jules Fisher lights the show.

Graciela is striking. Born in Buenos Aires, she looks like my mother and speaks a fractured English like my father. She is a welcome remembrance of both.

"You will put measurements on the floor, no?"

"Of course, Graciela. Anything you need, just let me know."

"This is very momentous. A birth of spring. Like having many babies. The Rockettes will have babies right on the stage."

She sounds insane, possessed. When her brown eyes glisten and her Raphael-inspired cherub cheeks break into a smile, Graciela asks for anything and I get it done. I feel a natural bonding with Graciela. I begin to think I have South American roots. I love watching her direct. She is most beautiful when she is most intense.

"More, more, deeper, make passion, girls! Show me passion in your hips! You are having the babies of spring!"

She exudes a creative volatility that is stimulating, electrifying. Rehearsals become adventures. She is a refreshing experience to the highly structured Rockettes, who tend to be regimented in their choreographic moves. Graciela changes that. She gives them a dancing personality, making each individual dancer unique.

"Show me the rise and fall. Rise and fall!"

Just listening to her is seductive. I wonder how successful this production can be. She invents suggestive, provocative moves that no one had ever seen Rockettes perform. No

Rockette director or choreographer has ever brought out a dancer's sensuality like Graciela does in this production. Perhaps she is the saving grace for this Eastertime show.

Meanwhile, a renowned Trinidadian puppeteer arrives at Radio City and assembles six 25-foot-high puppets for the opening production number of *Carnivale*. Educated and trained in England, the puppeteer would be quite at home playing Admiral Horatio Nelson in a melodrama in the provinces. His demeanor accentuates his grandiose direction with British elegance. He instructs the puppeteers to telegraph the sensuality of the spring ritual production number.

He claims he does not *design* costumes. He provides the means for the human body to "express its energy." These lofty proclamations do not impress the wardrobe attendants in the costume shop.

Nineteen-time Grammy Award-winning composer Emilio Estefan provides the musical narrative. Mark Dendy, a brilliant young choreographer despite the signature mess of notes he tends to leave in his path, implements the moves inspired by Graciela for the opening. Mark can choreograph a stone, but he somehow cannot keep a coffee cup from spilling over his notes on a dance floor. Foy Enterprises provides the flying rigs for carrying two acrobats over the orchestra in the house. Though members of the stagehand's union, Foy employees focus on keeping things and people in the air, and they operate separately from any other show component. They never fail, and no one is ever injured under their supervision.

With these heavy hitters, this dream team of talent, management is only concerned with how to service the anticipated sold-out houses. There is talk of cancelling concerts to make room for the new Radio City as the home of two spectaculars: Christmas and *Carnivale*.

We are all looking forward to a new stylized Spring Show that identifies a new branding approach. Radio City has a real chance this time to own another season just like Christmas, and we all work especially hard to make this happen. The entire management structure of MSG Entertainment has a defining stake in its success. The first invited promotional rehearsal of the opening production number includes all the top brass and the usual executive management in tow. We are invited to bring our families to this presentation.

Joseph is in school, but I take advantage of the opportunity to bring Lauren along with Carol.

The production is viewed as a unifying gesture and an attempt to return to normalcy after the event of September 11th. It is November 6th, and the show represents the confidence to return to business as usual in midtown Manhattan.

Since we are still in the rehearsal stages of the production, makeshift tables made from four-by-eight plywood sheets lay over the tenth, eleventh, and twelfth rows of seats in the orchestra. Telephones, communications equipment, scripts, stationery, headsets are strewn across the expanse of ten tech tables. In the row in front of the production table, sits the CEO, the president of MSG, the executive vice president of public relations, and assorted business, sports, and entertainment execs. To my left are Graciela, Jules Fisher, and the entire design team for the show. Just behind me is twelve-year-old Lauren with Carol.

The stage manager backstage clears the checklist to start the rehearsal presentation. I cue the line producer to walk to the podium set on stage right. As soon as he appears onstage, I cue a follow spot operator to pick him up and remain with him for his introductory speech. The producer is not a natural, and his delivery seems unprepared. I wonder how long he is going to last in the heated executive cauldron of the 2 Penn Plaza dynasty.

Time spent on the 26th floor of 2 Penn Plaza is like an executive boot camp. He does not seem to understand the nuances of being invited to the 26th floor. I sense it is only a matter of time.

He finishes his introduction and exits the stage. I call the stage manager to begin and call house lights to half.

The orchestra begins. A bright, Caribbean calypso beat garners applause and is followed by stage lighting accenting the samba beat across the huge arches of the hall. The Grand Curtain rises to reveal Rockettes in figure-hugging halter tops and hot pants lying on their backs, undulating their hips toward gigantic skeleton puppets. The puppeteer operators mimic the movement as if to compel the Rockettes to undulate deeper and harder. Huge bony hands lure and encourage submission to the rite of spring. The music and the dance rise to a crescendo, as two flying Rockettes serving as representative spirits of the season hover over the audience. Sacks of confetti are released over the invited audience. As soon as the flying Rockettes clear the proscenium arch, I call the Grand Curtain back down on to the stage. The entire event is over in 20 minutes.

Thunderous applause ensues. Excessive self-congratulation among executives follows as they shake welcome hands vigorously over the aisles. All look around as if to evaluate reactions.

Behind me, my daughter, in a purely innocent inquiry and within earshot of the gaggle of executives asks, "Daddy, why were the skeletons humping the Rockettes?"

I have no words.

On November 9th, trade publication *Variety* runs an article announcing a postponement of *Carnivale*, citing an economic slowdown and reduction in the tourism industry in New York.

The show never returns.

All those wonderful concepts of dramatic structure, narrative arc, theme, story, message take a back seat to the driving culture of filling seats, regardless of content. A few years into this gig brings Radio City its own brand of operational challenges. Radio City is acquired by Cablevision and falls under a new CEO who manages to keep every senior executive on the alert. Preparations for forecast meetings force managers to study their profit and loss reports to the minutest details, from the cost of Ranger hockey socks to Rockette laundry. Details are where a manager is cornered, and his competence assailed if they do not have an answer to an overlooked item in the budget.

The 26th floor of 2 Penn Plaza overlooks the perennially gray west side of midtown Manhattan. It looks that way even on sunny days. Knowing the prevailing management style is the top agenda of every senior executive across the company. It does not matter whether you work at Radio City, Madison Square Garden, the New York Rangers, or the New York Knicks. For sports teams, concerts, and Christmas Spectaculars, the agenda is simple: fill the seats. The secret is merchandising. Play until the very end, so the fans spend exorbitant sums for refreshments, jerseys, and a host of sports paraphernalia. I learn that being aware of the cost of obscure budget items gives the savvy executive the advantage of preempting the conference room strategy.

Uptown at Radio City, all we must do is keep on filing in 6,000 patrons per performance four, five, and six times a day for the Christmas Spectacular and for more than 300 concerts and events over the year. I am sure to know the cost of glitz applications on hosiery, Rockette character shoes, and how many *Wooden Soldier* pants we go through in 230 performances. I learn these details in hopes of keeping my boss happy and keeping my job.

But there is another agenda.

My boss is in a band. Having the CEO of a premier sports and entertainment conglomerate having a little fun by picking up a guitar and dressing up like a Blues Brother adds a human element to the man.

It is the uncomfortable reaction of every senior executive to support, attend, and pine over the rehearsals that makes these diversions peculiar. High-achieving executive management types arrive at sound check on performance day and feign sublime enjoyment watching the boss man pluck and croon to rhythms, riffs, and progressions.

One of his assistants, a former stagehand and friend and now a facility executive, scurries around with the CEO's effects like a harried wardrobe attendant. I watch the demeanor of this assistant approach a near mayhem in setting up the requirements for the gig. There is nothing he will not do for the man.

The venue at B.B. King's on 42nd Street between 7th and 8th Avenues sports the usual gaudiness of a jazz club. I am drafted to be the host, the announcer. At showtime, when the crowd fills the room, I muster enough courage to make like an auctioneer and scream into the mic.

"Ladies and Gentlemen, wel…"

No one hears, no one listens. I am standing in the back, figuring I can survey the action and have some sort of control from that vantage point. Nobody is going to respond to the announcement. This is not an audience. This is a massive, boisterous crowd on its way to getting drunk. I must learn to be as ridiculous as they are. I make my way backstage and borrow a cowbell from one of the musicians. I return to the back of the house and grab my mic. I begin whooping and hollering nonsensical utterances while madly ringing the cowbell. I make my way to the control desk and finally got the attention of the crowd. The spotlight operator helps by illuminating me.

Wildly ringing the cowbell, I proclaim, "Yo, everybody! Put your hands together for"…Screams and cheers drown out my attempt to overcome the expected overreaction to our boss onstage.

I feel like Anthony Quinn in *Requiem for a Heavyweight*. I return the cowbell to the percussionist and realize that regardless of our title or position, we are in show business. I work for a peculiar impresario.

The first set begins. My stage manager's performer admiration sets in. Here is a multi-million-dollar man with every available asset and resource to achieve or buy nearly anything he wants, even a bunch of executives faking a good time to ensure their long-term employment. But he is out there, and like all performers, vulnerable to the audience.

Guarded gyrations from patrons continue as dancing couples veer as close as possible to be seen by their boss who is plucking away at his Les Paul guitar.

The man wants to be in show business, just like everyone else, just enough to be a player, a fellow musician, part of the crowd he hires all year long at the Showplace of the Nation. He has the venue and the theatrical addiction, just like all of us.

The unrelenting urge for recognition, to be somebody, the need for affirmation we get in one form or another from parents, from family, and from friends. When it's not enough you look elsewhere, and the stage waits for such a personality. One that is hungry for acknowledgement and willing to make a fool of themselves. The stage lure does not discriminate. From chief executive officers in New York noodling strings in a 42nd Street jazz club to Victor the main curtain hauler in Toronto, inches from the stage upon which he dreams to perform. The theatre is an emotional home that offers camaraderie, connection, or a place to hide a devastating miscalculation of one's talent. The lesson is to forget about the billing. Whether or not my boss ends up a rock star does not matter. He is enjoying himself, even if he pays for it.

I have little desire to act or dance, and I especially do not fancy the requirement of changing costumes three, four, and five times a performance. I like to organize, to serve the shape of sequence. That is enough for me. I think it wise to leave the performing to folks like Tony Bennett, Elton John, Billy Joel, regulars who visit the hall and do what they do best.

My boss puts on a good show, but I hope he keeps his day job.

Chapter 13

Bloody, Bloody Monday

A brisk morning brings vibrancy and energy to a gray cityscape and a daily commute. Emerging from the Concourse level of Grand Central, I take advantage of the 100 steps and climb them, hoping to balance last night's order of New York cheesecake at Del Frisco's.

Rather than walk the usual route up Park Avenue then over to 6th, I work my way through the Broadway theatre district to find a decent toasted bialy.

A bialy is the ideal marriage of Italian garlic and Jewish bread.

I think of David Merrick, my first Broadway employer. I miss the theatrical neighborhood. Rockefeller Center is becoming trendy, selective, and cold-hearted. Expensive restaurants and boutique hotels cater to big spenders sporting keffiyehs and driving Mercedes. New York is losing its title as capital of the world, and the world is buying its real estate. I walk into my stage manager's office just off stage right. The only wall decoration in the windowless office is a 3'x5' blowup of the familiar "Radio City" vertical neon sign glaring over 51st Street. I sink into the worn leather couch and unwrap my bialy. For a moment, I contemplate my good fortune.

The power switch on my computer screen produces a large red exclamation point next to an email demanding attention. It is from the line producer of one of the Christmas Spectacular road shows. I think about opening the link and prepare for anything. But the morning has the promise of a special comfort, and I prefer to extend it by enjoying my morning coffee and delay the unavoidable onslaught of change, adjustment, shock, concern, worry, and trepidation. I decide to keep the email closed. I sit back and finish my toasted bialy. I take in the scenery of 6th Avenue street traffic and wish for the good old days of David Merrick.

Meanwhile, another executive at Radio City is experiencing a different change of scenery. The email I finally open reports the executive's termination at the executive offices of Cablevision at 2 Penn Plaza. The email reveals that a long-time veteran of stage and production management storms out of a forced exit strategy meeting. No one expects it, but the news comes as no surprise to me. The individual is an institution, a go-to person for all things Music Hall. Cablevision brass thinks otherwise. The executive happens to be my direct boss.

This refreshing morning in February assuages the fact that being employed in this environment is beginning to make me feel like a character in a video game. News like the email I open transform offices into a bunker. Entry doors are locked like cages holding senior executives in corporate captivity. Put the asses in the seats, feed fresh meat to the lion and sell out the merchandise made in China at exorbitant prices. Charge for every breath. Hope for the best.

A restructuring of the executive staff occurs on a regular basis. This "cleaning out" happens unexpectedly, literally at a moment's notice. It is never process-driven. It is a reactionary tactic to maintain control.

I am still managing every event from rock bands and broadcast award shows to the Christmas Spectacular. The frontline managers of show production follow the routine of loading in concerts daily. A few are promoted to the now-empty executive positions. I am part of this transition. I feel a hollow seediness in all of this, an ascendant evil that leaves broken careers and irreparable damage to work relationships. I am informed of this transition during one of my boss's blues-guitar-playing performances at BB King's. The new assistant, now our boss's new right ear, crony, and truckler, summons me to a corner behind the nightclub's dressing room and announces that I am now the executive producer of the Christmas Spectacular. This is not an offer I can decline. This has already been processed by human resources without my knowledge.

At the next strategy meeting, without the former executive of Radio City, the day continues with a rather contentious first-quarter meeting of all divisions of MSG Entertainment. Representatives of Radio City, Madison Square Garden, the Rockettes, the Knicks, the Rangers, Liberty, MSG network, and Cablevision fill the green leather swivel chairs around the conference room table at 2 Penn Plaza.

The usual refreshments of oversized cookies, sodas, coffee, and chips wait for the arrival of the CEO's first touch. I do not dare partake of the refreshments until after the CEO has first dibs.

Upon his arrival, tenuous greetings mumble forth.

"Good Morning, sir."

"Great to see you." Yeah, right. There is no cutlery invented that can cut through the tension.

The content of the conversation is irrelevant. The mood is ominous. Whether the Rangers blow the playoffs, or the Knicks are losing only intensifies the expectation that this meeting has a high potential to devolve into an unpleasant afternoon. Being in a patriarchally centered environment, it does not matter if the Liberty, the women's professional basketball team, wins or loses. The only female member of the executive team has recently sued some of her colleagues in a sexual harassment case and is awarded a multi-million-dollar settlement. *The Christmas Spectacular*, a single-digit percentage of the entire MSG budget, has increased its profit margin from the previous year. I feel confident I have nothing to worry about.

I do not anticipate the next assignment.

Following this formal first-quarter meeting, which sees vilification of three established executives, rejected proposals and reports, and sets the tone of the day on a continued pallor of doubt and concern over one's future, the outcome of the meeting manages to be a rather unproductive and fractured event. It seems to me to be dysfunctional business as usual; the best one can hope for. Personally, a few scratches but no mortal wounds. At these salaries, many do not mind being called incompetent in front of their colleagues. In fact, it seems to be a rite of passage on the 26th floor to be belittled, harassed, and repudiated for just coming to work. Almost everyone expects it; many tolerate it; some and a few inherit the tactics. Then the announcement comes.

I am summoned in my new role as the Executive Producer to a breakout meeting with the president of MSG and the executive vice president of production. On the agenda is corporate restructuring and repurposing. In other words, termination, firings, whack time. Reporting charts delineating position title, job descriptions, reassignments all leading to letting people go. In all, we are assigned to terminate employees by noon. The meeting is about who is going to fire whom. I have close working relationships with all the candidates and terminating their employment would almost certainly sever their friendships. This may be a business decision, but it never stops being personal.

Especially now.

There is no nice way to tell people their services are no longer required. The process requires calling up the intended victim into my office, assisted by a human resources psychcopomp and informing them in a carefully worded script that they are terminated for a myriad of obscure reasons. The deliverer of the bad news is pushing for the recipient to accept the fact by introducing the HR representative into the morbid discussion, who then soullessly details their severance package. Immediately following the initial conversation, the recipient of the day's unexpected consolation prize gets to return to their office escorted by a security officer, one whom they have greeted every day when showing their ID badge and having had small talk greetings. They are now told, "Have a nice day." The newly liberated former employee gets up to three hours to collect their personal items, attend to their emails, set aside any personal belongings for later delivery, and then is escorted out the building by the security officer. End of story. End of day. End of career.

I am assigned to terminate the employment of a 20-year veteran of Rockette choreography. I follow the suggested scripted terminology.

"We are moving in a new direction, and we will no longer be needing your services."

"We will assist you in this process of separation."

"We appreciate the years of hard work and thank you for your continued efforts."

The HR representative takes over.

I wonder how many shoes the choreographer has worn out performing and teaching the precision of the world-famous dance troupe. There she sits, facing me with that "How could you?" look of betrayal. I recall my childhood memory of the Feast of Our Lady of the Seven Sorrows, the grotesque representation of the statue with a grieving Mother of God bearing seven knives through her heart. The former employee has a similar look.

I feel like a murderer. The experience of snuffing out the productive work life out of someone is appalling. It is an irrevocable act of destruction, a violation of trust, a cold-as-death heartless rape of self-esteem. There is never a good reason given for the terminations, only a generalized, generic excuse for cost-effectiveness.

I recall the musician's issue back in December, and I am sure I would have been on the other side of this bloodletting today if I had not resolved it successfully.

Meanwhile, over in the office of the executive vice president of production, a creative director of the Rockettes is meeting his corporate demise. The knowledge of 15 years of branding the storied dance group lay meaningless as an anxious VP follows the fractured script of forced departure. Utterly surprised and upset, the director's visceral response prompts him to walk out before the HR representative completes his separation process.

The termination skirmishes continue throughout the day. Avoidance/avoidance conflicts proliferate throughout the hallways. No one wants to accidentally run into a newly fired employee or a newly assigned executioner. Evasive action ensues behind closed office doors, extended lunches outside the building, unanswered ringing phones. No one answers emails from HR.

Over at Madison Square Garden, in one of those oddly shaped offices hugging the perimeter of the arena downstairs, the production manager of special events meets his personal day of infamy after 18 years of service. A friendly HR representative in a short-sleeve white shirt with pen protector completes the separation process resembling a disembowelment. The manager is gone. At 56 years of age, one can only imagine his prospects for new employment in a business that eats people in their 30s and 40s and a corporate culture that runs on insensitivity.

On this bloody Monday at the *World's Most Famous Arena*, numerous positions of senior executives, managers, and supervisors are being restructured. Repurposing, job description clarification, corporate restructure become death codes for another goon squad culling.

I do not know of a rougher room than the *Showplace of the Nation*.

Two weeks pass. I try to grapple with the disturbing indignity of firing colleagues and the lifetime opportunity handed to me. Both require a perspective I am not prepared to accept. Both require compromise of my integrity. I think I am better than this, but it is merely that my price has been met.

MSG corporate philosophy redefines the concept of micromanagement. Before becoming executive producer of the Christmas Spectacular, I never attend a forecast meeting or review a budget beyond a top-sheet profit and loss statement. I am more interested in a three-inch spacer to increase resiliency in dance surfaces or if skin parts of costumes are being properly cleaned. But here I am, the guy in charge of production, elbowing with the executive vice president of finance, the general manager of the Rangers, the president of MSG, the president of the MSG network, the vice president of the Knicks. More VPs, more execs. A cadre of super-achievers, accomplished players in their respective fields, sitting around a maple table with green leather chairs and wood-paneled walls 26 floors above the bland, monolithic structure next to Madison Square Garden. The view outside, straining to be impressive, overlooks the mediocre, urban railroad yards of midtown. The CEO enters the room sporting a goatee of questionable fashion, a style repeated by many sitting at around the table.

I take the second seat from the head of the table. I sit next to the MSG president. The seat is usually left vacant, I discover later, because it seems to have a reputation for being the location for accusatory fury from the chairman. Newbies trip over a thousand traps a day. I have inadvertently placed myself in the hot seat for accusation. I inadvertently find the corporate version of Michael Price's Goodspeed barber chair. The cross examination begins.

"How much do the musicians cost us for Christmas?"

No one answers, and eyes turn to me, the new guy, the new potential piece of raw meat to feed the lion at the head of the table. I did not review the three- hundred-page production budget that morning. I do not expect to be thrown into the ring so soon. Forty-five seconds of silence passes. I must make a move that can go either way.

"I have to review the budget that I just received it this morning, so I don't know, but I can get back to you by end of day."

Silence. Preparation for an explosive moment. A hurl out the window to meet the gray west side pavement. My family would be taken care of. Perhaps just a forced exit, escorted by security. Well, it was nice working here. I bet I could have made friends with this $500,000 a year club. Not that I was making that much.

"You don't know?"

I surmise this is it. Vesuvius. The San Francisco Earthquake. The Great Chicago Fire. Armageddon.

The question is repeated, now emphasizing as if in preparation for the final salvo. Everyone braces for emotional outbreak, for the levee to be compromised. Eyes narrow, pens twirl wildly through nervous fingers, throats attempt to clear repeatedly without relief.

"No, sir, I don't. I started this new position just two weeks ago and I have been familiarizing myself wi…"

Executives surrounding this massive corporate conference table freeze.

"That's the first honest answer I've heard today."

The palpitations subside. Breathing resumes, and we continue to the next potentially fatal pitfall, this time in sports finance. The Rangers are on a one-game winning streak, so the GM of the Rangers is the hero of the day. The Knicks are surviving, and the Knicks president gets a break. But rummaging through the three-hundred-page budget proposal, I realize there are thousands of possible "gotcha" facts and the stomach-churning fear of not knowing all of them creates a panic I try to suppress.

A question is asked about the unit cost of paper hot dog folders. All eyes move down then back up to the VP of house operations. He is stymied. He knows the overall cost of the merchandise operations, but he has no idea of the unit cost of a paper plate. No one thinks such a minute calculation is relevant at this level.

"Probably two or three cents. I'll look into…"

He is interrupted in the middle of his sentence and waved away. Oversized chocolate chip cookies are being consumed and washed down with Diet Coke.

At this point, I realize this is on-the-job training norm for corporate executives in sports and entertainment. Enduring the usual mortification, the VP excuses himself. The meeting resumes with some mumblings of a healthy first quarter, meager attempts to diffuse the unsettling feeling in nearly every stomach and those with hearts still left beating. And then the meeting ends. No budgets are approved, and nothing moves forward. I ask for time to present a rendering for a new costume. That is not going to happen today. Nothing productive on my agenda comes from the 26th floor of 2 Penn Plaza that day.

The operating structure of Radio City is comprised of three elements. Cablevision dictates corporate policy and procedure, Madison Square Garden manages financial reporting for all divisions, and the Christmas Spectacular is a property within the MSG portfolio, along with the hockey Rangers, basketball Liberty and Knicks, and the MSG network. This creates a complex fiscal reporting procedure, since the fiscal year of MSG is in one timeframe, and the operating schedule of the Christmas Spectacular is sits between two fiscal year timeframes. That requires two separate unit budgets, one which coincides with MSG and the other with Radio City. Expenditure approvals must follow this line, so a single costume approval must be initiated no later than January of the year in which it was intended to be introduced into the show.

The chancy, haphazard forecast meetings force me to create a different path in acquiring timely new element expenditure approvals. I know the CEO has a special affection for the Rockettes, and he protects both the brand and the dancers with personal attention. He is impulsive, petulant, and unpredictable, but his awareness of their workplace is a top priority, and he is an enthusiastic proponent of improving sexual harassment training for corporate employees. This is vitally necessary, considering our newfound association with a sports-centered management operates with an ingrained sexist worldview.

Attempts to present a new element budget for approval through a normal process are abandoned. The new MSG president of the quarter is little more than a reactionary vizier working his own survival tactic and monitoring the temperament tolerances of his micromanaging the *Chairman-cum-Oracle*. I finally receive word of an opening on a Friday afternoon in May, already a month late for actual new costume production.

I walk in with a $5,000, full color rendering of a proposed new costume for that year's Christmas Spectacular. I think the rendering is enough of a visual aid to elicit a decision. But it doesn't matter. The subject is never brought up and the meeting ends early. Meeting completed. Moving forward to getting in line to accept two steps backward.

I have just spent $5,000 on a rendering and I have no decision. The timeframe for a new costume is closing in, fast. A costume approval is apparently not a high priority, until it becomes an issue. I find a way to prevent it. I decide to build a prototype.

I contact the costume house that had been tentatively awarded the bid and ask if they could come up with a prototype. They have just begun to shop around for the materials needed so they were not prepared to create anything yet, but they want the contract, so they proceed to gather remnants of the materials needed.

This is not the normal operating procedure for a costume tailor. It affects their process and takes people out of their routine, which then affects their business's bottom line. Costume designers deal with people who have a visionary capability in decision-making without having to see the real thing. They ask for a model size, so they can create the prototype.

I think about this dilemma. I must create a fail-safe opportunity for approval. The decision-making that is delayed because of a host of priorities costs time and money. I do not want it to cost my job. I think of his genuine regard for the Rockettes, which at times is manifested in an almost shy, diffident manner.

I need to find a way to coerce this lion in his own cage. I email Amanda, a dancer who had just recently become a Rockette, and ask if she would support me in speaking to the advantages of the prototype. She agrees. She is measured, the prototype is created in five days, and I have a costume to show my chief of disruption.

I finally have an actual costume to close my deal and get this costume made and a Rockette to accompany me to speak to the advantages of the costume. Amanda has a suggestion.

"Why don't I just wear it to the meeting?"

"You'd do that? Walk into an office in costume with a bunch of sports entertainment executives?"

"Let's do it." Amanda agrees to accompany me to the corporate boardroom office. She is engaging and her attitude is refreshing. She has common sense, style, and leadership. She can certainly handle the man cave of the 26th floor.

I arrange a meeting the following week. Amanda dons the costume under a raincoat, and we both cab down 7th Avenue to 2 Penn Plaza.

I share many cab rides with dancers in costumes. My destinations are not social hot spots of Manhattan. They are hospital emergency rooms and clinics that treat dance injuries. Sprained ankles from wearing bear costumes in *The Nutcracker*, lacerations after running into Santa's sleigh, burns from errant sparks spewing from the "Magic of Christmas," torn ligaments from slipping over falling fake snow in "Christmas in New York." I cannot effectively describe the experience of escorting a limping dancer dressed in silver lamé tights, street sneakers, and a military-inspired bodice sporting oversized epaulets with braided aiguillettes waving randomly as she hobbles into the emergency clinic of NYU Medical Center.

Amanda has yet to experience a date at the clinic, and the joy of being hired as a professional dancer in an iconic production is expressed in her enthusiasm and energy. She is the right individual to pull off this pitch.

We enter the elevator and ride to the 26th floor. No street noise is heard up here. There is only the low hiss of air transferring in an environment of sealed windows, like a recovery room. A separation from the reality of the street. We walk into reception and are given the usual imposed-upon look by the receptionist who displays a knee-jerk mistrust of greeting someone she does not recognize.

"Can I help you?" she says, not meaning a word of it.

"Hi, Wendy, we have an appointment with executive management."

Sure you do, her eyes telegraph unbelievingly. An intercom call confirms my statement.

"Go through that door; make a right."

I am in this reception area six times a year. But since my office was at Radio City and not 2 Penn, I am as familiar to Wendy as a one-time messenger.

I approach the conference room, knock, and Amanda and I walk in. A roomful of executives look up. I look at Amanda for reassurance that she is still comfortable with doing this. She nods.

"Hello everyone. This is Amanda who has volunteered to model the proposed costume for the new production number for the Christmas Spectacular." I am amazed I did not mess up this introduction.

Everyone nods, with most trying to conceal their delight at the sight of an attractive young woman in the room.

"Amanda volunteered to model the costume, so you could get the full effect."

I hold her raincoat, and Amanda immediately takes the iconic position of a performing Rockette, with bent knee, favored opposite hip, arms close to her sides, beaming smile.

The execs around the table applaud, responding in the way corporate executives guys ogling a dancer in a virtual bathing suit usually do.

Approval is granted to build the costume.

Amanda shakes some hands and puts her raincoat on to exit. A 30-second meeting for a decision that needed to be made three months before.

On the way out, the vice chairman gestures to me.

"John, you really delivered. Great job."

I'm thinking it was Amanda who delivered, but no one here thinks that way.

I acknowledge him, and we leave.

Great job. I had to resort to a near peep show to get approval. Almost 3 months behind schedule, we now had to rush to get these things created when production could have been on time and on budget. But things do not work that way in the Land of Impulse.

A few weeks later, the back page of *The New York Post* features a near full-page photo of my boss at a Knicks game. The banner reads, "Head Case Fires Head Coach." I take the paper home and show Carol.

"This is who I work for. My boss made the papers. Again."

Glen Livet 12, neat, becomes the relaxation of choice, making the hungry lion disappear at least for now.

My boss is used to the punching bag jabs of sports journalists. He is an easy target. But despite any shortcomings he is accused of, he is honest and straightforward, and he gets a chance to prove it on a grand scale.

Chapter 14

The Rodent and the Cougar

"City sidewalks, busy sidewalks, dressed in ho-li-day style…"

I watch the 50-foot steel mesh grid sitting atop the theatre's marquee swing precariously around the corner of the building. The frame carries the 5,000-diode lamps that illuminate midtown 6th Avenue as Radio City's official Holiday Christmas tree. The project requires closure of the easternmost lane of 6th Avenue to accommodate the 26-wheel crane hoisting the steel supports. Construction crews from the American Christmas Decorating Company are already busy at various establishments in midtown between 5th and 6th Avenues. Fred Schwam, the owner of the holiday decorations company, developed his father's artificial plant business, M. Schwam Floralart, into the premier corporate seasonal design company for midtown Manhattan. Fred is virtually the only game in town. He knows it, and he is worth it, but I must show some negotiating prowess to keep my job. We come to an agreement that places the yearly 2% increase in another line item. That gives Fred the fees he asks for and the ability to keep the increase hidden in a

$36,000,000 budget. Most of the familiar holiday decorations that adorn iconic 5th Avenue businesses are American Christmas installations. Before Halloween and Thanksgiving, Fred and his team are busy installing the background work for transforming midtown into a holiday destination. Huge metal starbursts of light emitting diodes, or LEDs, are being hoisted on the front facade of Saks Fifth Avenue. A giant, off-center ribbon of blazing red, weather-resistant fabric wraps two sides of the structure that houses Cartier on the corner of 52nd Street and 5th Avenue, creating a gigantic Christmas package of the entire building. Towering reproductions of those familiar 18th century German dress parade troops are fashioned after the military uniforms of Frederick the Great, better known as Wooden Soldiers. They stand guard at 1285 Avenue of the Americas. Fred, along with his Creative Director, Kent Fritzel, roam the streets of midtown like North Pole ambassadors transforming the gray concrete of the Manhattan grid into an outdoor holiday cartoon.

The pair double-handedly define the holiday as a New York institution and their craft is displayed throughout the plazas, lobbies, and front doors of midtown Manhattan. Office workers, tourists, and foot cart vendors cannot help but smile.

In an ideal world, there would be no negotiation with Fred, and I envision giving him full reign to create magical realism all over New York. I know he can.

"It's beginning to look a lot like Christmas…"

Directly below this iconic display of holiday cheer and facing the Art Deco marquee of Radio City Music Hall stands an inflated, vinyl balloon resembling a threatening, hungry rat publicizing the protest of the American Federation of Musicians of Greater New York, AFM Local 802. The scene in midtown Manhattan does not slow the traffic on 6th Avenue and 50th Street. It is the inflatable cougar perched on the Radio City marquee itself that draws the most attention. Its rear rubber paws are secured to the edge of the iconic, landmarked, wraparound canopy extending over the street. The installation allows a bobbing motion over the traffic with the right wind direction, feigning a potential jump toward the bulbous overweight rubber rodent sitting in front of the Time-Life Building across the street. Noisy electric blowers support the 15-foot-high rat and the 10-foot-high cougar's needs for constant replenishment of air. The decibel level from the air compressors used to maintain the integrity of both balloons sound like an Osprey landing on the deck of an aircraft carrier. These units of protest have seen political battles on many a New York street, and patches are visible from rips developed in the seams of the balloons hint at the end of their utility. The patches no longer share the same color as the body of the units holding the things together, looking more like bandages from wounds received from impassioned opponents of some cause. The inflated obstacle is too attractive a target when placed on a city sidewalk for pranksters seeking to deflate the balloon with a stab to the belly. The rat is a familiar visitor at many labor-related protests claiming unfair management practices allegedly responsible for everything from unsafe working conditions to lack of hazard pay to reduced break times.

We are conducting negotiations for a new collective bargaining agreement between Radio City management and Local 802. I represent management along with a killer labor lawyer who is lethal but mesmerizing to watch. The union's representation includes three or four musicians, depending upon the day of the meeting, and a legal representative who could be an understudy to Joe Pesci's misplaced attorney *Vincent Gambini* in *My Cousin Vinny*.

As day three of the negotiation meetings begin, I peer out onto Sixth Avenue and wonder if the vinyl cougar will lose its footing and fall onto midtown traffic. Worse, I begin to contemplate an upwind that might make the massive balloon airborne and send it directly into the steel-mesh tree structure above it and rip the delicate diode lamps being hung on the mesh. I imagine shards of metal and glass, spilling over the 1,000-people-a-minute sidewalk traffic. I anticipate damage, injury, a class-action lawsuit, and where my new job would come from after I am fired. The reality of the situation is that I am not directly responsible for the event, the cougar, the tree installation. I approve the budget for them. My job, for now, is to get musicians to shake on a three-year agreement. But the menacing cauldron of impulsive and reactionary management makes every executive a paranoid gerbil running as fast as we can to ensure no misunderstanding, no blip in operations comes to hunt us down and whack us out of our jobs. We hear it every day.

You know what's his name?

He was terminated an hour ago.

Yeah. Escorted out of the building.

Looked like he was going to have a heart attack.

Probably got him out of there quick so it wouldn't happen onsite.

Don't want lawsuits, you know.

I turn away and walk toward the stage door entrance. Let it begin, again.

Avenue of the Americas is a favorite spot for many protest groups exercising their right to dissent for all to see, especially with major network television stations close by. Not to be outdone, Radio City Music Hall joins the fray in staging an outdoor carnival of high theatrics announcing the ongoing negotiations between the musicians of Local 802 and the management of the Radio City division of MSG Entertainment.

"He knows if you've been bad or good so be good for goodness' sake…"

Such is the scenario for one of the more challenging events at the Music Hall.

The newly elected president of Local 802 sees the upcoming holiday season prior to the Christmas Spectacular engagement as an opportunity to strengthen the archaic rules of employment for music hall musicians and establish himself as the new union advocate with whom to be reckoned. But that strategy only works with opponents who are sane and share the same prodigious agenda. To the new #802 president, my boss is a malleable candidate for establishing his formidability as an upstart union boss. The starry-eyed union president does not bargain for my boss, a seasoned reactionary who operates within his own strategy and works his impulse to his own advantage. The issues at hand are productivity, cost control, and management of the quality of performance. Existing rules allow tenure for each musical instrument position played, or *chair*. The currently employed musicians refuse to give up control of how many times they could play a Christmas Spectacular. The show runs four performances a day, Monday through Thursday, five performances Friday, six performances Saturday, and five performances on Sunday. In theory, any currently playing musician has the right to play all thirty-two performances if they desire. Musicians are compensated at time and one half for the third and fourth shows every day, and double time for every fifth and sixth show in a day. The issue here is that it is the person occupying the *chair* receives the compensation differential, meaning that regardless of whether you play the first two performances, you still receive the differential even if it is your actual first performance of the day. Musicians who are assigned chairs would sub at a Broadway show matinee, then run over to the hall and do the last three or four performances at the hall at premium time.

JUST OFF, STAGE RIGHT

If I double-dipped ice cream coatings like a musician, I could develop a sugar dependency in just one Christmas week.

Making a yearly salary for ten weeks of work is an offer no musician ever refuses, and the timing is tempting. Break your butt for the holidays then off to Florida and cocktails in January. Return in March to your chair in a Broadway show until Christmastime and that music degree your father scoffed at pays off handsomely.

Being a working musician and developing industrious work strategies are admirable and sometimes greedy. That greed gets out of hand when the 802 negotiating team members, all of whom are chair-assigned musicians at the hall, fight against management's proposal to acquire the right to limit the number of performances a musician can play to three a day. The point behind the limitation is to maintain productivity, profit margin, and performance quality. Ever hear a trumpeter play the last show of the day? That is the time when musicians are paid double the normal rate to play flat notes. Do you know what a flat note sounds like in the middle of "Oh Come All Ye Faithful?"

Essentially, theatre audiences are getting a lackluster performance and producers are paying a premium for the service. But that does not matter to the chaired musicians and their plans for extra mojitos at their Florida retreats.

Enter the strike.

As I pass one of the corporate assistants, a newly anointed truckler, I realize the boss is on the other end of the cell phone attached to his ear. I could tell it is our boss on the other end by the assistant's face, now alabaster and matching his deforested pate. The hairs on his head stand up like antennae on an insect signaling stress and worry, or mating. He tepidly gives me the phone.

"Hey, Barzini," the newly minted corporate henchman growls, "It's for you." There is something subliminally alluring in being anointed a nickname from a character in *The Godfather*.

The nickname is bestowed upon me back when we walked the same stage endlessly throughout the day, me as a stage manager, he as a stagehand, setting up act after act as they pass through the hall. The camaraderie is infectious and privileged. We are a team, a family, and trust flourishes, always with an eye for our collective safety and well-being. We speak of our families, our wives, our children. We lament about the lost opportunities we miss in not being around to bring them up, to attend their soccer and baseball and hockey games. Those conversations, that camaraderie are now in the past.

I take the phone as I walked into the Rockette collective-bargaining-agreement negotiations in progress.

I am ordered to stop the Rockette negotiations and have security escort them out. I am told the Christmas Spectacular is cancelled this year. I have no need to respond to the suddenly dead phone line.

This is a first for me. I do what I am told. I remember thinking how the Yankees might have felt in 1972 when Major League Baseball experienced the first walkout in its history. There is a celebratory nature to this impending corporate disaster. I am invigorated by the sense of this never having happened in the history of Radio City. Christmas in New York without the Christmas show? Unthinkable. And I am in the middle of it.

"Ho, Ho, Ho…" Oh, no.

We are all beholden to the bigger-than-life tactics of our part-time band musician/boss and his full-time impulses. I glance at the assistant. He seems blank, indifferent. The affability is gone, the approachability severed. His stare is expressionless. He looks like a reconditioned configuration of a newly minted, evil authoritarian, a hastily assembled sycophant in a Fred Perry end-of-season special. The suit does not become him. I remember him always looking better in jeans and a sweatshirt, running the load ins, directing the crews. Now he fills an off-the-rack suit with purchased allegiance as a hired hit man. He does what he must do. We all do to keep our jobs. This is the brand of show business on the other side of Broadway.

By late afternoon, a new plan emerges. I prepare for the Spectacular but without musicians. I arrange to record the entire show on tape and run it without actual musicians. The technical and logistical nightmare of running a show that is designed to operate under a Society of Motion Picture and Television Engineers, or SMPTE, time code management system requires resequencing every element of physical production—lighting, scenery, stage elevators, music "sweetening," and musical tempi. While the musicians are locked out, I gather the music sheets of 40 parts—brass, strings, percussion—all of it—and make copies of the entire musical library of the show, more than 3,000 individual sheets of music. I then send it to Ireland to have a Dublin-based orchestra play the entire score for recording. Local 802 jurisdiction has no authority outside the United States, and no one knows I have made a second copy of every sheet. The show's sound designer, who also has conducting experience, flies to Dublin and runs the recording session. Nightly 4:00 a.m. phone calls to tweak out issues occur for a week. By Thursday, I am beginning to fall for the soft, honeyed tone of the Dublin coordinator. I am a sucker for her Gaelic inflections. Early morning is a most creative time. I imagine catching glimpses of her through flowers I cannot name, but it does not matter. If I continue this distraction, nothing will get done. I pick up the phone and dial her number, stirred by hearing her again. Her voice is electric. I try to maintain my focus, and my integrity.

"Yes, love, cut the first twelve bars of 'Here Comes Santa Claus.'"

"Repeat the refrain of 'Joy to the World' at the curtain call."
"Yes, of course."
"Me, as well."
"And you, too. Someday."
"Thank you, my love."

If she looks anything like how I feel, I am undone. I cherish and relive every call over again.

I never meet my charming Dubliner. I am relieved to keep it that way. Seeing her may destroy what I imagine of her. I would not want her to be disappointed at the sight of me. It is safer to imagine her as a goddess, an enthralling siren, and I, a willing object of her affection. I keep my fantasies intact. They are too sweet, unspoiled. Unrequited illusions have the irresistible advantage of endless invention. I do not want to taint the calm reassurance of her voice, so safely far away. Nor I do wish to live in deceit, manipulation, exploitation, coercion. I honor the partnership with my wife and my integrity. I realize my job is becoming an obsession, a dark and dangerous place for the soul, and my 4:00 a.m. phone calls provide a rendezvous, a gentle immersion in illusion.

Reality lands us hard on a runway, ending our wandering flights of bliss. But we savor those dreams and keep them inside of us. Their seclusion preserves innocence, maintains beauty, remaining unblemished by any hint of reality.

It is 5:30 a.m. on a Friday and the first dress rehearsal is scheduled for next week.

At 8:30 am on Tuesday morning, the day of the first dress rehearsal, I enter the theatre to prepare for the rehearsal day. I have no music, no musicians. I begin to wonder why I showed up in the first place, conceding to some fractured hope that somehow all this will work out and I still have a job by the end of the day. I wonder who will do the dirty deed of whacking me from my job and which grim human resources representative will accompany the event. Rehearsal is scheduled for 10:00 a.m. At 9:30 a.m., there is no word on the sound designer's return.

At 9:45 a.m., I receive a call from our attorney, the overbearing, killer labor lawyer, the legal mercenary shark, who informs me that the designer has landed at JFK. Crowded disembarking, baggage claim, traffic, bad taxi drivers all run through my head. I hope for a savvy cab driver and no accidents on the Van Wyck Expressway to further bollix up the day. I order the stage manager to call half hour to show time at 10:00 a.m.

At 10:30 a.m., the sound designer arrives, CD in hand, and runs it up to the second balcony to the sound engineer. By 10:45 a.m., an acceptable delay for a first dress, I instruct the stage manager to cue the sound engineer and hear the downbeat of the overture. Cheers from the cast and sneering, gloating smiles from MSG brass prompts my new legal buddy to high-five me in the 15th row of the orchestra. We pull off the *gotcha* of the century. The new Local 802 president is tripped by the rug pulled out from under him. The assistant stands by, or just behind, ready to serve, to pounce, or to perform any trick conjured up by the whim of his new master. My boss, regardless of journalistic gibes, prevails and sets the musician's agreement on a new track.

A week of performances later, Local 802, without their impetuous president, signs a three-year agreement with Radio City, enabling musicians to return to work. I live for another day, fully employed and gainfully in possession of a CBA agreement. Live music played by musicians is back for Christmas at the Music Hall.

"Sleigh bells ring, are you listening?"

Chapter 15

Those Rockettes

It is Thanksgiving morning and Mary hugs me in full costume, right in front of Macy's.

This is significant, since Mary, in her two-and-one-half-inch-heel, beige character shoes handmade by La Duca and her three-foot, red-sequined, drum majorette garrison helmet designed by Bob Mackie, towers over me like a sparkling, breathing Christmas ornament. It is not her bright hazel eyes adorning her face like smiling twin sunsets or her statuesque form that soars beyond six feet that overwhelms me. It is the fact that this iconic representative of an historical tradition recognizes my support, my service to her performance right there in front of thousands of people, right in front of Macy's main entrance. In that moment, Mary is every woman I have ever met, and she approves of me. I earn her trust, and that is more thrilling than any float, any Middle America dance team, and any artist lip-synching to recorded music that make up the Macy's Thanksgiving Day Parade.

I ask my daughter Lauren if she would like to be a Rockette.

"Absolutely not!"

"Why not?"

"Because I don't ever want to do anything that everyone else does."

My understanding and acceptance of her comment contributes to my approach to effective fatherhood.

The first Thanksgiving Day parade began in Newark, New Jersey, in 1924 by Louis Bamberger, who owned a general store bearing his name. Macy's acquired the parade and relocated the event to their flagship store on 34th Street and 7th Avenue in Manhattan.

I am on the job for less than two weeks before we begin rehearsal for the parade. The Rockettes rehearse for the two scheduled appearances that include the latest production dance number from the Christmas Spectacular as well as the "Opening of the Gates" routine, which is comprised of lining up 36 Rockettes across 7th Avenue at 35th Street to await the arrival of the traveling parade. When the first parade float arrives, the Rockettes split the line at the center, allowing the parade to pass through and continue to 34th Street. This act signifies the official beginning of the holiday season. This simple, 12-second formation creates more consternation due to its branding significance and broadcast exposure to national television. Three and a half million people line the parade route from 79th Street to 34th Street. Fifty million television viewers watch this move representing the iconic precision of the Rockette dance team and positioning them as the chosen ambassadors of a New York Thanksgiving and Christmas celebration. It needs to be perfect, and every Rockette needs to be precisely costumed regardless of the weather. I carry heat packs to assist the troupe with the challenges of single-digit-degree weather. They dance in frigid temperatures. They dance in rain. They dance in flurries. They dance on asphalt pavement made slippery by the festive coat of paint in front of Macy's on Herald Square. No rulebook protects them from making their appearance seem sublime and effortless despite the hardships and discomfort of the cold, hard environment of a New York City street. Through pain and injury, Rockettes maintain that well-rehearsed smile. They look happy, but I learn otherwise.

Every Rockette endures costumes not fit for humans. There are in a constant struggle to maintain endless variations of a bathing suit.

Regardless of piping, appliqués, pleats, smocking, or netting, leg exposure to the hip is the costume standard that all colors and fabrics support. Rockettes get cold, especially in outside events during the holidays. They wear coats until just before their scheduled performance, requiring me to collect the coats in a quick run down the line as they drop their outerwear into a rolling wardrobe bin. The synthetic materials used in their costumes are durable, cheaper, and washable, but they irritate the skin. When dancers perspire in unbreathable materials, rashes, chafes, skin reactions take center stage.

That is why I carry Neosporin.

When dancers wear out the rubber layer on their shoes designed to prevent slips, foot muscles work harder to compensate the balance required to execute a dance move.

That is why I carry Tiger Balm.

Precision dancing is brutal exercise. While the famous eye-high kickline appears to be a line of smiling women holding on to each other in a group kick, the reality is that every individual is balanced on their own and there are inches between their arms and the back of the dancer next to them. No one is holding on to anyone. Emotional tempers heat up.

That is why I carry Midol, Excedrin, Kaopectate.

Preparation for the parade performances require a visitation from the broadcast director televising the parade. Gary Halvorson, a veteran television and opera broadcast director, employs a theatre director's point of view when reviewing the dance routines. Group patterns, taken from a bird's eye POV, or point of view, accentuate the precision combinations of the production number. Gary has a Busby Berkley approach, televising the Rockette experience as a total event and focusing on patterns rather than individuals. Finding this perspective requires Gary to climb a stepladder with his head inches from the ceiling of the rehearsal hall to grasp the scope of patterning in the number. Gary's ability to transfer a stage presentation into a television screen is proven every year with flawless live coverage of the Rockettes in full performance.

My routine on Thanksgiving morning is to take a 6:20 a.m. train from Goldens Bridge to Grand Central Terminal and gather the 40 Rockettes and their needs on an Academy Bus for the short trip to 35th Street, the talent holding area. Manhattan streets are already blocked off by 7:30 a.m., so the bus needs a police escort to run through the restricted streets. While most people are just getting up for breakfast, I am travelling with 40 fully outfitted Rockettes and a delirious bus driver who cannot get over his luck on this assignment. I tell him to get over it and stop looking for a date. Past the Saks Fifth Avenue store, now fully adorned with an electrified, pulsating snowflake light show across its façade, and St. Patrick's Cathedral, all hollied up with evergreen wreaths and a hint of red ribbon, the bus ride seems magical. The Rockettes are the prime ministers of the holiday, and they are initiating the celebration for New York, for the country, for the world.

One Thanksgiving Day parade and three Christmas Spectacular performances later, I have my fill of dead turkeys, freezing temperatures, angelic-looking Rockettes with their smiles removed and in real complaint mode. So much for the last Thursday in this November.

A directive is initiated to enliven the Rockettes in the Christmas Spectacular with new elements. I reach out to experts in other media to seek enhancements that would relate to contemporary tastes. The challenge to find new blood to pump up an anachronistic tourist show leads me to film.

Jeff Madoff is a video director and producer with a client list that includes Ralph Lauren, Gucci, Victoria's Secret, Godiva, and in 2007, Radio City. When I hire him to create a short film to cover a scene change in the Spectacular, he responds by reintroducing the dance troupe brand as a uniquely New York institution that identifies the Rockette as a modern woman in charge of her destiny. The three-minute retrospective rejuvenates the Rockette brand into an inspiring standard for young women. The film could have been a trailer for a feature-length film. Jeff's talents matches the historical and iconic value of the music hall. He captures its storied past with panache and transforms a tourist tradition into a viable performing art.

He is a superb video artist with an uncanny sense of the stage. Jeff connects with the Rockettes as if he had been working with them for years.

This is not surprising since he is a crucial element of the yearly *Victoria's Secret Fashion Show*. While I am busy with a side gig industrial show making Maytag refrigerators look sexy in Newton, Iowa, to sell appliances, Jeff is busy in New York superimposing fashion models dressed as angels in silk intimates to catapult off iconic skyscrapers to sell underwear. He does it with class and style. And art. Jeff and I become close colleagues and friends, punch-lining one another in the middle of every conversation. Thanks to him, the Rockettes are dreamy and trendy once again, but an odd realization soon comes over me after I wisecrack a one liner to Jeff.

"Bottom line, Jeff, is I work with bathing suits; you work with underwear," I quip during a shared dinner.

Then the realization hits home. We are in the business of objectification.

I oversee the workplace for scores of women over the course of a theatrical career. I learn a lot being in service to the female performing artist. The supply of Halls Eucalyptus, safety pins, Velcro, and hair ties I keep in my desk reveal my expertise.

I am around a woman's workplace in ways others can only imagine.

Interaction with women is a common occurrence. You would think that everyone engages in a workplace social structure, but few of us spend our working life amid dance clothes, leg warmers, uncomfortable costumes, and young women dragging dance bags, sheet music, and script sides up the stairwells of old rehearsal halls to face another day of rejection. Few of us watch the hope in bright faces lining up at a dance call fade in full view of their colleagues. Years of dance and acting classes, months of preparation, days of travel, a moment of rejection.

Those Rockette auditions, rehearsals, and performances prove that women are indeed unique. There is no experience or situation to suggest they are inferior, unequal, subservient, or incapable of anything they set out to do. They share successes and failures like everyone else.

Somewhere along our life's work and living, we make the mistake of insulating ourselves within a gendered commonality of experience. We create brotherhoods, boys' clubs and fraternities on one side and cheerleaders, sororities, and Ya-Ya Sisterhoods on the other, separate and unequal entities, all under the categories of gender and beauty, power and sexuality.

This taxonomy in any workplace promotes inequality and danger. As performers, the dancers endure costumes that accentuate their form and present their parts instead of their persons in an objectified environment from the moment they enter onto the stage. On the street, or subway, or cab, they are aware of every look, response, or suggestion from others, evaluating the incidents as harmless, awkward, or menacing threats. Carol, as a Broadway performer, once shoved away an oddball who had suddenly appeared between her legs upon exiting the subway stairs. I worry about this threat. It no longer matters who they are. I imagine my wife or my daughter in their places. The threat becomes real and uncomfortable.

I learn that beyond their costumes and the lascivious imaginings of a groggy patron, there is an artist, a powerhouse who possesses leadership. The Rockette is a master multitasker, managing discomfort, balance, sweat, and endurance with a learned, fixed smile.

She wants to live unencumbered, uncategorized, and not subjugated by restrictive rules, hurtful intentions, prurient interests, push-up bras, and poorly designed shoes that titillate the viewer and injure the wearer. She wants to dance.

Adoration for her looks is for her to accept, not for anyone to impose.

The new Rockette is every woman reassessing social assumptions and traditions that perpetuate inequality and encourage indignity.

She is questioning the cultivation of subliminal assumptions that is a defining operative in how we engage with her sex. In the holiday show, dressing up like a Christmas present is somewhat disconcerting.

She is a mother, a sister, a daughter, a wife, a business partner, a friend. But especially a daughter, for she represents the longest span of the future.

But most importantly she is herself, fully engaged in her own self-determination. And as a father, a brother, a husband, a colleague, a friend, I learn to support that common equality.

Rockette dance discipline, and especially the rigorous routine of patterning and drill combinations, requires a focus and commitment. In ownership of their destiny, the Rockettes epitomize the distinction of a modern woman with craft, professionalism, and dignity.

Despite the work environment of bathing suits and underwear, Jeff and I work consistently to make the work experience healthy and reflective of the peerless quality of the women's contribution as artists and not as a commodity.

Being a part of the Rockette environment places me in the tiring position of admitting what I do for a living. The question inevitably arises at every social gathering I attend. There are times I wish I could claim to be one of the IBM execs who lives in the neighborhood. I could say I am in finance or an attorney or even a real estate agent. The conversation would then move on quickly to something else more exciting and I would be off the hook. I always feel like a walking carnival. All I want to do is refill my glass and be onto other topics or other people with a refreshed drink to journey through the relentless, phatic exchanges of the evening.

Thanks to Carol, whose ebullient, bubbly party reconnaissance guarantees revelation of my job in show business, I end up explaining my job and workstyle. Over the din of party banter, I could hear Carol blurt out "Broadway" and "Radio City Music Hall" headlining her social outreach. That generates the spiraling slide of gossip, innuendo, and backstage stories being elicited, begged, and pleaded. The "R" word comes up and the press conference starts.

Carol is very proud of my accomplishments, and she thinks it unimaginable I would ever cheat on her. She is right. She is a stay-at-home mom, and that is a different kind of objectification.

Some of her friends who have managerial and retail careers are jealous of her being able to afford the same lifestyle on one salary, so she is getting pressure from all sides. But all I see is the belief from all her friends that Carol is a fool to think that I have not taken advantage of a single performer in the possibilities presented in my work environment every day. I now employ a solution whenever I socialize at one of these events.

I hear the inevitable invitations.

"You ran the Rockettes?"

"Tell us more!"

"What's it *really* like?"

"It's gotta be heaven with all those women."

With no option to refill my glass, my mouth runs dry explaining the truth. To help facilitate the interview, I utilize stock answers and use them in conversation. This works for every social gathering. My talking-point vocabulary becomes a series of innocuous responses. They satisfy every gawky, peeping-tom urge to know the inside scoop on managing 200 women dancing in expensive costumes and not screaming at one another in the process.

"Unbelievable!" I say.

"Something else!"

"A treat!"

"It's all like family, really."

"It's a hard job, but someone has to do it."

This last response usually produces guttural snickering, which is where the men in the group always want to take the conversation. Their wives eventually wander off, disillusioned and subliminally miffed, and I am left to stoke a false heat under the monkey-boy anticipations of the remaining group.

One party evening, after 9 years, 2,500 performances of the Christmas Spectacular and 3,000 one-off concerts, the Tonys, the Grammys, the Emmys, *Cake Boss*, the Dali Lama, Metallica, 50 Cent, Pavarotti, et al., I stop working the room. I begin to tell the truth.

It starts with what I overhear Carol say in a cluster of wives empathizing by the three-bean salad.

"I know, I know. It's difficult being a single mother," Carol admits to the group of wives, the ones who never believe that Carol's producer husband could maintain marital fidelity. How simpleminded, how myopic can she be to assume a show business personality could be trusted?

One Talbots-clad suburban wife offers, "You can never be sure what happens when they get on that train." The remark burns me.

Increasing the volume in my corner gives these gold coast, boutique shopping women the opportunity to overhear my conversation. I clarify my job description. I say I do not *run* the Rockettes. I oversee their workplace. I am their stage manager and their executive producer. I protect their work environment. I manage their brand.

They are my colleagues. I honor them. I am indebted to them. They educate me.

Carol looks over in my direction. She is listening.

I do not sleep with any of them. Even if I want to, no one ever asks.

And if I ask, I would have been fired. I learn a lot being in service to a gender-based performing artist troupe.

When I try out this new truthful tune, people reserve their punch-line interruptions.

I say working with Rockettes is just another job.

"Don't you work with women at your team leader job at Mastercard?" I continue.

"I thought interaction with women was a common occurrence in any workplace, being that half the population consider themselves female in some form, variation, or degree," I say.

I realize everyone has a misconstrued idea of show business life. We, the chosen and lucky few in this stage-show business, spend our working lives amid dance rehearsal halls that reek like gymnasiums and costumes that retain the steely aroma of repeated dry cleanings.

I admit to having secret dates with Rockettes, and some listeners begin to lean in for the juicy details. I do not let them down. I deliver.

I tell them my favorite meeting place in New York is the emergency room at the NYU Medical Emergency Center, where my date and I await treatment for a sprained ankle, hamstring pulls, or an eye injury due to the fake falling snow in the "Christmas in New York" scene. Or a bruise from a reindeer hoof. A burn from a firework display in the *Nutcracker* segment.

I tell them how I see young hopeful faces line up on 50th Street, just outside the stage door, after having traveled across the country or directly from the airport with American Girl luggage and the archetypal stage mother, she herself pathetically out of place in this midtown Manhattan urbanity sporting an *I Love NY* tee shirt purchased that morning at the hotel gift shop.

I propose to my party friends that auditions, rehearsals, and performances prove that women are athletes. I dismiss conversations about whether they *put out* or not.

I bring up that some Rockettes are bisexual and lesbian, and the tone of the conversation changes immediately.

Then I say to them, "Could you just imagine your wife or your daughter in their place?"

The boys get uncomfortable. I suggest they think of their own wives or daughters serving up their wares in front of 6,000 people, four, five or six times a day.

Just try dancing in a spangled Lycra bodysuit and balancing an 8-pound headpiece without falling on your ass. And smiling through it. Some Rockette costumes tax the wearer's ability to move safely on a slippery stage.

Had enough, Carol? I think to myself. Her earlier comment refuses to leave my resentment.

By now all the suburban wives are clustered in the kitchen. They get the message. They also know I can be confrontational, and suburban housewives are never confrontational. They sustain their lot by maintaining a subliminally lethal attitude delivered with the sweetest raspberry drizzle. A lot of leg shifting happens here, and many drink glasses are refilled as I continue my assessment. That's what usually happens when a sidebar discussion of the gritty details of show business is above your IBM management performance incentive program competency level.

"What? You're kidding, right?"

"Well," I said, "I'm sure you'd be proud to see your daughter up there, but would you be comfortable with your buddies ogling her?"

"I learned that calling them a 'bunch of gorgeous dames,' as you say, only enforces their desire for self-determination, ownership of their destiny, not just as women but as individuals, as human beings. This can't be legislated. It is the very essence of human respect, connection, and engagement."

I tell them the next time they gaze upon 36 pairs of legs kicking eye-high in unison, they should try to fantasize on the troupe's good talents before their own private fantasies.

"Just imagine your wife eye-high kicking in front of your buddies. Now, be honest, what do you think they have on their minds?"

That comment receives a unified, collective guffaw.

"Look, this is what I learned. Stand up with them, not above them. Hold the door open for them not because they are female, but because they are human beings and you are not a social ingrate. Don't be a predator. Be angry at the piggish creeps who are ruining the genuine expressions of affection for all of us. When Rockettes hurl eye-high kicks 18 times in a row, they perform a dance tradition, not a burlesque of bouncing bodies."

I give my listeners fair warning that this dance troupe may not survive as an entertainment of the future. I tell them that my idea of partnering the Rockettes with male dancers was met with threatening responses suggesting termination of my employment, compliments of a pervasive boardroom culture.

Silence. Then I come up with a unique ice breaker.

"So, is Claire working out? She looks stunning, a real hottie."

Claire's husband turns white and stiff. I respond.

"See what I mean? What if Claire were a Rockette?"

In fact, they are all speechless, embarrassed, and displeased. I feel relieved just like an IBM account executive. Carol knows where this might lead.

"Where did you learn all this? An HR sexual harassment training at work?"

"No, from all those intimate relationships I have with every Rockette."

"Wait. What are you saying?"

"I don't touch them, Keith. I listen to them."

My attendance at these parties becomes less frequent, but I feel satisfied in delivering a warning shot in my fight for moral credibility.

They still think I sleep with all those Rockettes. Not every executive has a showgirl friend they kiss goodbye under the arches of the Oyster Bar before departing for New Canaan.

I think I will succeed as my daughter's father.

We finally leave the party. Carol's single mom comment is hurtful and cutting. I do not let it go.

"So, just how much do you receive in food stamps in your role as *single mother?*"

She dismisses my comment as an annoying jab. I have no intent of joking. This is an accusation.

"If you are holding down two jobs, who takes care of the kids while you are out mopping the floors at the nearby MacMansion?"

"Oh, right,' I say, feigning correction. "You don't mop floors in other people's houses, do you?"

Carol looks straight ahead.

"You don't work at all, I understand."

I ask her where her audacious, insensitive comment comes from. I ask her where did she think her children's father was every day. She fires back.

"You think bringing up the kids every day is not a job?"

There is silence for the remainder of the trip home. I wonder if I have been the fool here, not ever having delivered a departing kiss to some gold-digging intern on her way to Poughkeepsie on the Hudson line. My only indiscretion is a black and white from *Zaro's*.

Our conversations in the morning become brief and efficient. Our topics are merely necessary. I profess my daily "I love you" as an agreement, not a commitment. I arrive at the theatre. I watch the "Parade of the Wooden Soldiers" in a new light. I do not see their beauty, their precision. I see another 80 pair of white soldier pants getting wrinkled, scuffed, another set of complaints between dancers not getting along, another charade of the holiday tradition sold at premium prices. Everything smells counterfeit.

I am acting like a jilted boyfriend. Making a city-centered, unconventional career work by pegging it into the square hole of a late century suburban lifestyle not only costs money. It requires me to rethink our lives and establish priorities. If we are to survive, I must establish new priorities beyond taking out the trash and running for the train.

    The Rockettes teach me a lesson. I am not Carol's keeper. I am not in charge of her happiness, as she repeatedly reminds me. I am her partner, and she is mine. We invent new ways to replace those cracks that are becoming too frequent in a deteriorating American Dream of Stepford wives and Grey Flannel males.

Chapter 16

And the Award for Best Supporting Instructor Goes To…

Show business hysteria does not always involve hard-edged, substance-abused personalities bent on trashing hotel rooms. Variants of those egotistical traits are equally prevalent within the academic administrative crowd.

When a private university chooses Radio City Music Hall for their commencement ceremony, the Development Relations Office sees the event as a major opportunity for cultivating long-term financial support for the school. They do not want to be outdone by last week's university's School of Business event the week before. They push the envelope of physical production requirements. The school produces a stellar theatrical event that includes a state-of-the-art laser-projection system at a time when such a special effect is more likely found in underground, celebrity-laden discos or overproduced wrestling matches. This is a separate expense from the cost of just being in the theatre.

Something comes over educators when get the chance to address an audience of students, parents, and colleagues. They lose their ability to edit. They succumb to their desire to make the podium their permanent home. Budgets burst open, spilling overtime costs onto extra hours and technical toy rentals. Tedious procedures are implemented to fashion a well-rehearsed event with no allotment for cost overruns. Alas, it's showtime, and PhDs are at the helm or, in this case, the podium, capitulating to their addictive propensity for loitering near every phrase, extending their time under brilliant light and brilliant crimson regalia. Every professor a person of letters, transforming every letter into an acting moment, every syllable pronounced as if they were speaking to the elitist- challenged.

Onstage, colleagues of equal stature are assigned the most prominent seating positions, followed by the rank and file of associate, assistant, adjunct, and nontenured personnel taking their positions according to pedagogical hierarchy.

Through endless hours of supersized inspiration, the deadening and repetitive drone of mispronounced candidate names is captured by a hired camera flashing a staged handshake and distribution of 1,200 blank, ochre scrolls, neatly adorned with acetate ribbon in official university blue—Pantone 281. Bleary-eyed candidates pose for the forced moment with the dean they have not met until this moment for this rushed photo-op moment. But the climax of the event is yet to be presented.

The retiring president of the university offers the final speech aimed at the parents and families of the candidates, who are sitting 180 feet from the stage in the second and third balconies. He speaks of their wisdom in contributing substantial portions of their wealth to this revered university. He reminds the group that the institution was founded in the tradition of a revered saint, and their continued support celebrates the saint's conversion to Christianity. Cultivation of mind and wallet is the theme of this and every convocation ceremony. Sanctification and soul-saving available through philanthropy. Online giving encouraged. Bless you.

Toward the end of the banal delivery of academic claptrap, I cue a stagehand to roll out a velveteen-draped rolling cart to the president's right side carrying a lever switch. The unit, waving its pleated dress of university blue, is connected to nothing. The stagehand manages to keep a straight face while executing the move despite the hazing his coworkers are bestowing upon him from offstage. He dons a cap and gown for the event. The stagehand is a hefty, towering individual and the only available gown embraces his rotund middle like shrink wrap. The gown does not hang past the tops of his knees. I think of Luciano Pavarotti in a teddy. Audience snorting begins midway through his journey of 40 feet. Unaffected by the reaction, the stagehand delivers the prop and returns. The president increases his vocal projection to overcome the tittering audience and continues with his rosy annual report. He announces the results of the year's funding campaign by instructing the audience, especially the discretionary income-producing second and third balcony, to stand and turn around to view the back wall of the theatre. A moment passes, and the president then flips the switch, which, you recall, is connected to nothing, and concurrently I cue another stagehand to ignite the expensive laser rental, illuminating the numbers "$750,000" in shimmering St. Patrick's Day green against the back wall of the theatre. This is done to the underscored accompaniment of a recorded version of Queen lead singer Freddie Mercury's "We Are the Champions." Ten automated Vari-Lites "ballyhoo", which is the art of moving a lamp in a continuous figure-eight configuration over orchestra patrons. All these theatre toys emphasize a dramatic moment and the serious financial investment for the Board of Directors. The revelation of this very expensive 30 seconds of disco triumph initiates the exit underscore. Wild applause ensues, as if a seismic benchmark in the financial health of the institution has been met. Twin Wurlitzer organs roll out of the side walls of the 6,000-seat theatre to play the infernal Elgar refrain once again, repeatedly, until the last parent savors the last costly moment in the limelight. I am lucky they do not want to drop fake snow from the grid.

If tuition and the student loan industrial complex are a university's loan sharking, marketing is its chief accomplice. Commencement is a corporate, promotional show, and it is uniquely designed to loosen what is in your wallet. But it needs casting help. Not every doctor of academia inherits the confidence of public speaking, especially from on the stage of a 6,000-seat theatre.

Many are called to show business, but few should enter it.

Not to be outdone by private-school panache, another institution better known for its basketball coaches than its spiritual ministry presents a lavish commencement spectacular at the Showplace of the Nation. No laser shows this time but a discussion to play a few of the college's basketball games at the music hall, onstage. The school's development officer along with the director of university events, presents a disjointed plan to infuse a college-centered sports event as part of the commencement ceremony. This idea comes from an inspiration taken from an event that occurs on January 16, 2000, when the Music Hall decides to present a first-ever sports event onstage. Some school board members attended that boxing match between Roy Jones, Jr. and David Telesco on the Great Stage. It was to be the inaugural event to mark the sale of Radio City Music Hall Productions to Madison Square Garden. The new corporate entity, MSG Entertainment, is the beginning of the formation of the new entity as a R.E.S.T. conglomerate—an acronym for recreation, entertainment, sports, and tourism. The three massive, 72-foot-wide stage elevators are sunk 10 feet below stage level to accommodate the boxing mat, the press ring, and broadcast equipment. The reviews for this first-ever event results in an MSG executive management staff restructuring to reduce head count. That is the official corporate term for termination. Wallace Matthews of *The New York Post* describes the evening as "the kind of affair that is best conducted in privacy of one's basement or gymnasium, or best of all, favorite back-alley." The school's plan fails approval and is never executed. Months later, I hear that a staff restructure initiative like the one implemented at MSG occurs in the administrative offices of the venerable educational institution. Commencement costs for a day at the Hall equal that of mounting an Off-Broadway show.

The religious order in charge of this institution was organized for the care of abandoned infants, beggars, and wounded soldiers in 17th century France. The 20th century mission is different from those core values of enabling the least of our brethren. Courtside adoration becomes the vesper of the day.

This is not to suggest that a spiritual malaise permeates these venerable institutions. The good fathers merely adjust their propensity for veneration and enter it in the profit and loss report as a line item.

Secular colleges also contribute to the theatricalization of educational events. In one spring, a Manhattan university celebrates their graduate classes with a pricey one-off that includes onsite catering for the faculty. In this university adventure, sandwiches are ordered by some professors an hour before the start of the program. The faculty *always* needs refreshment for every faculty-attended commencement event, I am told.

The food arrives and the professors have little time to chomp down on their wraps before reporting to the stage and occupying their assigned seats.

The plan is to place the entire faculty, seated, on three stage elevators and raise the units separately to provide an unencumbered view of the faculty for the students and family members seated in the audience. The faculty chairs are positioned across the three large stage elevators with 45 chairs on elevator #1, 25 chairs on elevator #2, and 55 chairs on elevator #3. Some professors succeed in grabbing a turkey wrap for lunch before boarding the stage elevator to their assigned seat. Levels range from 6 feet above stage level to 12 feet. The program begins, as the Mighty Wurlitzers of the Music Hall whoosh forced air to the familiar refrain of the first of Elgar's five "Pomp and Circumstance Marches." Students begin the stroll down past the 52 rows of red seats. This continues for 30 minutes.

Elgar's work was originally composed for the coronation of King Edward VII. The now familiar tune acquires a libretto, added in 1901 by Arthur Christopher Benson. Known as "Land of Hope and Glory," the lyric addition accommodates the king's request. The grandeur of the piece has nothing to do with academic achievement, and the King never hears it. The first academic performance of the piece occurs at the commencement at Yale University in 1905 when an honorary Doctor of Music degree is conferred upon the composer by Yale president Arthur Hadley. As a sign of gratitude to his friend, Hadley orders Elgar's catchy tune to be performed as a recessional in his honor. Every Ivy League institution adopts the piece. Now we even play it for kindergarten.

Like in show business, it's just about who you know.

Elgar's refrain takes approximately 56 seconds to play, which, for the size of the graduating class, requires playing the refrain 32 times before every candidate completes the march. Two professors, reacting to the rushed lunch and the unexpected, unrehearsed reaction of sitting high off the ground, become ill. They request assistance to leave the elevator. At 12 feet, the elevator is too high to jump down, and access is only at stage level. I carefully plan to lower the elevator back down to the stage level to allow the stricken professors to exit. I wait for the professor to return, and then plan to send the elevator up again to its preset level. However, the remaining 73 faculty members on #3 elevator complain that they were missing too much of the ceremony and request to go back up before the ill professors returned. I am responsible for the safe operation of these mammoth units. I search for the director of events to approve the move, and he complies. I proceed to cue the elevator back up. Just when it finally reaches its prescribed height of 12 feet, the afflicted professor makes a timely return, demanding to return to his seat, now back at 12 feet in the air. Upon a second approval from the director of events, I again cue the #3 elevator to stage level down to collect the professors, and then return the unit again to its 12-foot height.

Rumblings and snickers from the audience distract the speaker, and she stops for a moment. By the time she turns around to investigate the disturbance, the stage elevators are at their prescribed height, and everything seems normal. Perplexed, she returns to her speechmaking, periodically throwing a darting look toward me off stage right as if I had just allowed a practical joke to be played on her. This elevator dance occurs once more during the ceremony. A second professor demands to be returned to stage level. I accommodate the individual but this time I do not wait for the ill professor and return the elevator back immediately. The professor, now disgruntled, is stopped by the hulking stagehand who had become a regular house prop man for commencement events in the theatre. The academic thought better than to contest the physical barrier the stagehand had created between the stage elevator and the professor. I am glad. Even I am embarrassed. But at least our hefty stagehand did not have to don another cap and gown.

Moving a scenic element that contains 75 occupied chairs is not an event that can be hidden during a ceremony, especially when the only other activity is focused on the learned individual expounding at the podium downstage. When the elevator moves down and out of sight of the audience, it looks as if the entire grouping of people have suddenly become disinterested in the subject and opt to take a break.

My most outrageous and entertaining commencement experience ever at Radio City is for a highly respected design school. The instructors are out-of-the-box creatives who truly celebrate the efforts of their constituents. There is an engaging, comfortable intimacy between student and instructor, the feeling that they are all in this together. The chevrons on the sleeves of the faculty do not impact their approachability. There is excitement in the air, a sense of liberation more than accomplishment. There is little of the touchy-feely affirmations of achievement. It is a reality check. The student body seemed fully prepared to express creativity every moment of their lives moving forward.

Once again, the Mighty Wurlitzers grind out the familiar refrain of "Pomp and Circumstance No.1," but this time the candidates shimmy, bop, dance and *dervish* their way down the four aisles of the music hall wearing the most original and colorful adornments to their mortarboards. Their creativity is their regalia, beautifully displayed on top of their heads. Each is unique, and there is not an undecorated head in the group. When all are finally seated, six huge beach balloons appear and continue a bouncing trajectory throughout the ceremony.

At the close of the spectacle a group of students and professors approach me and ask if the organist can play something other than Elgar. There is no event director in sight, and we are nearing the end of the last speech. I ask George the organist, a man who had been playing there for more than 30 years and could have been understudy to Santa Claus for every one of those years. He thinks a minute, then offers, "Just cue me, and I'll see what I can do." Usually in show business, *see what I can do* is just north of *buzz off.*

The speech ends. The "go forth" moment is proclaimed. I flip the organist cue light off and George lets out all the stops and cyphers of the Mighty Wurlitzers, grandly filling the house with Jack Norworth's and Albert von Tilzer's 1908 classic "Take Me Out to the Ball Game."

Nearly every mortarboard flies into the air with screams of delight. Most of the faculty remains on the stage to finish out the vocal rendition of the baseball ditty. George accommodates the faculty who request an encore. Some try their hand at a solo, standing directly down center stage and bask in that wonderful elixir of performance.

Many are called to show business, even teachers.

The realization from these experiences reveals that teachers are indeed human, and some are even loveable. Sometimes the administrative individuals in charge of these educational extravaganzas are unique personalities who belie the assumptions of level headedness, decorum, and procedure. Albeit they contend with three unique groups made up of students, instructors, and parents/families, all of whom can prove to be unreasonable at one time or another. They are also called on the carpet for budget overruns and not the students or the professors.

I remember one manager, a wiry, raspy individual who chain smokes even when I inform her it is not allowed on the premises. She is called the program director (the position title always changes) of a prominent New York City institution. She would have been at home being the production manager for a rocker tour. Gruff, expletive-laden instructions are her vocabulary, and to hell with where professors sit. I expect her to be replaced every year, yet she always returns, appearing through a foggy waft of poisoned air, like an unwelcome, unhealthy apparition. She is a toxic individual, and she spreads her joyless demeanor like a noxious bug spray, destroying all attempts at propriety, professionalism, or engagement in her path.

Beyond the fractious demeanor of the program manager, these gifted instructors improve the social mobility of their students. They elevate their aspirations to a level of reality. They introduce them to things they may not have had an opportunity to experience.

The students and teachers of this city college event at Radio City are different than most. Coming from more unique and different walks of life than many other institutions, the graduating candidates seem animated, enthusiastic. There is laughter and many boisterous moments, and it seems as if they look forward to the pomp and circumstance of the event to reflect the importance of their hard-earned efforts. These are city kids, commuter students, studying on the N train to Brooklyn or writing an essay at lunch break at work. Their capacity for frivolity is unrestricted, flamboyant. The focus, for most, is taking in as much as possible of the experience without wasting it on an excessive, platitudinous orations. Their party is onstage at a venue where they might have seen a favorite concert or event. This time they are the headliner, and the music is playing for their entrance. They amaze themselves, not quite believing what they are undertaking, and they are awed by the outcome. I am captured by the humanness of the day. I recall that feeling in my college life a long time ago.

The faculty exhibit a similar reverence, honoring the caution tape around the stage elevator system while I cue the elevator units 27 feet down to the basement to onload risers and chairs. They watch the operation, like an interactive museum exhibition. There is genuine appreciation here.

I remember my own undergraduate experiences fashioning my future. Many of my professors are accomplished theatre professionals. They know more about the building blocks of live presentation than any Broadway director I meet in my career.

These public university professors provide the connection and agency for change with their students. My 20-minute discussion with a science professor turns to a 19th century point of view. He makes it relevant. There are no banners, no laser effects, no fancy props. He refers over 100 years ago, when the good old days were not all that good and delivers a message that secures the best performance of an academic in the role of teacher. It resonates in me to this day. He quotes the following passage:

The dogmas of the quiet past are inadequate to the stormy present.

The occasion is piled high with difficulty, and we must rise to the occasion.

As our case is new, so we must think anew and act anew.

We must disenthrall ourselves, and then we shall save our country."

A. *Lincoln, 1862.*

The eloquence of Dr. Stephen "Mitch" Wagener, Biological and Environmental Sciences, is pedagogy at its finest. It is not costuming that makes the actor. Many professors delight in their regalia, but a choice few are real teachers.

Chapter 17

Fire at Will

No one is safe.

It's 10:00 a.m., and the person I report to is nowhere to be found.

The vice president of production, a former stage manager better versed in theatrical play production than event supervision, does not hear the phone ring over the laughter of the television audience on the morning *Martha Stewart Living Show*. He never misses an episode, and I suspect he schedules meetings around the time slot to ensure he views the half hour show. His direct report, the director of production, does not think highly of him. He is a gentle soul, and the position calls for an unscrupulous son of a bitch. He is not capable of filling the bill regardless of his efforts. He is a single father of two adopted children, rearing them both to adulthood. His former teaching background helps his parenting, and the executive position helps pay for a comfortable lifestyle in New York.

But he is no shark.

A different animal manages the myriad of needs, wants, and desires of concerts, business meetings, special events. The game is played with a nonnegotiable financial bottom line, and one had better understand what battle to fight over, from ordering too many stagehands to awarding an unqualified vendor not vetted by a bid session. The venue makes money regardless of whether the show clears its costs.

Most of the time, he would maneuver his responsibilities to let more qualified people manage production decisions, which he would edit, and the engagement would proceed uneventfully. In other times, especially with large award shows that included a broadcast element, his lack of experience would create an awkward moment at production meetings. It became evident that he could not contribute to planning a scheduling strategy involving more than 300 technicians, performers, support personnel from our own staffing and the televised support groups. This fact captures the attention of the newly assigned executives seeking to make their own impression upon executive management. The monthly meat must be fed to the lion, and he is on the chopping block next.

Being on the passenger manifest for the helicopter ride from the West Side Heliport to Cablevision's Bethpage headquarters impresses many director-level managers at the Garden and at Radio City. But vice presidents know better. It can be the defining ride of death of one's job security. Death by firing or torture from repeated exposure to accusatorial tirades of complaint and incompetence are a regular occurrence. A potentially incendiary question is posed, and executives are forced to answer. There is no right answer. The question is merely to start the process of dismantling one's corporate stature. The experience is likened to being held hostage by a gun-happy delinquent forcing one to dance as they shoot at their feet. Then, the helicopter lands, and one enters the Cablevision headquarters transformed, being escorted to a new meeting or a new job.

The VP of production secretly fancies the attention, thinking he can hold his own during the 30-minute ride in the noisy, twirling torture chamber clipping over northern Long Island.

But on this Monday in spring just after another failed Spring Spectacular extravaganza, I walk into the VP's office fully expecting to overhear Martha Stewart expound on using gathered corn husks as holders for eating cob corn. I arrive to see the television off, and what appears to be a newly appointed *Irish Westy* now in charge, on the phone setting up the crew call for the next concert. This scenario is no longer a surprise. Bloodletting is an operational fact of Radio City life, and its halls are filled with the debris of broken careers, terminated bonuses, and recalled Management Performance Incentive Programs.

One survival tactic of corporate restructuring is the realization that work is not your whole life. In the game of revolving doors in corporate management, a reentry door is taken away with every turn just to make it interesting.

I was no exception.

One day, after 14 years of Radio City culture, I could not find the door back in.

Like my own experience in terminating colleagues who had become friends, my present boss, the Executive Vice President in charge of production, enters my office unannounced. He walks in my office as he had in the past, so there is no surprise. It is the person who follows him, the EVP of Human Resources. The message is simple, bland, known to every HR rep as the standard termination vocabulary designed to diminish the threat of a lawsuit. In February of 2008, after having achieved a record $80 million dollars in gross sales for the Radio City Christmas Spectacular, and receiving the largest bonus of my career, the management seeks to "go in a new direction." When human capital becomes too expensive, one's achievements became a liability. I had made the grade.

The EVP assigned to this task displays a familiar look on his face, the same sense of embarrassment and revulsion. The ugly realization is that the termination process is not as devastating as the destruction of a friendship, a severing collaboration. He is the hatchet man of the day just as I had been two years earlier. I wonder how much he will drink tonight.

Oddly, I am unexpectedly relieved. I had had enough of corporate theatre, sports entertainment, and protecting Rockettes from roving eyes, sticky hands, and splintered dance floors. Some who experience a downsizing or termination seldom recover from their corporate identity loss. They wait on the side in the shadows, mimicking their learned practice of emails, lunches, follow ups, desperately seeking reentry into familiar territory. They sneak in corners of coffee shops watching people enter and exit from the stage door they frequented in the past. They are looking for another day, just one chance to have good reason to walk through that door again. Just to feel it again.

They live at Linkedin.

Termination is unnerving at 58 years old but not devastating. In fact, it is just as familiar as another day in the schoolyard facing the bully of the week.

Denny the Irish bully from Bishop Ford returns to my psyche, the story of the uncollected refuse in front of my grandmother's apartment in *Salita Scudillo* lures me back into a feeling of ineptitude, a sense of incapability, of not being good enough. My father not being good enough. I think that all the corporate buzzwords of being on top, *proactive, out of the box, on it, consider it done,* are no longer relevant to me, a half-breed of first-generation immigrant offspring. Some days, the hurt falls deep until I refuse to let it run my emotions. I wonder what my children think.

Then I think of my father, Colombo Angelo Mariano, the monk who set himself free, and my grandfather Vincenzo Pasquale, the coppersmith who took a boat ride one day from Porto Sezione and never returned. I think of Giacomo, the third-generation grandfather, a coachman at the Palace at Caserta who walked away from opening doors for kings and queens and chose to make shoes by the Neapolitan shore. I shed the pity from my ego and realize that peril and opportunity in life are equal partners. If your head is not sopping in remorse and knee-jerk sympathy, you just might get by. Radio City is corporate boot camp, and I survive for 14 years. If I make it here, I make it anywhere, just like the John Kander and Fred Ebb love song to New York.

Then I face the real issue of Carol and the dreadful task of breaking the news to her. This phone call, more than anything else, is the hardest thing to do. I feel I failed my part of our agreement. Finding another six-figure salary is a challenge.

I sit in my office for an hour before I get up the courage.

The call is inevitable, but the opportunity is perfect. Carol, as usually is the case in my defining career transitions, is in Florida. Unbeknownst to me, Carol is enjoying her mom's hosting a farewell dinner party. Carol answers my call.

"Hi Carol." Carol senses trouble. I rarely address her formally.

"Hold on, I'm going out on the lanai."

I am glad she takes the lead.

"What's wrong? Should I be sitting down?"

"Well, I have good news and bad news."

"What happened?"

"I'm done here. It's over. No more Radio City for me, Mom."

It was the best attempt at humor I could muster. There is silence.

"On a lighter note, I am receiving a fabulous severance package. We could take off for a year!"

"So, what are you going to do next?" She treats it as just another show closing.

I am out of creative responses. I reiterate my best shot. There is a generous severance, so we don't have to worry about that, at least for now."

"Pick me up at LaGuardia tomorrow at 4:00 p.m. Then we'll talk."

Carol returns to her dinner party nursing another mojito, maintaining her well-honed discretionary skills. She adds a helping of key lime pie, wondering what other surprises she will have to harbor. That is the last time she has key lime pie.

These are the moments in your life that define the depth of a relationship forever. Carol's voice, her simple assessment smashes through the walls of doubt growing within me every moment I waste reflecting on what had just occurred.

Severances get you out the door. They do not continue your career. They are like winning Power Ball. They feel great for a very short time and can change your demeanor from euphoria to depression in a week. How much of my life is my work, and when it stops, how much is left that is alive? I feel hopeful.

There is a silver lining thicker than ever in this cloudy career ambush. I never again need to feel the clammy stickiness of a starched collar at a board meeting. I am free of the debilitating stress of quarterly meetings where accomplished executives are thrown to the wolves because of a wrong choice of words in responding to inane questions. I am free to appreciate women again for their beauty and intelligence rather than protect them as an objective commodity.

In my four years as Executive Producer, I slash a large chunk of the mounting budget, restructure the live entertainment division, incorporate a state-of-the-art LED cyclorama wall into the Christmas Spectacular, and produce new elements for nearly three-quarters of the show. Some of the sharpest, nicest people I ever meet work at this showplace of the nation, and as the years go by, many of them leave. The day I walk out the stage door is the last time I am on 51st Street. There is no after shock. There is no longer a reason to return. Just like my mother's funeral. Just like Patty. Just like my father's failures. Everyone I cherish moves on, and so do I. Going back is like visiting a dead horse. Besides, there is no restaurant on the street worth frequenting, and that fact is decisively important.

The addiction never leaves. It can only be treated with a new show.

I find myself free and fully funded for years to come with a generous severance, 401k, MPIP bonus, and nowhere to go. I could go to Florida, don my madras shorts and white sneakers and stand first in line for my complimentary blueberry pie at the local Sweet Tomato's as an introductory offer to retirement.

Given the choice, I would rather die and rather quickly, too.

I decide it is time to cross back over 6th Avenue, revisit Little Tokyo on 48th Street, where stage managers and actors dine on sushi between shows. Being away for 13 years from the theatre district is like a lifetime in a Broadway life, but there are still people around who recognize me, and it is good to see them again. Susan Bristow, an engaging, sharp theatre executive who had taken over as company manager for *Crazy for You* during my stage manager stint offers a room rental in her office located at 260 West 44th Street above John's Pizza. The daily reminder of baked-tomato pies wafting up the stairwell answers the question of lunch every day. The office is next to the St. James Theatre, the place I first saw when exiting from the Eighth Avenue subway 40 years ago.

I start a company and name it for my father-in-law who had recently passed on. Big Fish Big Pond, Ltd. produced off Broadway shows, and I am contracted for production services for the FIFA Awards in the Bahamas. The highlight of having this Broadway office is managing the purchase and delivery of 250 soccer balls made in Iran, and the attendant security issues of getting the balls delivered to the Bahamas in a post 911 environment. In the middle of all this big time producing, Susan asks me to cover the absence of her stage manager on one of her shows while he directs a touring version of the show she is producing. It is *Grease*. I had not stage managed a Broadway show for about 15 years, but when I walk through the stage door at the Brooks Atkinson, the loneliness of producing fades immediately and the intimate joy of working closely with actors returns like I had been gone for just a weekend. The show is a blast. Tacky, fun, innocuous, and filled with nostalgia. I am fully engaged on both ends of the theatrical spectrum, kind of like increasing the dosage of a good medication. An office on Broadway and a Broadway show as well. I am a happy addict. I feel 25 again, and my Equity card, that defining verification of my worth in this business, is still in my wallet. I would have traded 1,000 Christmas Spectaculars for a Broadway show. I have a theatrical family again. I am a father again, and my stage children are getting younger.

There is a comforting familiarity in contributing to the goings-on in a creaky 80-year-old building. So many hopes and dreams and disappointments lie dormant in the corners of every old theatre waiting for a sensitive soul to bring them out again. Forgotten moments of thunderous applause, eloquently delivered soliloquies, mesmerizing performances captivating an entire sold-out house. Declarations of war, announcements of victory, privilege, tragedy, finality. It is the act of assembly, bearing witness to the human condition, with every grief, every triumph exposed, desperately hoping for recognition, for that welcome and familiar sound of palms slapping that comforting noise of acknowledgement.

There is life after Radio City, and I no longer think about those who are still there wondering what it would be like to stop running and start living.

Chapter 18

A Cauldron of Community Theatre

Twin hurricanes follow each other like alluring sirens delivering their fury in angry waves of rain upon Main Street in Torrington, Connecticut. It is August 1955, and in one summer's day the town transforms into a graveyard for 88 residents with over 600 homes and nearly 600 businesses destroyed. Local law enforcement, fire protection, state and federal agencies including the Coast Guard attempt to curtail the devastation. The bustling manufacturing town dies a civic death. The town never recovers. The industry, social fabric and economic function is irrevocably damaged.

In the spring of 2011, I become aware of Torrington, Connecticut from a wrong turn off I-84. I discover time has stopped on Main Street. I do not think Torringtonians have ever forgiven the rest of the world since 1955. Once a manufacturing hub, now it claims the dubious achievement as the chief purveyor of inertia, myopia, and provincialism. Commerce is the last departing element of the town. Nothing else leaves Torrington. The debilitating status quo manifests itself and festers in every moment of daily life in a town too reclusive to know it is dead.

The one remaining shining sign of life is the completion of a rescue and restoration program to preserve an Art Deco movie house on Main Street built by Warner Brothers in 1931. I discover that the governing board is looking for an executive director. I had never been one before, and this is a nonprofit venture, but after 15 years as a stage manager, 14 years at Radio City, and additional years as an independent producer, I do not think there is much more to learn about putting on a show. It seems like a good fit. For 14 years, I heard the Radio City tour guides begin their presentation, "Built in 1932…" I only had to adjust by a year here. Funny how little tidbits like that fill in for defining moments of decision, especially when there is no other compelling reason to act.

Six months of arduous interviewing by a 36-member board of directors finally results in a phone call from the president whom I address as Eddie because his smirk demands it and his irascible, grating personality deserves it. He offers me the job. He is sure to mention that I am not his first choice. He has apparently been outvoted by a remaining majority of 35 members of the board and is forced to implement their decision.

I never have so much fun in my life. Working with someone who is not totally behind me can be unnerving, until I recall the experience I bring working with corporate tyrants, little dictators, borderline cons, and Broadway producers. I find it difficult to return a professional courtesy to this senior executive at the local construction company. He is overdressed for his work. Somewhere in his brain there is brilliance, beyond his inappropriate public manner and his inadvertent misogyny. For a moment I believe we can do great things together. This is short lived. It is not something worth a concern or a second thought. Eddie lives in the anachronism of the heady days of downtown Torrington. He loves this Northwestern Connecticut city, and he is the driving force in the restoration campaign for the breathtaking theatre.

He is not a programmer. All he wants in an executive director is someone to count the number of sold candy bars. He wants a venue manager, not a producer. I am a producer. A good portion of the board wants to see the organization grow, and one of the challenges in Connecticut is that there is more theatre per square mile than any other state. We develop a unique programming strategy that competes with the Bushnell in Hartford, 30 miles away, the Palace Theatre in Waterbury, a restored and renovated Beaux-Arts emporium which enjoys the advantage of a major campus installation of University of Connecticut just across from its main entrance. This 3,000-seat auditorium is just 15 miles away. Dotted within a 20-mile radius of the Warner are no fewer than ten regional and community theatre companies vying for talent and audience.

One significant change I attempt to implement involves treating the audience as if they are attending a special event instead of a local hangout. Carol has a great idea. We claim a beautifully restored atrium behind the rear balcony and furnish it to be the point of engagement for high-end subscribers. These donor patrons are given special access with refreshments before attending a performance. Carol names it Café Moderne, which evokes the art deco ambiance of the heyday Hollywood era and creates a discriminating environment that speaks to their generosity. My socially challenged president's action proves my assessment of his eloquence beyond his well-earned efforts in the restoration campaign.

His contribution is drawing up a hastily written signs that announce "TOILETS, THIS WAY" with an arrow to the hallway.

Carol loses it. Her face bares the warning signs of a pissed-off bulldozer. Carol, in one look, becomes a mother chastising an errant child.

"Are you serious? We just created an attractive incentive for cultivating development money, and you are worried about toilets? In New York, we call them restrooms."

She continues as Eddie's eyes narrow. He is not used to this kind of reaction, especially from a woman. Eddie is an inadvertent sexist, more a product of upbringing than intent. Carol is on a roll.

"I think you have no idea of how to utilize the value of gathering potential donors in a space conducive to loosening their wallets. This is not the construction business. This is a theatre."

I am impressed. I welcome Carol's expression of leadership.

For the first time since I meet him, Eddie looks intimidated. He is always frustrated with me. I never buy into his bullying. Receiving a reprimand from the wife of the executive director initiates my eventual departure in his brain. He says nothing. The rest of the development committee tries to move on. I pursue the project as planned.

After the meeting, Carol and I walk a block to dinner at The Venetian, Torrington's only restaurant of worth. Michael DiLullo, the owner, saves the evening by offering his specialty, a Caesar salad created tableside complete with anchovy paste, egg, pecorino romano, and leaf lettuce. The joy of eating freshly made pasta is enhanced by his personable touch. His restaurant could serve as the Disney locale for a sweet Italian romantic comedy, complete with his pleasant and coy daughter, Marilena, dutifully serving exquisite dishes and harboring an underlying desire to be an actress. The Venetian is the only storybook experience in an otherwise morbid downtown streetscape.

Somehow, the quaint eatery, the exquisitely restored theatre, the significant Main Street architecture cannot not resuscitate the spirit of this dysfunctional town. Entrenchment, made most visible by an anachronistic board president and a recalcitrant town planning and zoning board, prevents rejuvenation and derails any attempts to revitalize interest from the surrounding affluent communities. Well-heeled folks living just over the town line want nothing to do with Torrington.

I make numerous attempts to pump professional blood into the organization. Roger Goodman, a longtime colleague and ABC vice president of production, accepts my offer to spend a day onsite discussing possibilities. He has a brilliant idea. He recognizes the quirky strength of the organization and its connection to the community. Aside from the smattering of B-level acts and concerts, the Warner Stage Company mounts three to four major musical productions a year, casting as many as 100 people, friends, sons, daughters, and cousins of extended families. This is a success story that needs to be told. The opening scene of one musical boasts 110 people onstage belting "Godspeed, Titanic" with the strength and volume of the Mormon Tabernacle Choir. Roger sits down in the middle of the theatre under its signature six-pointed center chandelier forming a glittering star.

"John, you have a reality show here that can transform the design of future television programming."

He begins to detail an idea to produce weekly coverage of mounting a show with people who are in the theatre for the love of it, regular people playing characters. The local pharmacist, a university professor, tradesmen, merchants, the local church organist all combining forces to put on a show.

The board shows no interest in the proposition. They like things just the way they are.

The board abandons the opportunity to place the Warner Theatre on a national visibility level as a standard bearer of community theatre life.

Roger moves on. The following season, network television is inundated with reality shows of every taste and quality. Eddie returns to counting candy bars.

I produce *Curtains*, a show that had been originally produced on Broadway by Roger Berlind, whom I worked for during my stint as a stage manager at *City of Angels*. Roger is also a contributor to the Warner, and he is pleased to see one of his show properties being produced regionally. One of the founders of the Warner Stage Company is hired to direct, and Carol decides to join the Warner's despotic culture and audition for a major role that is age appropriate for her and speaks to her professional expertise.

At a morning audition, Carol chooses "Broadway Baby" from Follies, the number made famous by Elaine Stritch and is a standard known by just about everyone in the theatre. The conversation leads to Carol's Broadway experience in *A Chorus Line*. The director responds with a request that reveals the dearth of his own experience.

"Can you do 'Tits and Ass' for us?" the director asks.

Carol has a powerful and effective response.

"You want to see a 61-year-old audition for a role that has nothing to do with what I did 35 years ago on Broadway? Just what will that prove?"

The director withdraws his request.

Most of the Torrington experience is disappointing but never overwhelming. But I never expect what is about to happen.

I receive a call from a board member later that evening reporting that federal officers had raided the home of a senior member of the Warner Stage Company currently involved in the present production of *Curtains* and arrested him on charges of exchanging pornographic images of minors over the internet. The director is taken into custody.

My first reaction is the realization that the Warner conducts acting, dance, and voice classes for children. The second reaction is managing damage control of the organization, the community, and the future of the school.

The last thing I worry about and the first thing to be affected is the first scheduled rehearsal day the following morning. After issuing a statement to the press, immediately firing the director and barring him from the theatre property until his legal issues are resolved, I publish a statement assuring theatre supporters and parents of the school that there were no opportunities for this director to have had any direct contact with the school population.

Incredibly, some board members feel my words are too severe and judgmental before the events take its course. This is head-in-the-sand governance at its best.

I must find another director, and a long shot enters my mind. My friend, Rob Schiller, an accomplished and highly successful situation comedy writer, director, and producer in Los Angeles, is just the ringer to grab this show and make it happen. I call him, not thinking he would even answer. I hear the phone pick up.

"You know, if you were here now instead of on the phone, you could be sharing a martini with me by the pool, Johnny." Somehow, knowing Rob, I do not think he is alone at that pool.

Rob is an old, dear friend. A mentor, a mensch, a man with a great heart. I first hire him because of his first girlfriend, who happened to be in a Goodspeed show so many years back. Through three marriages, two divorces, and literally millions of dollars, Rob never lets go. We are always friends. Rob is characteristically LA, and I always admire that. I respond rather creatively, if not as coolly, taking his cue. I give it my best, desperate shot.

"If you were here instead of sweating by a pool, you could be directing a big Broadway musical." It is a stretch, but I gamble on him hearing "musical," his favorite theatrical genre.

Despite his broadcast TV successes, Rob is a theatre guy at heart, and he jumps at the opportunity to do a stage show. I know this, and I play the card, the only one I have.

"I have a crazy request. A creative staff member just got arrested; I will tell you why when you get here. I start rehearsal tomorrow for a musical that will be attended by the Broadway producer who originally mounted it. And if I can publicize that I just contracted a Hollywood director, they just might forget the soon-to-be con who had the job in the first place. Interested?"

"Johnny, are you serious?"

"Never more, in my life."

"How long is the rehearsal period?"

"As long as you like. I'll delay the opening if I have to."

I did not know if I could do that, but I knew Rob was on a roll, and I didn't want to trip him up with an opportunity for an out.

"Pay my airfare. I'm on my way."

Could this be true? Is he really going to do this? I had no guarantee this scheme would come to fruition. The following morning is going to be here very soon, and my only hope is to get Rob here.

"Do you need directions? Probably a good idea to fly into Hartford. I'll pick you …"

"Johnny, Johnny, I have a manager for all that. Relax. Talk soon."

Rob hung up. Was he loaded? Another babe by his side? What is it with directors and sex?

The next morning, at 7:30 a.m., my phone rings. It is Rob. I figure this is the apology.

I am sorry. What was I thinking? I was a little tipsy, etc. I look at the scribble of a speech I must make to the cast later that morning.

"Where are you? Aren't you going to buy me breakfast?" Rob loves punch lines. It is his trademark to set you up then watch you come through or fail miserably.

"Where are you? I ask.

"At the Nutmeg around the corner from the theatre. There's still time for a bacon, egg and cheese. Weird little town you got here, Johnny."

Rob, as he has always done since I have known him, proves his friendship.

The show goes off without a hitch. Most of the younger folks in the cast love the idea of working with an accomplished Hollywood pro. Some cast members are frightened to death. Others want to make love to him. Community theatre has a secret society syndrome that protects its own mediocrity. The film *Waiting for Guffman* best depicts this autocratic assumption of theatrical privilege based on the last brilliant nonperformance of the local thespian sage who happens to be your local grocer.

Rob has none of that. He shakes up his cast with inspiration, creativity, and joy while they are expecting attitude, condescension, and flippancy. At first, the cast has a hard time believing Rob's sincerity. By opening, Rob transforms the pettiness of community theatre culture into a working acting company.

The only downside is the unprecedented amount of suck up being exhibited by the cast and staff. The accommodation and patronization is so invasive it promotes tooth decay. So much for community theatre.

I have a great time with my old friend doing the thing we love best. Show business.

I discover one significant hope in this village of provincial inertia. At the northern end of Main Street sits a modest home of mentally challenged individuals who go about their day in an environment of support, productivity, and self-renewal. Lisa Lynch, the executive director of Prime Time House, proposes a collaboration which results in mounting an original play about the challenges of mental illness with original music. The excitement of casting the show with community actors and members of the Prime Time community is a transforming opportunity to define true community engagement. The feeling is not unanimous, but I go ahead with the project.

The first day of rehearsal reveals trepidation of the community actors feeling the discomfort and fear of being out of their comfort zone and engaging with individuals who have never been onstage. The Prime Timers have challenges being in a social environment and that is the point of the exercise. Two clusters form on stage, separate from one another. The reading begins. Tepid and strained accommodations are offered by the community members as quiet, awkward responses emanate from the Prime Timers. Missed lines and long pauses lend to the fragile rehearsal. Suddenly, a loud proclamation from a Prime Timer member interrupts the tentative environment.

"I want to say something. To everyone! I feel I just got my life back again!" The line is not in the script.

The group breaks into applause, laughter, and cheers. The ice is broken, and the cast becomes one group. The show provides visibility for mental illness and raises the bar on defining the power of inclusion beyond the recurring revivals of summer stock fare. But the community members prefer to return to *Gypsy* and *Annie* and *Grease*. At the Warner, social conscience hitched a ride with commerce on its way out of Torrington 50 years ago.

After nearly two years of entrenchment, endless Rotary Club summits, production meetings, pizza seminars, and planning and zoning conferences to rebuild sidewalks in front of the theatre, I am informed by a small board committee that they can no longer afford my salary and need to terminate my contract. I feel like they are apologizing. I could have done a much more efficient job firing myself. I had been ready to leave for weeks. My reaction is akin to having missed a mediocre lunch. Regardless of the menu, the outcome is never surprising. I throw in my executive director towel and head back to New York. Heading south on Route 8, the weather forecast calls for a series of hurricane-level storms in the area.

Transitions in life produce plot twists in memoirs, and phone calls usually initiate the next chapter. This time it is Neil, my old friend from high school, and he has an idea.

Neil Callari's actual first name is Aniello. I suspect he prefers Neil because he is tired of being mistaken for an olive oil salesman and a racketeer. Neil is an artist by talent and a graphic designer by trade, and I first meet him in the auditorium of Bishop Ford High School when I stage-manage a play for which he created the artwork. He has the same appreciation for the director, our favorite Franciscan brother Jonathan, as I do. He is an artsy guy, and frankly, I am in high school to meet girls and not artsy guys, but we become solid friends and have so much fun in the remaining two years in high school we decide not to meet up again until 40 years later.

Having acquired some discretionary income from his successful graphic design business, Neil decides to get in contact with me and play producer. Neil helps me produce *Under Fire* for the New York Musical Theatre Festival, then *Slow Dance with a Hot Pick Up* for the Boulder Theatre in Colorado, and becomes a partner in Big Fish Big Pond, LTD.

Neil and I are producers. Neil and I make no money. Neil and I are happy.

This time, however, the classic show comes along. They always do. The right business model, a sure thing. Two characters, one set, no music and a mind-bending rate of return. The plan is to hire two stars for a short run, gain visibility, and franchise companies on the road.

As is customary in most show business stories, something unexpected happens. People react; then people resign themselves to realizing no matter how seismic the change may be, things really do not change that much.

In the whirl of mounting this sure thing, the author dies. Of course, this is not the first time the author of a play in production has died, but great things can occur to a dead author's property after they pass on, so we, after a brief sorrowful moment, are thrilled at this new predicament and anticipate the projected windfall of a sure thing now being virtually guaranteed by a heart-stopped author.

Moolah! is a great vehicle for franchising. After surviving height-challenged demagogues, impulsive, reactionary tyrants, self-serving artists, starry-eyed visionaries blinded by ambition, and the ever-present addiction to succumb to another show, I sign on.

The first reading of the script registers 200 vulgarities uttered in various stages of anger, humor, panic, and frustration. There are more fornicative references per page than a squiffed mate's parley aboard the *Black Pearl*.

I shudder at the perceived reaction of my invited audience. The realization prompts Neil to request some changes. His suggestions become so numerous he essentially rewrites the play. Neil the producer becomes Neil the new author, replacing the departed original.

I am glad for my old friend. I give him an opportunity to be a player, and in the gritty theatrical environment of 8th Avenue and 47th Street, Neil Callari, my investor angel and buddy, becomes the artistic voice that is inside of him. *Moolah!* lives to this day and may resurface in a trendy new web-based format, cleaned up and funnier than it ever had been after Neil put his artistic hand to the project. But a realization occurs that moving scenery with a cargo van in midtown Manhattan is for 25-year-olds. It is time to grow up and grow old.

I fulfill my father's dream of securing a "nice city job, Johnny!" I am hired as an adjunct and meet theatre students who are overflowing with passion and parched with confusion. Their excitement is invigorating, their experience is translucent. I can see right through their arguments. They are like the Satsies from under my childhood dining table, and I have an opportunity to play along, maybe this time to teach them.

I have children again.

Chapter 19

No Worries, No Filter

*Can you forgive a pig-headed old fool
with no eyes to see with
and no ears to hear with all these years?*
— *Ebenezer Scrooge*

I know why I chose this business for a living. Why would I think growing up in lower middle class urban streets make me eligible to work in an elite cottage industry? Living in a world promising fake social mobility in 30-second commercials may have fooled me into thinking I could succeed in a business requiring discretionary income from patrons for its very survival. In my growing years, I dressed in *Robert Hall* bargain clothes. I fed on *Hamburger Helper* when my father's paycheck did not cover the whole week's expenses. *Chicken Delight TV Dinners* were considered a luxury. I had no knowledge of, nor did I seek to understand, the nuances of dramatic theory. My theatre bug, unlike so many others fascinated with their own enlightenment of the performing arts, did not evolve from training or exposure.

It was the only available tunnel of escape. The longest of long shots. The winning lottery ticket. My incentive was the brutal and sometimes foolish reaction to the fact that somebody must win, and I may as well take a shot at it, since I do not have that much to lose anyway. It was a reactionary and impulsive act of courage.

The older I get, the less important everything is. Reflection becomes a daily exercise in a septuagenarian's agenda. I reminisce and regret at breakfast, apologize and hope at lunch, reflect by mid-afternoon, and pour a drink at dusk. Conversations remain the same and much of it is insignificant. In this era, I assume I have not become the crotchety old man I am expected to be. Carol sets me straight and assures me that I achieved that persona years ago. I wonder why I am still here. Why I still care. I do not have a bucket list. I emptied it along the way while living.

I do not miss show business.

On Christmas Eve, I watch a transformed Ebenezer Scrooge evoke a comforting sense of reconciliation and good will. I am cured of my career addiction of a holiday extravaganzas. My expectations are downsized now. My Christmas lost is now found.

The comfort of simple living through this consumptive holiday has its advantages. No wood to cut, no pine needles to sweep, the mimicking warmth of hearth and home managed by the flip of a wall switch or the voice command of my new protector and overseer, Alexa. The only new indulgence is fruitcake. I have a lot in common with fruitcake. Mocked, dismissed, retreaded as an unwanted gift re-sent to someone who is not on your A-list of friends. I revel in the gummy density of it all. With filters slowly eroding, I command Alexa to deliver two pounds of the candied dessert. A day later, the hearty tin of sweet and sticky arrives.

I use my last remaining contacts to secure choice house seats to *Hamilton,* but not for me.

"Thanks, Dad, you really came through," Joseph claims after I give him two tickets for a Saturday matinee. He is proud of his father, at least for the moment. He walks 46th Street as if he owns it, and he basks in his girlfriend's adoration. Carol and I wave them off, and meander under the Marriott Marquis, Shubert Alley, consolidating 45 years of memories in a five-minute walk. I wonder if Joseph will think of this day beyond this matinee. I wonder if he will ever see how those 40 years of his father and mother earned this moment. We walk the same blocks back to Grand Central that I had walked for a lifetime and go home. It is my children's world now, as it should be.

This is not the retirement I anticipate. I miss the significance of my old life.

The year 2020 changes everything.

We are in the 11th month of the coronavirus pandemic. The historical club of medieval bubonic plague, 19th-century cholera, and 20th-centrury flu has a new and improved member. It changes dinner plans and social activities. My home becomes a sanctuary, my computer, my office. The future is in the hands of people half my age whom I hope are twice as smart. Maybe my generation did not produce the great parents we assume we are.

Theatres are closed. Arenas are empty. For the first time ever, there is no Thanksgiving Day Parade. No concerts. No Metropolitan Opera. I realize every categorization that identifies me is becoming an anomaly. We claim laws, governments, social assignments and throw in location, color, gender, and age to define ourselves, to qualify for recognition. But all we have, in the end, is ourselves in the present tense of living.

My entertainment is home-spun. My age labels me compromised. The photographs in the curio cabinet depict

Joseph, once dreaming of planes and cookies, now married with a pilot's license and a vintage townhouse, and Lauren who wished *Good Night, Moon* to a starry sky, who dreams of a better world. I wonder who will end up an anachronism.

It is now just the two of us, and the fruitcake.

I learn more and remember less. I transform myself.

No more losing. No more climbing. No more achieving.

The bargain of a senior citizen ticket on Metro North is inviting, but I am out of commuting practice. The need no longer matches the desire. I am determined to smell the flowers right here at home.

The virtual classroom of theatre students grappling with a new brand of 21st-century intimacy within a laptop screen becomes my workplace. I am dismayed that my tactile lifetime experience is unknown to young students. My expertise becomes a memory of the way things used to be. I am more a living museum than a source of professional advice. I see worry and confusion on their faces. I am confident that they will persevere. They are creating their own knowledge history.

In the quiet of my evenings, I find comfort on a blank page. I find it in a refurbished fountain pen, a delicate mechanism controlling a release of colored liquid that inevitably stains the fingers in refilling despite my best efforts. The pen gives me a voice. It speaks to me. I create my own drama. I imagine a conversation, admiring the sleek resin of the barrel.

"Don't let me catch you with another!" the handmade *Pelikan 205* warns.

She glides away, leaving indelible streams to remind me. Every stroke spills purpose.

Her smooth flow, a dance on point. Indigo bleeding in rivulets, bending, wiping words like a paintbrush. She implores contemplation with her eloquent nib. I place a final touch to a work of connection.

"Sail away until you run dry," I say. "I will replenish your life blood before I hold another less worthy to grasp."

Writing is such a torrid, personal affair.

I become a purveyor of creative commerce. An inventor instead of a facilitator. In these days of insignificance, I learn to be truthful to myself.

I am not famous. I am rich. My working theatrical life is a priceless memory, and it is a great place to learn storytelling. We no longer fit easily into other people's memoirs. People exist mainly in our complaints. I fall for the condition as well. In the aloneness of chronological age, I am my own supporting character in a self-serving monodrama. I do not want to lose those elements that make me complex and interesting: my past, my experiences, the people I have met, how they have affected me. But the age in which I live, tolerance does not allow dialogue; politics does not permit discourse. Exchange is replaced by censure, truth by agenda. We are like the players of an ancient Mesoamerican ball game, where the losers lose their heads, literally.

A photo of Lauren with Ranger goalie Henrik Lundqvist adorns her bureau. It is a perk for enduring the rough room of MSG. A memory of the big job. She remembers it to this day. It is something I can no longer arrange. The photo is a trophy of a happy childhood.

The Music Hall looks different. There is a brighter, more festive tone to the place. A huge garland of flowers, hundreds of them in large circles of bright color festoon the arched proscenium. I feel its freshness, like a festive Polynesian event. Clean, untainted by the experiences of the past. Pleasant, caring folk run the place now. The glow seems to come from within, and I am happy to be there once again. Technicians mull about their prep work, a little older but no wiser. I stand around like a memory from another time, ready to give my opening greeting to a new group excited for the new program to begin. I have not written anything, but I know what I will say.

I will promise them the time of their lives. I will make them feel special, since they are the attendees of another opening night. I assure the safety and quality of the workplace for my performing artists. I await my cue to enter the stage to deliver the opening night speech, just like the other times. I am wearing my favorite suit.

But is only a dream, a "What if?" of my mind. There are no more shows in my life. The theatres are dark, and the restaurants are dying.

For the first time in its performance history, the Radio City Christmas Spectacular is cancelled to prevent the transmission of the coronavirus.

Victor the curtain hauler was right. His compromise was an act of maturity. The curtain man's contribution to his passion reflects closure. He commands a flying drape better than anyone, and he dresses for the occasion. He serves the show. He manages his dreams, so they do not overcome him.

We are losing sight of who we are. Algorithms fail to identify the wonderful stories behind our resumes. Analytics fail to engage the human heart. In protest, I read instead of surf, listen instead of pontificate, connect instead of judge. When in doubt, I embrace humor.

What is left of Carol is her brain, her heart, her warmth, her compassion, her commitment. What is not left is her right shoulder, her left hip, her right hip, her left knee, and her right knee. She has had more replacements than a *Chevy Vega*, a car she was once proud to own. She is on a first-name basis at the Brookfield Orthopedic Group. She can tell a shady physical therapist from a mile away.

Carol and I sit on the couch, pinot noir and scotch in respective hands and watch *A Christmas Carol* to its ending credits. The story is filled with all those good things I have been gifted. Home, warmth, true and lasting love, fatherhood, a meaningful career that stole time away from two crazy beautiful children and served them a secure environment in which to grow.

It is a story of transformation that reconciles a selfish heart and enlightens the life of the young with paternal compassion.

This is the fatherhood I speak of. One based in service to human dignity, not patriarchal authoritarianism. To touch a searching heart where one's thoughts are understood and acknowledged by another is thrilling. No agreement is necessary.

"Tell me a story, Grandpa."

"Look out the window. What do you see?"

"It's dark. There are lights in the sky."

"What kind of lights?"

"Little lights and big lights.".

"Are they moving?"

"No. Wait! There's one!"

"Where did it go?"

"It went away. It looked like it was coming down."

"It is. It is coming for a visit."

"To us?"

"To someone. They only come if you want them to."

"From where?"

"A happy place, Palenti Tempi."

"Where?"

"The moving lights are stars. I call them Satsies. They come from Plenti Tempi, and they like to visit us."

"Will they come here?"

"Only if you believe they will. That's the fun with Satsies. You can wish them over anytime."

"Did they come to see you?"

"Many times."

"How did they know to come to you?"

"Well, first you have to believe. Then you must keep it a secret from everyone. They only visit if you prepare a place for them…can you gobble like a turkey?"

I am ready for grandchildren. The dialogue is already written.

I flip the gas fireplace switch. I turn on the plastic Christmas tree. The ceramic village under the tree lights up, and once again, once a year, it is where I live.

I glance at Carol. I sit back and enjoy the quiet of nothing important to say. Whatever was bigger than the two of us is still intact. Whatever compelled us to spend each other's lifetimes together is still there. The peace between us confirms our purpose.

When I look back, I never stay there.

And neither does she. The years pass without question.

Without bogus therapists who need their own help.

Without the flirtatious secretary who dresses her front end like a midcentury Buick.

Without quick trysts with a willing intern under the Oyster Bar arches at Grand Central.

Or that soft sack with groping eyes who passes himself off as a sensitive artist.

Him with his greasy guitar. Not everyone is *Easy*.

There is life beyond the champagne spaghetti straps of youthful appearances.

We walk the walk, down the aisle, down the road, watching calendars become worthless,

And each other become useless.

Going beyond dreams and taking stewardship of one another.

John Bonanni

Truth and peace are not elusive. They are found within the integrity of one's conscience. They are not in possessions, achievements, or position. May my children discover them in the pursuit of their purpose.

JOHN BONANNI - ©2020

Works Cited

Dick Smith, Felix Bernard Bregman, Vollo, Conn, 1934. Lyrics to "Winter Wonderland."

Meredith Wilson, Plymouth Music Publishers, 1951. Lyrics to "Beginning to Look a Lot Like Christmas."

Jay Livingston, Ray Evans, 1950. From the Paramount film, The Lemon Drop Kid. Lyrics to "Silver Bells."

Charles Dickens, Neil Langley, 1950. From the Renown Pictures film, Scrooge

Douglas Cross, George Cory, Lyrics.com, STANDS4 LLC, 2020. "I Left My Heart in San Francisco Lyrics." Accessed July 27, 2020 https://www.lyrics.com/lyric/2326802/Tony+Bennett.

Matthews, Wallace. https://nypost.com/2000/01/16/jones-wins-radio-city-mismatch/?utm_source=url_sitebuttons&utm_medium=site%20buttons&utm_campaign=site%20buttons

Acknowledgements

This is a big hug to the folks who have influenced, supported, and encouraged me.

People like Henry Aronson, composer and comrade in the pit; Ken Aymong, Supervising Producer at Saturday Night Live, who assured me my job was better than my wish to be his page on SNL; Bob Bennett, Broadway PSM and VP at Radio City, who shared antics on both sides of Broadway; Neil Callari, an Evil Genius and angel, who made my producing bug possible; George Greczylo, whose Emmy Awards prove that good people finish first; Peter and Sarah Maniscalco, my extended family and financial wizard; Arturo Porazzi, Broadway PSM, who taught me how to call a show and keep in touch for a lifetime; Michael P. Price, for creating a jewel of a theatre and inviting me to play in it; Rob Schiller, West Coast TV director, who stood by our friendship through earthquakes, divorces, and regional theatre house arrests; Nicola Taylor, stage manager from Bora Bora, who brought class to a rough room; Joseph A. Onorato and Kathy Hoovler, whose stage manager voices in a head set assured me the 240 technicians, performers, musicians, and exotic animals backstage were safe and ready; Eric Titcomb, technician at the Music Hall, the very best wing man I ever had the honor to know; Steven

Zweigbaum, Broadway sage, who kept my theatre career alive simply by hiring me over and over again.

The mentors of the MFA Creative and Professional Writing Program at Western Connecticut State University: Anthony D'Aries, author, friend, for his encouragement and literary fatherhood; Dr. M Jackson, author and scientist, who forced me to get real and vulnerable; Brian Clements, who took the bogeyman out of poetry; Mike Perrota, who cut to the chase; Jane Cleland, the Queen of Structure, Kateri Kosek, who taught me to write what I meant to say; Ron Samul, the media maven; Erik Ofgang and John Roche for unrelenting encouragement.

Authors Lisa Peterson, Ron Farina, and Diana Payne, classmates, writers, friends who labored through revisions, critiques, and prompts together as a team, as family.

Nancy and Joe Marik, proofreader sister/brother-in-law, who sloshed through this first book; Joseph, the son fathers dream of, Lauren, my warrior daughter who forced me to walk a mile every day and succeeded most of the time.

My gratitude to Stevan Nikolic and Adelaide Books, an organization true to their motto.

Finally, to Carol. She lived this book. Thank you to all, and to all a fun read.

About the Author

John began his theatrical career at 16 years old in the offices of Broadway producer David Merrick. The advantage of being a subway ride from the Broadway theatre district helped him bypass the usual trek of summer stock gigs. His first stage manager assignment was a Broadway musical, *Very Good Eddie,* which lasted six months. Actor's Equity card in hand, John worked his beginner's luck in hopes of finding another show. The opportunity came, but the summer stock life he thought he avoided claimed him for eight years at the Goodspeed Opera House in East Haddam, Connecticut.

It was at this postage stamp-sized theatre where John honed his craft, met Carol, and began his career. The little theatre in the woods was a magical place, and every year its charm became harder to resist. Twenty-six shows later, one Goodspeed production took him back to New York.

For six months, John and Carol had their own Broadway gigs, he at *Whoopee* and Carol at *A Chorus Line,* beating the odds of a shared working life in the theatre. The short-lived bliss forced John to work hotel ballrooms and street fair gigs. After resorting to painting his former boss's apartment for cash, John's luck turned, thanks to colleague Steven Zweigbaum, who hired him on a string of Broadway shows. A career blossomed from *Singin' in the Rain*, *Me & My Girl*, *City of Angels*, *Crazy for You*, and a few one-nighters. Throughout the experience, John and Carol raised a family in the most traditional mid-century fashion despite the challenges of a theatre career. He spent 13 years at Radio City Music Hall, eight of them as Production Stage Manager for the Christmas Spectacular and Resident Stage Manager for over 1000 events from the Grammys, the Tonys, the Daytime Emmys to Tony Bennett, Bill Clinton's 50th Birthday Celebration, Eminem, the MTV Awards and the Dalai Lama.

As Executive Producer of the Radio City Christmas Spectacular, he produced the 75th Anniversary production and supervised four touring companies across eight cities. As independent producer, he introduced the *International Playwrights Festival* and partnered with Prime Time House, a transitional mental health facility in Connecticut by hiring their clients as actors in a production entitled *Truly Dually*. John's latest venture is "Moolah," a two-character comedy about two misunderstood gangsters written by Broadway author Arje Shaw.

It is in this environment of actors seeking a standing ovation or dreading the next morning's cutting criticism where John's perspective on work and life in the performing arts is formed. He illustrates that good theatrical management also requires a healthy dose of genuine, non-patriarchal fatherhood. He discovers the mix supports the artist, balances the inequality of gender, and serves in the rearing of his own children. *Just Off, Stage Right* is a personal, compelling narrative of how self-importance becomes meaningless in the wake of compassion, empathy, and the universal need for connection on and off stage.

John lives in Connecticut with Carol and a very fussy orange cat.

Made in United States
North Haven, CT
18 December 2021